THINK ABOUT THESE THINGS: PONDERINGS AND PROMPTINGS

Norman D. Holcomb, Jr., PhD
Virginia Beach, Virginia 2024

Copyright © 2024 by Norman D. Holcomb, Jr.

Published by Amazon Books

All rights reserved. Printed in the United States of America. No part of this book may be reproduced in any manner whatsoever without written permission except in the case of brief quotations.

ISBN

Cover design from licensed Adobe Stock.

Illustrations page iii, v. and vii from licensed Adobe Stock.

Illustration Silhouette for chapter headings from licensed Adobe Stock.

The cover illustration is a likeness of the famous bronze sculpture by Auguste Rodin (1840 – 1917) depicting a muscular man lost in thought. While sitting on a large stone, he ponders over the mysteries and realities of human existence. Rodin's "Thinker" is a symbol of the strength and power inherent in the act of thinking.

Why should we think upon things that are lovely? Because thinking determines life. It is a common habit to blame life upon the environment. Environment modifies life but does not govern life. The soul is stronger than its surroundings.—William James

Man is but a reed, the most feeble thing in nature, but he is a thinking reed. –Blaise Pascal

People demand freedom of speech as a compensation for the freedom of thought which they seldom use . – Soren Kierkegaard

We are the product of our thoughts. What we think, we become. – Gandhi

One ought to look a good deal at oneself before thinking of condemning others. – Moliere

No problem can withstand the assault of sustained thinking. – Voltaire

Thinking is the talking of the soul with itself. – Plato

Thinking is not agreeing or disagreeing. That's voting. – Robert Frost

Dedicated to Mary Beth:
my childhood sweetheart,
my high school cheerleader,
my wife of more than a half-century,
the mother of our children,
and the one with whom I now share
"the last, the best, for which the first was made."
I find in her everything the poet must have meant when he wrote,
"A thing of beauty is a joy forever,
its loveliness increases,
it will never pass into nothingness."

(John Keats, Endymion)

AUTHOR'S NOTE

All scripture quotations in this book are taken from the Revised Standard Version of the Holy Bible except where otherwise noted. The reading of Luke 9:49-56 that begins Chapter Twelve is printed as found in the King James Version of the Bible (KJV). In this instance, I chose the KJV version as translated from the Textus Receptus manuscripts because of contextual probability and support by many ancient sources.

New Testament translation references are from *The Greek New Testament* 3rd edition, edited by Kurt Aland, Matthew Black, Carlo M. Martini, Bruce M. Metzger, and Allen Wikgren. United Bible Society, 1975.

Textus Receptus comparisons are based on texts contained in *The Greek New Testament, Textus Receptus: Reader's Edition*, Grange Press, 2022.

Latin translation references are from *Biblia Sacra Vulgata (Vulgate): Holy Bible in Latin*, 5th edition, edited by R. Gryson. Published by The German Bible Society, 2006.

Throughout the book, I use the era designations of AD, *anno domini* (in the year of the Lord), and BC (before Christ). There are other systems of designating eras, but these are the most common designations.

A list of abbreviations is not included. Abbreviations referring to books of the Bible seem to me to be self-explanatory and readily identify the book referenced.

TABLE OF CONTENTS

PREFACE i
CHAPTER ONE WHAT HAPPENS WHEN YOU DIE? 1
    Prayer: 53
CHAPTER TWO THE NECESSARY PRELUDE 54
    Prayer: 64
CHAPTER THREE THE PROCESS OF BECOMING 65
    Prayer: 74
CHAPTER FOUR WHY DOES GOD CARE? 76
    Prayer: 101
CHAPTER FIVE SPIRITUAL MYOPIA 102
    Prayer: 112
CHAPTER SIX LEST WE FORGET 113
    Prayer: 117
CHAPTER SEVEN OUR TIMES ARE IN HIS HANDS 118
    Prayer: 122
CHAPTER EIGHT ACTION VERBS 123
    Prayer: 126
CHAPTER NINE NOT WHY? BUT HOW? 127
    Prayer: 133
CHAPTER TEN BUT NOW, A NEW BEGINNING 134
    Prayer: 138
CHAPTER ELEVEN TO GOD BE THE GLORY 139

Prayer: 143
CHAPTER TWELVE FORGIVEN, LOVED, REDEEMED 144
    Prayer: 147
CHAPTER THIRTEEN MANAGING THE STORMS OF LIFE
.... 149
    Prayer: 160
CHAPTER FOURTEEN GOD'S GREAT ABILITY 161
    Prayer: 179
CHAPTER FIFTEEN YOU CAN'T GO TO HELL 180
    Prayer: 247
CONCLUSION 248
    Prayer: 253
ENDNOTES 254
BIBLIOGRAPHY 277
INDEX 299

Ask and it will be given you; seek and you will find; knock and it will be opened to you. For everyone who asks receives, and he who seeks finds, and to him who knocks it will be opened (Matthew 7:7; Luke 11:9)

PREFACE

Philosophers of every age have emphasized the necessity and value of thinking in the pursuit of all human endeavors. Descartes assured himself of his own existence through his first principle of philosophy, which we know as "I think, therefore I am" (*cogito, ergo sum*). Socrates, Plato, and many other ancient philosophers constructed their teachings on the belief that "The unexamined life is not worth living." While we may find the study of philosophy to be laborious, confusing, and often incomprehensible, Socrates, and probably others, said that all of philosophy can be summed up in just two words—know thyself.

Our involvement with each other and the business of our world requires disciplined thinking. While I respect and appreciate the work of the great philosophers and thinkers of the world, I have recently been prompted to consider the role of thinking in the lives of Mary, the mother of Jesus, and the writings of the Apostle Paul. I take my lead on this from Soren Kierkegaard's parable of the prompter.[1] The prompter was an important participant in theatre productions and operatic performances. He sat in a box in a hidden position on the stage and helped the actors and singers with their lines. When performers forgot what to say or became disoriented regarding their relationship to what was happening, the prompter whispered instructions and reoriented them to the flow and action of the performance. I believe that prayerful thinking plays the role of the prompter in our spiritual lives.

It came as a surprise to me when I realized that Mary, the Mother of Jesus, was a perfect role model as a thinker. Luke's account of the birth of Jesus tells us that an angel of the Lord appeared to some shepherds and told them that Christ the Lord was born in Bethlehem. They hurried off to the city to tell everyone what they had seen and heard. Those who heard the story were amazed and wondered about the details of the shepherds' report. They were astonished and curious, but they failed to understand the significance of the event. As is usually true with crowds of people, curiosity and amazement are temporarily exciting, but they fall far short of functioning as faith. Wonder can turn to doubt and disbelief as it ages and is replaced by other temporary excitements. Astonishment at one event can quickly be overcome by another unusual event.

Mary was listening to all the talk about what the shepherds had reported. There were probably as many responses to the news as there were hearers present. There was no shortage of explanations that rationally and irrationally described what the shepherds thought they had heard and seen. Luke portrays Mary as keeping silent through all of this. He says that she "kept all these things, pondering them in her heart" (Luke 2:19). Although I had read this story hundreds of times, the word "pondering" jumped out at me and fully captured my attention. It became a prompter that forced me to look deeper into this simple sentence.

When did you last hear someone use the word ponder in a sentence? We find the word in poetry, hymns, and religious jargon, but seldom do we hear it used in our everyday conversations. The word Luke used for "pondered" is the combination of two Greek words, one meaning "with or together," and the other meaning "to throw or toss."² Mary was silently weighing and considering what she was hearing. She was identifying the thoughts, feelings, and concerns about what she had experienced in the past and how it related to the report of the shepherds. She pondered about the coincidence of two women in the same family, one beyond child-bearing years and the other a virgin, both becoming pregnant. Had she really been told that "with God nothing will be impossible?" (Luke 2:37). Mary "Kept all these things, pondering them in her heart," which means that she was tossing/throwing all these things together and was trying to make sense of them. She treasured them in her heart and constantly tried to make the pieces add up to a sensible and recognizable whole.

Pondering is not an act of split-second thinking. It can be prolonged, one moment being accepted as conclusive and certain, and in the next moment presenting as inconclusive and threatened by doubt. Mary argued and debated with herself about her understanding of all that had happened. She knew that she would have to live with the unpleasant consequences of her predicament. Her virtue and morality would be questioned. Her son would be accused by friends and relatives of being out of his mind (Mark 3:21). He would be criticized by the religious authorities and viewed as an enemy of his own country. Finally, she would have to watch him as he was ridiculed, mocked, tortured, and crucified. Across thirty-three years, she argued and debated with herself about her own understanding of all that had happened. Nevertheless, she stood by her son and believed that God was at work in some way in His life. She won the long debate with her doubts when she learned that God had restored his broken body and raised it to a glorified exit from the tomb.

Mary's many years of pondering prompted me to think about what might be locked away in the vault of my memory. I was certain that it housed events that were not completely understood at the time of their deposit. As these memories came to mind, I began to toss them around, pondering as to how all the various pieces could possibly fit together in any harmonious pattern. Have you ever pondered over your life, trying to make sense of how God has been at work in your journey? As people on the move from birth to death, is it possible to ponder over our experiences of life and get some idea of how God has accompanied us on the pilgrimage? Have we been traveling on a merry-go-round, a carousel that does nothing but go around and around in the same old rutted circle? Have we lived lives of endless circles, or have we been traveling in a caravan that is going from somewhere to somewhere else? Have we had the faith and courage to go forward through stretches of desert, all the while trusting that God would provide an oasis of refreshment, peace, and joy? Can we ponder over our lives and see what the Psalmist saw when he said, "The Lord will keep your going out and your coming in from this time forth and forever more"? (Ps. 121:8).

We all have known and will continue to know times of good and bad, victory and defeat, sadness and happiness, grief and joy, gain and loss, and of times yet to come that will affect us in ways not yet known. Can all of these opposing emotions, these ups and downs of life, fit together and become complementary parts that form the whole picture of our going out and coming in? As we seek an answer, perhaps we can benefit from the story of Joseph, Jacob's younger son. He was the victim of his brothers' conspiracy and was carried off into slavery. He was denied the support and comfort of a loving family. He was falsely accused of sexual assault and thrown into prison. In the end, he became Pharaoh's administrator over all the land of Egypt. When all the pieces of his life fell into place, Joseph could look back over his shoulder and say to those who abused him, "You meant evil against me, but God meant it for good" (Gen. 50:19).

Mary's pondering did not produce an immediate answer to the how, what, when, and why of what was happening in her life. She had to live by faith during the shifting circumstances of that period of time that we identify as "now." Our "now" often produces anxiety and impatience. We find ourselves in the uncomfortable grip of a failure to recognize that our "now" may be God's "not yet." Stephen Hawking, the brilliant theoretical physicist said, "It is no use getting furious if you get stuck. What I do is keep thinking about the problem but work on something else. Sometimes, it is years before I see the way forward. In the case of information loss and black holes, it was 29 years."[3] Regarding our prayer requests, we may have to wait, often times with impatience and doubt, but we can be assured that God is never late. Using the language of some business models, we can trust that "God is always just in time, with just as much as is needed."

Our going out and coming in is not a one-and-done event. It is a moving stream of action until we finally close our eyes in death and immediately move into the re-created dimension that God has prepared for us. In the meantime, we can be sustained through our pondering over the many events we have experienced, both good and bad. I am certain that each of us can arrive at some sense of meaning for our lives if, under the influence of prayer and God's Word, we ponder over what has happened and is happening to us.

We could not ask for a better prompter than the Apostle Paul. He provides a list of characteristics that should always be in our thoughts and serve as the motivating principles of our relationships with other people. He says, "Finally, brethren, whatever is true, whatever is honorable, whatever is just, whatever is pure, whatever is lovely, whatever is gracious, if there is anything worthy of praise, think about these things" (Phil. 4:8). The interesting thing about these characteristics is that they are not specifically Christian characteristics. Truth, honor, justice, purity, loveliness, and graciousness are appreciated and recommended among people everywhere. Recognizing and respecting these qualities in anyone, regardless of their religious orientation, promotes peaceful existence among all of us.

Paul prompts us to closely consider these personal qualities. He is referring to thinking about them as being more than a passive act. He wants us to think of the value of what each of these words represents. In the world of food and nutrition, we say, "You are what you eat." Concerning the content of our thoughts, may we not also say, "You are what you think"? Pessimism breeds more pessimism. Negativity turns every thought into an impossibility. Thinking about nothing but the ugliness and despair that we see in the world can turn our lives into defeatism and depression.

Paul prompts us to think about positive, uplifting words and says, "Do not be conformed to this world, but be transformed by the renewal of your mind" (Rom. 12:2). We are responsible for the maintenance of our thoughts. Thinking about truth, honor, justice, purity, loveliness, and graciousness involves considering their power to create harmony and goodwill. Holding the power of these words in our thinking will leave no room for the petty selfishness that disturbs and destroys our peace.

In the following pages, I am daring the reader to become more intimate and more personally involved with the Bible. That involvement reaches beyond the fifteen selections that I have presented. I challenge you to take this approach in every encounter with the Word of God. Dare to be provocative. The God who responded to Job's provocations will have no trouble in dealing with any challenge or line of questioning that you can initiate. Recruit yourself to be an active character in the stories and parables as you read them. Become both protagonist and antagonist, and let the prompter speak to you from both perspectives. The appropriate question to ask yourself in every situation is not "What would Jesus do?" We are given the answer to that question. The question that confronts us is, "What am I going to do?" Listen for clues from Kierkegaard's "prompter in the box." Ponder with Mary over the actions and events that are taking place. Think with Saint Paul about the relationship of the Father, Son, and Holy Spirit to the past and present details and the future possibilities of your life.

Pondering and thinking are wonderful ways of satisfying our hunger and thirst for communion with that spiritual world that we cannot see but are sure that it is there. It is okay to talk aloud to God. I long ago abandoned the formalities of liturgically structured prayer in my personal prayer life. I talk to God every night (at least). And you know what I have found? I look forward to it; it has become a time I love and treasure. What is more, I believe that my prayers are heard. It is not necessary that I get an immediate answer in a way that gives me what I want. It is enough to know that God knows about my concerns.

We must understand that pondering is not the same thing as worrying. Worrying exhausts you, frightens you, upsets you emotionally, and creates a sense of hopelessness. Pondering brings power and control, new streams of thought, and new perceptions of what is happening, and it makes you aware of how you are being affected by whatever you are facing. Worrying creates a list of insurmountable "what ifs" and gasps for a breath of life as it flails around in a thought pool of impossibilities. Pondering creates solutions and identifies possibilities.

I arrived at the somewhat cumbersome title of *Think About These Things: Ponderings and Promptings* because I believe that pondering and thinking about the things that matter in life draw us closer to communion with the Great Lord God. It moves us beyond our own selfish awareness of ourselves and creates an inward relationship with the Word of God. When we ponder, think, and listen for the prompting clues provided by the Spirit, we experience more than just an accumulation of information. We are drawn into a participation in the power and majesty of "Thus says the Lord." This, in itself, is something worth thinking about.

CHAPTER ONE
WHAT HAPPENS WHEN YOU DIE?

Isaiah 34: *[1]Draw near, O nations, to hear, and hearken, O peoples! Let the earth listen, and all that fills it; the world, and all that comes from it.*

[2]For the LORD is enraged against all the nations, and furious against all their host, he has doomed them, has given them over for slaughter.

[3]Their slain shall be cast out, and the stench of their corpses shall rise; the mountains shall flow with their blood.

[4]All the host of heaven shall rot away, and the skies roll up like a scroll. All their host shall fall, as leaves fall from the vine, like leaves falling from the fig tree.

[5] For my sword has drunk its fill in the heavens; behold, it descends for judgment upon Edom, upon the people I have doomed.

[6]The LORD has a sword; it is sated with blood, it is gorged with fat, with the blood of lambs and goats, with the fat of the kidneys of rams.

For the LORD has a sacrifice in Bozrah, a great slaughter in the land of Edom.

⁷Wild oxen shall fall with them, and young steers with the mighty bulls. Their land shall be soaked with blood, and their soil made rich with fat.

⁸For the LORD has a day of vengeance, a year of recompense for the cause of Zion.

⁹And the streams of Edom shall be turned into pitch, and her soil into brimstone; her land shall become burning pitch. ¹⁰Night and day it shall not be quenched; its smoke shall go up for ever.

From generation to generation it shall lie waste; none shall pass through it for ever and ever.

¹¹But the hawk and the porcupine shall possess it, the owl and the raven shall dwell in it. He shall stretch the line of confusion over it, and the plummet of chaos over its nobles.

¹²They shall name it No Kingdom There, and all its princes shall be nothing.

¹³Thorns shall grow over its strongholds, nettles and thistles in its fortresses. It shall be the haunt of jackals, an abode for ostriches.

¹⁴And wild beasts shall meet with hyenas, the satyr shall cry to his fellow; yea, there shall the night hag alight, and find for herself a resting place.

¹⁵There shall the owl nest and lay and hatch and gather her young in her shadow; yea, there shall the kites be gathered, each one with her mate.

¹⁶Seek and read from the book of the LORD: Not one of these shall be missing; none shall be without her mate. For the mouth of the LORD has commanded, and his Spirit has gathered them.

¹⁷He has cast the lot for them, his hand has portioned it out to them with the line; they shall possess it for ever, from generation to generation they shall dwell in it.

Isaiah 35: ¹The wilderness and the dry land shall be glad. The desert shall rejoice and blossom; like the crocus

²it shall blossom abundantly, and rejoice with joy and singing. The glory of Lebanon shall be given to it, the majesty of Carmel and Sharon. They shall see the glory of the LORD, the majesty of our God.

³Strengthen the weak hands, and make firm the feeble knees.

⁴Say to those who are of a fearful heart, "Be strong, fear not! Behold, your God will come with vengeance, with the recompense of God. He will come and save you."

⁵Then the eyes of the blind shall be opened, and the ears of the deaf unstopped;

⁶then shall the lame man leap like a hart, and the tongue of the dumb sing for joy. For waters shall break forth in the wilderness, and streams in the desert;

⁷the burning sand shall become a pool, and the thirsty ground springs of water; the haunt of jackals shall become a swamp, the grass shall become reeds and rushes.

⁸And a highway shall be there, and it shall be called the Holy Way; the unclean shall not pass over it, and fools shall not err therein.

⁹No lion shall be there, nor shall any ravenous beast come up on it; they shall not be found there, but the redeemed shall walk there.

¹⁰And the ransomed of the LORD shall return, and come to Zion with singing; everlasting joy shall be upon their heads; they shall obtain joy and gladness, and sorrow and sighing shall flee away.

Chapters 34 and 35 of Isaiah belong together. A reader should not try to understand anything in one chapter without reading both chapters and thinking about the "big picture" message of the prophet. Too often, I hear preachers picking a favorite verse of scripture for a sermon without considering context, translation and document issues, and sound theological principles. Martin Luther's advice (and warning) was, "Whoever wants to read the Bible must make sure he is not wrong, for the Scriptures can easily be stretched and guided, but no one should guide them according to his emotions; he should lead them to the well, that is to the cross of Christ, then he will certainly be right and cannot fail."[1]

On one occasion, quoting a single verse of scripture from Isaiah 35 brought me uncomfortably face-to-face with the inadequacy of that single verse at that moment in time. I was concluding a funeral service at the grave of a young Lieutenant Colonel. *The Book of Worship of the Methodist Church* gave the following instructions for the graveside service: "*At the grave, when the people are assembled, the minister shall say one or more of the following sentences.*" Several one-sentence verses were suggested, including Isaiah 35:4, "Say to those who are of a fearful heart, Be strong, fear not! Behold, your God will come and save you."[2]

As I stood at the grave on one of the coldest January days I had ever known, I looked into the broken-hearted faces of a wife and two little daughters. In what I now remember as a presumptuous, sanctimonious voice, I read: "Be strong, fear not; your God will come and save you." I suddenly felt a wave of doubt and shame sweep over me. I immediately felt as though I was the cruelest hypocrite and the biggest liar the world had ever known. Here was a young wife whose world was split down the middle by the loss of the love of her life. Here were two young daughters who would never again feel the loving touch of their father's arms around them or hear that precious fatherly voice say, "I love you girls more than anything in this world." As I stood with them on the edge of a cold, dark hole in the frozen earth; a place where all that was dear to them would soon be buried, it suddenly seemed unthinkable to say to them, "Be strong, fear not; your God will come and save you."

Through the eye of my mind's memory, I watched a carousel of death turn before me. How many times had I seen death on the battlefield? In how many hospital waiting rooms had I announced the death of a loved one to a waiting family? How many parents had I prayed with when they lost a child to sickness, disease, or accident? These were real events in my memory, but I asked myself, "When, in my memory, had I ever seen God really come and save anybody under those conditions?" The real answer to the question posed by the real carousel of death was an emphatic, undeniable, "Never!" As I looked into the faces of that mother and her daughters, I realized how foolish and inadequate that stand-alone one verse of scripture was in that moment of time and under those circumstances. How could they not be afraid? How could they expect anyone to save a person who was already dead? I felt the heavy weight of an unfulfilled expectation dragging my soul and spirit into a thick, black, disappointing darkness.

In the immediate company of death and doubt, and in the awareness of the roller-coaster carousel of death's seemingly unstoppable progress, I knew that I had to think about three things: 1) the devastation of my faith; 2) an assessment of my expectations; and 3) the re-creation of my understanding of resurrection and eternal life. In moments such as this, Saint Paul advised us to "think about these things," and "the God of peace will be with you" (Phil. 4:8-9). I determined that I would examine this single verse, Isaiah 35:4, in the context of both chapters, (Isaiah 34 and 35), and determine for myself how it complements "the peace of God which passes all understanding" (Phil. 4:7).

Isaiah 34 begins with a summons for the nations to draw near and listen to God. We must not overlook the fact that this summons includes the earth and everything in it, and the world and all that the world brings into existence. God is angry with the totality of His creation. Israel does not enjoy a status that exempts it from the effects of God's anger. While Israel has an identity apart from the nations, it is still counted as a member of the nations and suffers the same fate that they suffer.

While we generally think of Isaiah only in terms of prophet/prophecy, we must not ignore the role of apocalypticism in the Book of Isaiah. Briefly stated, prophetic eschatology is a recognition of the existing factors (e.g., political, sociological, economic, religious, cultural, leadership, etc.) that will be the cause(s) of the conditions declared by the prophet(s). Apocalyptic eschatology, a revealing of the end times, is a way of viewing God's plan in light of, and in relation to current reality.[3] Chapters 34 and 35 of Isaiah represent both prophetic and apocalyptic eschatology.[4] In chapter 34, the prophet gives us a picture of the horror and devastation that Israel and the nations will suffer as a result of the Assyrian captivity and fall of northern Israel (734 BC to 732 BC), and the Babylonian captivity of Israel and Judah (586 BC to 516 BC). The dead will be so numerous that their bodies will appear to be a rug covering the surface of the earth. The wild beasts will roam throughout the land and feed on the dead bodies. The sickening smell of decaying flesh will blow across the land. The fire and violence of war will ecologically destroy the natural environment. Isaiah prophesies that the death toll will be beyond imagination and the land itself will be uninhabitable.

In chapter 35, Isaiah moves from prophetic eschatology to apocalyptic eschatology. His intent here is to present God's plan for the redemption of His creation following the ghastly results of the prophecy. The redeemed creation, (humanity, animals, plant life, the earth, the world), will be at peace and exist in perfect harmony. All of the creation will rejoice with singing. Suffering and weariness will disappear. To understand this beautiful picture, and to resolve any disquietude with "Be strong, fear not; your God will come and save you," we must look to the medium of apocalyptic literature and enter the world of *The Book of the Revelation to John* (*The Apocalypse*).

I do not believe that the message of Isaiah 35 can be superimposed as a repaired picture of the world we live in. Simply put, the world that we have ruined and continue to destroy cannot be repaired. The picture presented by Isaiah 35 is too perfect to represent a repair or a remodeling project. What we are presented with is a new creation on a cosmic level. A reading of history tells us that neither Israel nor the nations have experienced any lasting semblance of peace and beauty, as is described in chapter 35. Deliverance from the horrible effects of sin cannot be built upon the old order of our fallen world. Jesus warns of the futility of trying to simply repair the old with the new:

> No one puts a piece of unshrunk cloth on an old garment, for the patch tears away from the garment, and a worse tear is made. Neither is new wine put into old wineskins; if it is, the skins burst, and the wine is spilled, and the skins are destroyed; but new wine is put into fresh wineskins, and so both are preserved (Matt. 9:16-17).

Both the Old and New Testaments speak of a "new heaven and a new earth." Some of the most notable references are,

Isaiah 65:17: "For behold, I create new heavens and a new earth; and the former things shall not be remembered or come into mind."

Isaiah 66:22: "For as the new heavens and the new earth which I will make, shall remain before me, says the Lord; so shall your descendants and your name remain."

2 Peter 3:13: "But according to his promise we wait for new heavens and a new earth in which righteousness dwells."

Revelation 21:1: "Then I saw a new heaven and a new earth; for the first heaven and the first earth had passed away, and the sea was no more."

A doctrine of two ages can also be found in many of the apocryphal writings. While some of these works cannot stand the scrutiny of literary criticism, we should not assume that others of them do not have any value for informing our Church history and Christian beliefs. Bruce Metzger says, "Though opinion has not been unanimous, a generally high regard for the books of the Apocrypha has prevailed."[5] Offering favorable support for the value of many of the apocryphal books, D. S. Russell says,

> One sign of the popularity of these books is the great number of languages into which they were, in due course, translated—Latin, Syriac, Arabic, Armenian, Ethiopic, Coptic, Slavonic, Georgian, etc. This wide range of translations no doubt reflects the degree of popularity they came to have among the Christians, but it also indicates the place they held within Judaism itself.[6]

The accounts from the apocryphal and apocalyptic writings typically identify the first creation as that given in Genesis, and the second creation serves as the redemption of the first, which has become beyond repair. The re-created world is one where the following characteristics will prevail: "Immortality, freedom from corruption, death, and infirmity. In it the evil heart will be removed."[7] As for the Genesis creation, the ravages of sin and humankind's inclination to continue to do evil cannot be fixed. The entire aggregate of life—human, animal, and plant—and the physical/natural environment from which sustenance for all things emanates must be re-created.

This idea of two creations is most clearly stated in Second Esdras.[8] The writer says, "The Most High has made not one world but two" (2 Esd. /4 Ezra 7:50). I personally accept the message of Second Esdras to be a dependable witness regarding the apocalyptic mysteries of the Judeo-Christian heritage. The book was written between AD 81 and AD 96. I find it interesting to note that Clement of Alexandria AD 150 to AD 217) supports his writings with references to Second Esdras alongside references from many of the canonical books, (e.g., John 13:33, Gal. 4;19, 1 Cor. 4:15, Deut. 23:1, Matt. 19:12, Jer. 20:14,18, Job 14:4,5, Ps. 1:7, Mic. 6:7, Gen. 1:28, 2 Esd. 5:35).[9] As head of the Catechetical School of Alexandria, Clement probably met some Christian disciples who had known martyrs such as Saints Ignatius (AD 50 to AD 117 or AD 35 to AD 107) and Polycarp (AD 69 to AD 155). It is highly possible that he also met some disciples who, as children, had met and heard Saint John (AD 6 to AD 100) preach and teach. Clement was the teacher of many of the early pupils of Christianity, including Origen, who succeeded him as head of the famous and influential Alexandrian school. Bruce Metzger, editor of the *Introduction to the Apocrypha of the Old Testament, Revised Standard Version,* includes Second Esdras in a collection of books written during the last two centuries before Christ and the first century of the Christian era. He says, "Many of the early Church Fathers quoted most of these books as authoritative Scripture."[10]

In keeping with the title of this book, *Think About These Things*, I have gone to great lengths to tediously think about the devastation found in Isaiah 34, the expectations of the people of Israel, and the resolution found in Isaiah 35. My thoughts have brought me to acceptance of the prophetic and apocalyptic claim of 2 Esdras that "God has made not one world but two." As I continue to think on these things, I want to expand on how and why I believe that the messages of Isaiah 34 and 35 are not restricted to just a single period in the history of Israel. Isaiah is addressing the fate of the entire world, and the fate of humans at our death. This will not be easy, but I ask you to think about these things with me as I proceed.

The devastation described in Isaiah 34 is the same kind of devastation described in the creation story: "The earth was without form and void, and darkness was upon the face of the deep, and the Spirit of God was moving over the face of the waters." Isaiah says that God "will stretch the line of chaos" and the "stones of emptiness" across the earth (Isa. 34:11). Both desolate conditions are described by the Hebrew compound term *tohu wabohu*. It is a term that always refers to desolation and emptiness, but it means much more than that. It includes emptiness, nothingness, trackless waste, lifelessness, futility, worthlessness, instability, and this list does not completely satisfy what *tohu wabohu* stands for.[11]

Basically, *tohu wabohu* describes the primordial state of chaos that existed before God brought order to the Creation. In Isaiah 34, the Creation has become a place where it is impossible for human beings to dwell. The result is doom and destruction for the earth and all its inhabitants. In the original Creation, God neutralized, tamed, and defeated the chaotic power of *tohu wabohu*. Having done that, as only He could do, God appointed man as manager of the entire Creation (Gen. 1:26). However, per the prophecy of Isaiah 34, through sin and disobedience, humankind has once again unleashed the power of *tohu wabohu* throughout the environment and has lost control of the ability to manage it responsibly. Commenting on the fate of the nations as represented in Isaiah 34, Otto Kaiser says that Yahweh has reduced the world forever "to a place just like chaos, to a real *tohu wabohu*, dominated by eternal fire and by plants hostile to men and animals."[12]

Isaiah 34 is a microcosm of the ultimate condition of the world/earth and all that is in it. Life as we know it exists in a state of *tohu wabohu*. We lurch from one chaotic situation to another. Nowhere is this chaos more visible than in the dissolution of the family. The nurture of families and raising children has been taken out of the hands of love and put into the uncaring, incompetent hands of hired agents. This act is but another example of the terrible decisions we make so that we can exercise the autonomy we think we deserve. In all too many cases, this is little more than a selfish convenience for those who are too lazy or too pleasure-mad to care for their own children. When we turn our children over to the government and to hired hands to provide education, care, and keeping, we can be certain that the result will be depravity and despair. Jesus said, "He who is a hireling and not a shepherd, whose own the sheep are not, sees the wolf coming and leaves the sheep and flees; and the wolf snatches them and scatters them. He flees because he is a hireling and cares nothing for the sheep" (John 10:12-13).

We think that we can save ourselves by bringing our modern-day resources to bear on the many problems we face. In our arrogance, we refuse to see that it is not broken things that cause our problems. We are broken ourselves, and our greed, pride, deceit, and selfish desires are at the root of the chaos that runs rampant throughout our world. I find a lot of truth in the observation of the novelist Arthur Koestler. He wrote, "We are a mentally sick race, and as such, we are deaf to logical persuasion."[13] If this observation is not strong enough, we might also consider the gloomy assessment of H. G. Wells:

> The viruses and pestilential germs will resume their experiments in variation, and new blotches and infections will give scope for pious resignation and turn men's hearts again towards a better world beyond the stars. There will be a last crop of saints and devotees. Mankind, which began in a cave and behind a windbreak, will end in the disease-soaked ruins of a slum.[14]

It is not the physical and natural aspects of life that have sent shock waves through our modern daily lives. We have learned how to make continuous improvements to the age-old invention of the wheel. Even most of those who resist change eventually accept the benefits of mechanical and scientific advantages as they are introduced into the mainstream of our lifestyles. It is the rejection and violation of the moral guidance and ethical disciplines proffered by the teachings of the sacred Scriptures that have created the environment of *tohu wabohu* that we now see threatening the foundations of civilization in general and America in particular. Each attack on God and religion is followed by an increase in the moral and ethical poisoning of society. Quantitatively, the increases are exponential; qualitatively, they are more lethal than at any other time in our national history.

Our methods of management seem to fail us as we confront the societal *tohu wabohu* that is growing dramatically in speed and mass. We try to deal with crime in our world through threats of punishment. Our politicians promise "swift justice, "strict law enforcement," and publicly proclaim that they intend to "teach lawbreakers a lesson they won't forget." On the opposite side, another group advocates for "more compassion and milder punishments." Desperately, we look to our public school system for answers to our problems, but there is no consensus as to what to teach and how to teach it. Self-help literature encourages us to promote "enlightened self-interest" and to respect the rights and viewpoints of everyone, but we remain divided and polarized as a world community. One could argue that, in many ways, we are constructing a social, cultural, and racial balkanization in America. Our peace of mind and mental health are under siege to the point that pharmacology, legal and illegal, has become our preferred remedy for the stressful lifestyles we have embraced.

Our human foolishness is exposed in thinking that we can understand God better from our reasoning than we can by being obedient to His Word. In trying to justify our desires to the exclusion of God's commands, we make ourselves superior to God. The proper posture before God in every circumstance is that of the creature before its Creator. This does not mean that we may not prayerfully and humbly ask questions and express our fears and doubts to God. I remember some students in one of my seminary classes who would frequently say that they did not understand why God did some of the things that are recorded in the scriptures. The professor would calmly answer, "You can't understand that particular situation because you are not God." There are times when we wrestle with difficult questions and concerns, but it is never our place to disobey the Word of God. Dietrich Bonhoeffer explained it this way: "When man proceeds against the concrete Word of God, he is in the right from the first, he becomes God's master, he has left the path of obedience, he has withdrawn from God addressing him."[15] In other words, when a person assumes this posture, they have become the lord of God.

In the beginning, God provided everything that was good and necessary, but it was not good enough for the man and the woman. The first decision that they made was the decision to decide for themselves, and that is what removed them from the circle of their Creator's divine protection. Since then, that same demand for autonomy has echoed throughout every age. It has proved to be the most complex burden we carry throughout life.

Upon acquiring autonomy, humans immediately began to make ridiculous decisions. They decided that they should not appear in a state of nakedness. Why? Was it because of a new sense of guilt and/or shame? Did they suddenly need to protect themselves against the weather? They made clothing out of fig leaves, which were rough and prickly and certainly would irritate the skin. That decision was akin to one that would think it a good idea to make undergarments out of sandpaper. They began to accuse each other and the Creator for their actions. Rather than improve their lives, their new-found autonomy brought distress at every level of their existence; physical, psychological, emotional, and relational.

When God saw that they had frustrated the intent of His great gifts to them, He knew that they would continue to make decisions that would bring more grief and pain into their autonomous lives. No longer accepting their role as creatures, humans became independent operators as though they were gods. If they lived forever, their flawed decision-making capacity would result in eternal misery. Knowing both good and evil, it was certain that man was just as capable of making evil decisions as he might be of making good decisions. Under those circumstances, one can only imagine the perpetual mess that would accumulate if humans could live forever. To insulate humankind from the ceaseless compounding of this eternal misery, God mercifully declared: "Behold the man has become like one of us, knowing good and evil;

and now, lest he put forth his hand and take also of the tree of life, and eat, and live forever"— therefore the Lord God sent him forth from the garden of Eden to till the ground from which he was taken. He drove out the man; and at the east of the garden of Eden he placed the cherubim, and a flaming sword which turned every way, to guard the way to the tree of life (Gen. 3:22-24). With this, the potential for immortality in this world was terminated by God, and the certain sentence of death in this world became a reality: "You are dust, and to dust you shall return" (Gen. 3:19).

Things did not improve much with the merciful introduction of death. The evil impulses of human beings increased every day. With renewed vigor, man demonstrated the capacity to turn everything that he could make, think, or imagine into an instrument or act that produced some form of moral or physical depravity. Finally, there came a time when in essence, God said, "Enough! You have found a way to frustrate every good reason or purpose for which I created you." The biblical accusation says, The Lord saw that the wickedness of man was great in the earth, and that every imagination of the thoughts of his heart was only evil continually. And the Lord was sorry that he had made man on the earth, and it grieved him to his heart, So the Lord said, "I will blot out man whom I have created from the face of the ground, man and beast and creeping things and birds of the air, for I am sorry that I have made them" (Gen. 6:5-7).

Having the life-giving breath of God in his nostrils, humankind had become totally depraved. Wickedness and evil prevailed wherever humans inhabited the earth. The crown jewel of God's creation, humankind itself, had become a race of unrighteous and immoral rebels. His initial thought was to eradicate humankind from the face of the earth as though he had never existed. Mercifully, God did not carry His disappointment to its logical conclusion of total annihilation. A man named Noah "found favor in the eyes of the

Lord" (Gen. 6:8) and he was chosen to continue the life and vitality of the creation. Scripture tells us that "Noah was a righteous man; blameless in his generation; Noah walked with God" (Gen. 6:9).

We are not told the content or extent of Noah's righteousness. Whatever it may have been, it was enough to satisfy God's righteous anger. Rather than extending a victory to the chaos, the *tohu wabohu*, that He previously tamed and neutralized, God opted to give humankind another chance to populate the earth. By an act of God's grace, humankind lived to sin another day. Ironically, the salvation of Noah from the drowning waters of the flood found him, to the embarrassment of his surviving family, lying in a state of an alcoholic blackout, unclothed, and exposed. The biblical accounts of the history of humans from that time forward show a continuous record of disobedience and rebellion. We moderns continue to contribute to this long history of crime, war, depravity, and disregard for the Word of God. Maybe, as never before, we have assumed a position of absolute superiority that excludes us from any accountability to our Creator. The news that screams from the speakers and screens of our technological inventions exposes our sin and presents a living account of what it means to resist God. Karl Barth said, "There is no time in which man is not a transgressor and therefore guiltless before God."[16] Borrowing from Kant's moral philosophy, he says, "Man lives by an evil principle, with a bias towards evil, in the power of a radical evil which shows itself virulent and active in his life."[17]

Because we are sinners and are earth-bound to this decaying fallen world (Rom. 8:21), this world as we know it is doomed to give way to a new world, a re-creation conforming to the original intention of the Creator. We have managerial ownership of the earth and everything in it, and we have mismanaged it in every way imaginable. The environment continues to be depleted of its vitality, and every day, thousands of us who are made in God's image are killed by others who are also made in God's image. The created world that we now occupy is moving toward destruction, and we cannot stop it. Our protests and programs to "save the planet" will have minimal temporary success, if any at all. The Green New Deal notwithstanding, and as far as our survival is concerned, all human efforts will ultimately result in dead ends and blind alleys. Living creatures and the natural world itself will pass away. We do not think of the world as suffering the debilitating effects of old age, but the writer of 2 Esdras says, "For the weaker the world becomes through old age, the more shall evil be multiplied among its inhabitants" (2 Esd. 14:17). Perhaps Saint Paul had this in mind when he wrote: "For the creation waits with eager longing for the revealing of the Sons of God; For the creation was subjected to futility not of its own will but by the will of him who subjected it in hope.; because the creation itself will be set free from its bondage to decay and obtain the glorious liberty of the children of God. We know that the whole creation has been groaning in travail together until now; and not only the creation, but we ourselves, who have the first fruits of the Spirit, groan inwardly as we wait for adoption as sons, the redemption of our bodies" (Rom. 8:19-25).

Do we humans groan and suffer under the burdens of our flesh and the curse of our disobedience? Yes, and so does the entire creation! We suffer in a world that suffers with us. Created entirely for our benefit, the world was pulled into the vortex of fear and misery, which resulted from our desire for absolute autonomy. Now, the creation shares our expectation that God has created another world for us. An accurate translation of Paul's words is that "creation is waiting with anxious expectation." The phrase is descriptive of one who bends the neck forward and strains to see what is approaching from afar. We describe the experience as "craning the neck."

This anxious expectation is accompanied by a constant state of "groaning in travail." Being in travail involves more than a single person or thing. It refers to suffering and agonizing together. Heraclitus, a Greek philosopher, says: "After the winter's cold, the groaning earth gives birth in travail to what has been formed within her."[18] In a similar fashion, we might speak of travail as a woman giving birth to a child. There is pain and anguish, but that is of no importance after the child is delivered, cleansed, wrapped, and placed in her arms for the first time. The travail of many weeks of carrying it is lost in the fulfillment of her expectation of the new life.

Paul assures us that the travail of life on this side of the new creation is but a necessary prelude "as we wait for adoption as sons, the redemption of our bodies" (Rom. 8:23). He has a confident expectation that the devastation resulting from our disobedience will be overcome by the love of a gracious God. Martin Luther said that Paul "urges us to explore not what the creature is, but what it expects."[19] Our expectations should be heightened when we consider that scripture tells us that this world is passing away. Paul tells us that even though we are living in this world, we should not be quick to let the ways of the world have control over our lives. The transactions that take place in this world have no permanence about them. Why is this so? Because "the form of this world is passing away" (1 Cor. 7:31). The word he uses for "form" is the Greek word "schema." This word has the theatrical application of "playing a role."[20] It always refers to the outward form or structure of the world. That is, it is something that can be seen and experienced by our sensory perceptions, and not just something that we think about. On the stage, it is a role that someone plays in one situation, and then, through a change of costume or scenery, becomes a different role in another act. As Paul sees it, the role that this world was first appointed to play is played out; is passing away and giving place to another form (world) that God has re-created.

Peter and the writer of First John also recognized that this world was destined to pass away. Peter wrote, "But the Day of the Lord will come like a thief, and then the heavens will pass away with a loud noise, and the elements will be dissolved with fire, and the earth and the works that are upon it will be burned up" (2 Pet. 3:10). He uses the apocalyptic language of his day to express the inevitable mortality of all created things. Our first response to an apocalyptic scripture such as this is to become fixated on the spectacular phenomena; the raging fire, loud noises, earthquakes, etc. It is natural to be curious about the language, but it makes no difference whether we accept every mysterious detail of the passing away of all that we have known during our brief span of life. The surest thing we can know is that the earth and we, along with it, are passing away.

The author of First John says, "And the whole world passes away, and the light of it; but he who does the will of God abides forever" (1 John 2:17). Is the world literally passing away? Is it passing away in terms of the passing of many years of human history? Is it passing away in the literature of mythological stories and tales as passed on by ancient cultures and civilizations? Is it passing away in terms of the erosion of morality and righteousness of the peoples of the earth, and are these peoples the successive generations of "all the nations against whom the Lord was enraged" in Isaiah 34:2? Is the world literally passing away as life on the planet naturally passes away through aging, accidents, disease, famine, and other forms of pestilence? It matters little as to how we understand these questions, or whether we understand them at all. The world is under the same curse of death as are we. However it goes, whether in a fiery conflagration, with a big bang, a whimper, or a silent passing into nothingness, it is destined to give way to God's re-creation.

The message of Isaiah chapter 34 is unpleasant in that it is devoted to the devastation of the earth and the slaughter of human beings. And yet, beyond the violent lawlessness and human savagery, it points to the care of a merciful God for rebellious and disobedient people. While we receive this story through Israelite history, it is really the story of the love of the Creator for everything and every creature He created. It is not easy for us to understand this kind of love affair. We encounter names that we cannot pronounce, periods of time that we cannot calculate, human disasters that we cannot imagine, primitive customs and laws that seem to be without any rational purpose, and many other religious idiosyncrasies. As much as we like to read and study the scriptures, we are likely to find the nationalism and political intrigue of ancient Israel and its neighbors to be perplexing. Even so, we are quite certain that all of this is an important part of who we are as Christians. After all, Jesus said, "Think not that I have come to abolish the law and the prophets; I have come not to abolish them but to fulfill them" (Matt. 5:17).

This statement by Jesus provides the perfect (and necessary), transition from the devastation of chapter 34 to chapter 35, which will lead to the fulfillment of expectancy and the re-creation of the world, including God's provision for life after death in this first world. Isaiah says, "The wilderness and the dry land shall be glad, the desert shall rejoice and blossom" (Isa. 35:1), and "A Highway shall be there, and it shall be called the Holy Way" (Isa. 35:8). Later, we learn that a "voice cries out" to announce the details of the re-creation of the devastation described in chapter 34 (Isa. 40:1-5). Isaiah also prophesies that "The ransomed of the Lord shall return, and come to Zion with singing; everlasting joy shall be upon their heads; they shall obtain joy and gladness, and sorrow and sighing shall flee away" (Isa. 35:10). We should not let the "return to Zion" confuse us as to place and time. Israel did return to Jerusalem (Zion) following the captivity in Babylon. However, that return did not result in permanent and everlasting joy and gladness. When the Romans destroyed the temple and much of Jerusalem in 70 AD, Israel's fate was once again one of "sorrow and sighing." The Jewish population was scattered across the world, and almost nineteen hundred years passed before there was any appreciable return from that diasporic event.

As I have indicated before, the history of God's relationship with Israel, Jerusalem, and the temple is but a microcosmic picture of God's greater relationship with all of humanity. Otto Kaiser says that Isaiah is speaking of "the conversion of the nations to Yahweh at the end of time."[21] Jerusalem (Zion) has become a symbol of the projected reality that will exist as the re-created heaven and earth. This means that the Creator's love for His creation is not restricted by geography, nationalism, politics, race, color, language, or any other accidental attributes of human existence. Notwithstanding its occasions of victory, majesty, success, and the protection of Yahweh, Israel/Zion/Jerusalem fell under the same curse as all of creation. Blaise Pascal referred to the destruction of Jerusalem as, "Jerusalem, a type of the ruin of the world, forty years after the death of Jesus."[22] Indeed, Jerusalem became a symbol for all the nations, and it was never going to be repaired and permanently established in the post-Noah world. Because of its rebellion and disobedience, it was numbered among the powers that were hostile to God and were subject to annihilation along with the rest of creation.

Autonomously mismanaged by humans, it was obvious that humans were not capable of repairing the original creation. We cannot fix the mess we have made of the world and our own lives as we find them today. Of course, we will try to repair the mess because our pride (hubris) will not let us think that there is something we cannot do without the help of anyone but ourselves. We are clever, (as was the serpent in the Garden of Eden, Gen. 3:1), and we have been able to make and invent many things. However, the one thing that we cannot do is create something out of nothing *(ex nihilo)*. Only God can do that, and all our inventions and the products of our hands and minds are composed of elements and "things" that God has already made. New beginnings come from God alone. The new beginnings (re-creation) of Isaiah chapter 35 do not describe the environment of this interim period, this world, in which we now live. It describes the reality of our hope for what comes next. It is an expectancy that can be re-created only by God's saving and reclaiming action. Georg Fohrer says that the re-creation and new beginning will be a "repetition of the creation of the world, so that the end of the world corresponds to its beginning."[23]

The connection between the message of the prophet Isaiah and the appearance of John the Baptizer became the necessary transition event between what we call the Old and New Testaments. John confirmed that he was the one that Isaiah identified as "a voice crying in the wilderness" (Isa. 40:3). As such, he became an extension of the voice and message of Isaiah. Jesus said, "The law and the prophets were until John; since then, the good news of the kingdom of God is preached, and every one enters it violently" (Luke 16:16). With this announcement, a new period of salvation history began. Regarding this transition, Otto Kaiser says, "In the end, both the Old and New Testaments are in agreement in looking forward to the acceptance of all nations into the fellowship with God."[24]

In the person and ministry of Jesus Christ, we find the law and the prophets fulfilled. Jesus showed that God was not slavishly tied to the customs of the Jerusalem temple and the ancient traditions of religious leaders. The obvious focus of his ministry was that God meets people where they are. He denounced the concept of exclusivity by virtue of birth or any other form of inheritance. He affirmed that every person created by God is a legitimate member of the people of God.

Jesus validated John's authority and declared that John was greater than any of Israel's previous prophets. He said that John was to be recognized as the premiere voice of God's plan for the reconciliation and re-creation of the world (Matt. 11:11; Luke 7:28). All four of the Gospels put the words of Isaiah into John's mouth:

Matthew 3:3: "For this is he who was spoken of by the prophet Isaiah when he said, 'The voice of one crying in the wilderness: Prepare the way of the Lord, make his paths straight.'"

Mark 1:2-3: "As it is written in Isaiah the prophet, 'Behold, I send my messenger before thy face, who shall prepare the way; the voice of one crying in the wilderness: Prepare the way of the Lord, make his paths straight.'"

Luke 3:4: "As it is written in the book of the word of Isaiah the prophet, 'the voice of one crying in the wilderness, Prepare the way of the Lord, make his paths straight.'"

John 1:23: "He said, 'I am the voice of one crying in the wilderness, make straight the way of the Lord,' as the prophet Isaiah said."

From the above four accounts, I want to consider the common references to "the wilderness" and "the way." In the Old Testament, the wilderness is a hostile and uninhabitable place. Any human entering it faced the possibility of inescapable death. To designate the wilderness or desert, the Hebrew text of the Old Testament uses the word "midbar," and the Greek text (Septuagint) uses the word "ἔρημος/e-ray-mos." The New Testament texts, of course, use the Greek word. These two words are strict equivalents in their meanings. Robert Funk says that they "are virtually tied to each other."[25] They describe a desolate area that has been reduced again to a primeval state of chaos, and this could include God's action as "divine punishment for human transactions."[26] The biblical writers refer to "the great and terrible wilderness," and identify it as a place that provokes horror and paralyzing fear (Deut. 1:19, 8:15; Lam. 5:9; Num. 20:2-5, 21:5). The "midbar" is an awe-inspiring, howling wilderness (Deut. 32:10). The elements associated with it are the same as those described as *tohu wabohu* in the Genesis creation account.

Job refers to the wilderness as a place "where no man is" (Job 38:26). Jeremiah calls the wilderness "a land where none passes through and no man dwells" (Jer. 2:6). It appears that the only thing the wilderness has to offer is fear, hunger, thirst, pain, and death. Its inhabitants are beasts of prey, scavengers, snakes, scorpions, and mythical creatures (Isa. 13:21-22; 34:14). It exists in a state of primal chaos and seems to be possessed of a demonic character. The ancient Mesopotamians identified the wilderness as the area that leads to the nether world; the world of the dead; no-man's land.[27]

Death is certain without divine deliverance from the chaos, devastation, and violence of the wilderness. Talmon says, "The civilized person will come to an inescapable and bitter end unless God helps such a person who has strayed into the 'midbar' to find the right path, or unless a desert dweller familiar with the wilderness terrain leads him to food and water."[28] Both these necessities for survival are found in John and Jesus. John was familiar with the wilderness, and Jesus was the Son of God. John was an authority on how to survive in the wilderness, and Jesus had the power of his Father and the authority to apply it as "a very present help in time of trouble." At this point, we must understand that neither John nor Jesus was preaching about being saved from the dangers of a literal wilderness. Their concern was for a different kind of wilderness.

It is not likely that any of us will ever actually or intentionally enter the Judean desert. The image of the wilderness serves as a symbol for the condition of humankind and the world following expulsion from the Garden, and the subsequent imposition of death. It is a metaphor, a figure of speech for what we have become, and the mess we have made of our world and our homes because of disobedience and rebellion against our Creator. In a recent conversation with my seminary Hebrew teacher, a wise man now in his late eighties, I asked, "What can we do to fix the mess our nation and our world are in?" He replied, "Nothing. It is completely in God's hands now."

Fortunately, God has prepared another world that restores our lives as He intended them to be. Jesus Christ, the Messiah of Israel, the Son of God, Our Lord, and Savior, did not go into the wilderness to fight with wild beasts, serpents, scorpions, and the many physical threats of that desolate place. He went there to be alone with God, to seek communion with his Father before beginning the work that would fulfill the heavenly mission that lay before him. The Tempter, using the same strategy he used to deceive Adam and Eve, tried to sabotage his mission (Matt. 4:1-11; Mark 1:12-13; Luke 4:1-13). John Lightfoot says that the Evil One endeavors to ensnare Jesus through "the lust of the flesh, the lust of the eye, and the pride of life."[29] These temptations, of course, are the ones that we humans struggle with all our lives. The arena in which they occur is the "wilderness" with which both John and Jesus were concerned. It was within this wilderness context of multiple temptations that Jesus defeated the assault of Satan, The writer of Hebrews says, "For because he himself has suffered and been tempted, he is able to help those who are tempted" (Heb. 2:18); and, "For we have not a high priest who is unable to sympathize with our weakness, but one who in every respect has been tempted as we are, yet without sinning" (Heb. 4:15).

Temptations came to Jesus in many forms and from many directions, just as they come to us. If life becomes so hard that you think you cannot stand another setback or piece of bad news, I challenge you to listen to Mahalia Jackson sing, "Nobody knows the trouble I've seen; nobody knows but Jesus." In this wilderness of life, things may seem so chaotic and unmanageable (*tohu wabohu*), that we are certain that we are losing the battle. As a young Marine, I lived in a barracks at Camp Lejeune that had a sign above the entrance that said, "The Japanese said it would take a million men one hundred years to capture the island of Tarawa. It took the 2nd Marine Division 72 hours!" During that horrific battle, Colonel David Shupe was the commander on the ground. While the outcome of the battle was still in doubt, he sent a situation report saying, "Casualties, many; percentage of dead, not known; combat efficiency, we are winning." As I have thought about my journey in this wilderness of life, I vividly remember that I have been a casualty of temptation too many times to count. There have been times when I shared the lament of Jeremiah when he said, "Cursed be the day on which I was born! The day when my mother bore me, let it not be blessed!" (Jer. 20:14). There certainly have been times when my will to resist sin has been near to nothing. However, when I take the fight to the Lord in prayer, I can say, "I am winning!" The Holy Spirit reminds me that the leader whom I serve has said, "In the world you have tribulation; but be of good cheer, I have overcome the world" (John 14:33).

The Greek word translated as "tribulation" is "θλῖψις/thlipsis."[30] In its Johannine context, "tribulation" is a good translation because it refers specifically to the physical dangers the apostles and early disciples might face as they witnessed their faith. Today, we do not yet face those same tribulations. In today's context of Christian discipleship, other translations of this word seem to be more appropriate for our daily lives. The word "thlipsis" can be translated as "trouble, distress, evil, affliction, oppression, and harassment." In today's world, we can all identify with a warning of, "In the world, you will have trouble." The "trouble" associated with "thlipsis" can be experienced externally, as in tribulation; or internally, as in fear, anxiety, stress, and worry. Describing his ministry in Macedonia, Paul said, "Our bodies had no rest but we were afflicted at every turn—fighting without and fear within" (2 Cor. 7:5).

Have you ever thought about why stress, worry, anxiety, and trouble have such negative effects on our physical and emotional health? Where do these threats against our health and happiness have their origin? There is no shortage of self-help books on this subject, but my experience has been that they offer little or no help. In my more than fifty years of pastoral counseling, I have listened to scores of troubled and suffering people who could quote from books that had promised them relief and healing from their misery, all to no avail. This is not to suggest that medical science does not provide medical remedies and plausible scientific explanations for many of our illnesses. However, it is a fact that many people suffer from emotional and mental conditions for which there are no physical symptoms or discernible psychological causes for the problem. It is not unusual for a human being to be deeply troubled without knowing why they are troubled.

Heinrich Schlier, a theologian, and biblical scholar, says the power common to all "trouble/thlipsis" is the power of death at work in whatever trouble is at hand.[31] Sigmund Freud, an atheist, concluded that the total reality of human behavior is reflected in the mutual antagonism of the life and death instincts common to all humans. In the final analysis, Freud's work is long on description and short on the effective prescription of relief from the troubles that beset us. Many years ago, Job told us that "Man is born to trouble as the sparks fly upward" (Job 5:7). Throughout our lives, the possibility of anxiety and depression hang above us like some foreboding cloud. Christians know that we are not exempt from trouble. We also should know that we are called to understand our lives, with or without trouble, in terms of our faith. The certainty of trouble in this world must be accepted alongside the divine promise of Jesus Christ, "But be of good cheer, I have overcome the world."

Death, and our awareness of it as an imminent event, is the last and strongest trouble of life. The awareness that we must die is more terrible for some people than the event itself. The anxiety and depression over the fear of death become so overpowering that they rob life of all its fulfillment and enjoyment. It places us in the grip of that despair of life that Kierkegaard called "sickness in the self, the sickness unto death."[32] It drives us into the wilderness of doubt and misery and denies us the abundant life that Jesus came to give us (John 10:10).

To have life abundantly means that we enjoy a dimension of life that is not usually or routinely encountered within the human population. Even in the wilderness where troubles abound, the abundant life given by Jesus is sustained by grace, truth, hope, and love. When the world tries to tell us that a situation is in doubt, the power of faith tells us that "we are winning." There is a voice that accompanies us and tells us that there is a "way" in every wilderness that will lead us to a life that is worth living.

From what we know of the wilderness environment, we can conclude that any passage into it or through it was a dangerous venture. The rugged terrain would determine the way of the route. Dangerous obstacles would have to be avoided, and the way would necessarily become a maze of turns and detours. A prescribed way was not regularly maintained, and there was no guarantee that it would be passable at any given time. Wild and uncontrollable growth could quickly reclaim previously cleared areas. A traveler embarking on a wilderness road would have to fend for himself in dealing with any unexpected problem or danger. The only exception to consideration for maintenance was when a king or royal personage wanted to travel. When the word was passed among his subjects that he was traveling through a certain area, it was expected that they would make that stretch of road as safe as possible. Obstacles were removed, and the way was redirected to remove dangerous curves and provide safe passage. The way had to be clearly marked because losing the way and getting lost meant certain death.

John's voice was not the voice of a crossing guard or traffic police officer who was concerned about travel on an actual road. The Hebrew word for "way" almost never means a literal stretch of road.[33] It means "conduct, behavior, and the direction of an individual's life."[34] New Testament Greek uses the word "ὁδός/hoedos" for "way." It is used in the Gospel accounts in the same figurative sense as the Hebrew word.[35] John was calling Israel to repentance. The people knew that "to walk in the way of the Lord" required them to keep the commandments and obey the covenant. Israel had stepped off the known road, lost the way, and was on a course that could only end in destruction. The voice in the wilderness of their failures told them that the King was coming, and they would have to make a choice.

All our lives, we must make choices about managing the way that will rule and guide our lives. Poets and novelists have written extensively about the inescapable necessity of making choices in life. Robert Burns wrote,

Two roads diverged in a wood, and I—

I took the one less traveled by,

And that has made all the difference.[36]

Carl Sandburg says that he came from the wilderness of creation and that he is responsible for all the choices that compete within his daily existence:

> O, I got a zoo, I got a menagerie inside my ribs, under my bony head, under my red-valve heart—and I got something else: it is a man-child heart, a woman-child heart: it is a father and mother and lover: it came from God-Knows-Where: it is going to God-Knows-Where—For I am the keeper of the zoo: I say yes and no: I sing and kill and work: I am a pal of the world: I came from the wilderness.[37]

Using symbolism and figurative speech, T. S. Eliot describes and defines the spiritual apathy, corruption, and temptations that have made a wilderness and a wasteland of society. He calls the great cities of civilization "Falling towers." The habitat of humankind has been reduced to a "decayed hole among the mountains." The chapels are empty. Unused and abandoned, their windows are broken, and the doors swing back and forth on unstable hinges. Eliot saw a society that had forsaken the physical and spiritual reference points upon which civilized decisions are made.

Lacking purpose and guidance, confusion became the order of the day, and the preferred choice was the choice of not choosing:

What shall I do now? What shall I do?

I shall rush out as I am, and walk the street

With my hair down, so. What shall we do tomorrow?

What shall we ever do?[38]

In the novel, *The Great Gatsby,* F. Scott Fitzgerald's character, Daisy, asks this haunting question: "What'll we do with ourselves this afternoon and the day after that, and the next thirty years?"[39] Although she is an educated and wealthy socialite, she has no idea of how to invest herself in any kind of meaningful existence. She has been successful in accumulating wealth and knowledge, but her lack of wisdom leaves her unable to make choices that bring stability, contentment, and hope to her life. She represents those of every age who try everything only to find that nothing satisfies them. The emptiness of their lives confirms Saint Augustine's discovery that "Thou hast formed us for Thyself, and our hearts are restless till they find rest in Thee."[40] Augustine's experience tells us that the restlessness about who we are and where we are going can find no resolution outside of acknowledging that God created us for Himself. We find our rest, our coming to terms with life and death, by choosing to submit to having been chosen by God. We can look toward God for guidance, or we can turn our heads the other way. The look toward God provides the faith required to calm the restlessness we experience in this life. Paul Tillich called this "the courage to be." He said, "Accepting acceptance though being unacceptable is the basis for the courage of confidence."[41] That is the choice of faith that provides the courage to live and die and to know that eternal life, and re-creation is God's will for us.

Throughout our lives, we cannot escape being confronted by a wilderness, a wasteland, or an intersection of ways. Choices will not always be easy to make, but the process by which we choose and decide has been simplified. The clarion call, the God-inspired voice from John, tells us to prepare our hearts and minds to accept the truth that will make us free. The law and the prophets served the purpose of God in their day, but the arrival of Jesus signaled the far greater presence of God in human history. We no longer must search for the way that we should live. Jesus said, "I am the way, and the truth, and the life; no one comes to the Father but by me" (John 14:6). We do not need to memorize volumes of rules and regulations. There is no value in arguing about petty moralities that represent manufactured traditions. Concerning travel on this "way" through the twists and turns of life, Saint Augustine said:

> Walk by Him as Man, and thou comest to God. By Him thou goest, to him thou goest. Look not out for any way whereby to come to Him, besides Himself. For if He had not vouchsafed to be the Way, we should have always gone astray. He then became the Way whereby thou shouldst come; I do not say to thee, seek the Way. The Way itself hath come to thee, arise and walk.[42]

And what is the content of that "way" by which we should walk? Luke says that a lawyer, a leader of the Jewish people whose job was to deal with the administration and understanding of the law, tested Jesus with a question. He asked,

> Teacher, what shall I do to inherit eternal life? He said to him, "What is written in the law? How do you read?" And he answered, "You shall love the Lord your God with all your heart, and with all your soul, and with all your strength, and with all your mind;

and your neighbor as yourself." And he said to him, "You have answered right; do this, and you will live" (Luke 10:25-28).

There is no ambiguity in the formula for life in this world, and for entry into eternal life. Jesus has removed all the curves and obstacles—love the Lord God and the neighbor as you love yourself. The way through every wilderness and wasteland, and the turn to take at every intersection has been made clear. The way itself has come to us. Arise and walk!

Death and the question of life after death have been concerns for all religions and civilizations of the world. Primitive humans buried their dead or disposed of them in some way that reflected a special concern for their remains. In some cases, they were buried or entombed with objects such as coins, tools, or weapons that they might need on their unknown journey beyond this life. The literature about death and eternal life is immense and represents many theories and conclusions regarding what happens to humans when we die. John Hick, a theologian who has written extensively on the subject, refers to death as a "tantalizing mystery."[43]

The lawyer in Luke's Gospel was curious about eternal life, and Jesus' answer confirmed that eternal life is a reality. He said, "Do this and you will live." Isaiah 35 provides a hint of what the biblical concept of eternal life promises. It provides a transition from the devastation of people, places, and things in chapter 34. The heartbreak and disappointment of the physical, emotional, and spiritual trauma give way to a sense of expectancy and culminate in God's victory and humankind's reinstatement through the process of re-creation. As I previously stated, repair of the mess we have made of things is beyond probability. God tells us, "Remember not the former things, nor consider the things of old. Behold, I am doing a new thing; now it springs forth, do you not perceive it? I will make a way in the wilderness and rivers in the desert" (Isa. 43:18-19).

Because God can do anything He wants to do, we cannot accurately say that repair is beyond possibility. However, God has made His intention known by telling us that He is "doing a new thing." The writer's word literally means "to be or become new." For Isaiah, this action does not describe a mere renewal, transformation, or re-working of something already in existence. C. R. North says, "On the contrary, God brings from nowhere a thing that previously had not existed at all."[44] God's promise is re-creation, an act that will be "brand new." Comparing this "new thing" to the Exodus from Egypt has its limitations. In that wilderness experience, God provided miracles of food and water to sustain the Israelites, but He did not make any physical changes to the wilderness itself. Likewise, when Israel returned from Babylonian captivity, God did not change, transform, or re-create any of the natural aspects of the Judean desert and the surrounding areas.

Isaiah chapter 35 paints a picture of a radical, supernatural re-creation of humans, beasts, and the earth itself. This comes as no surprise since we know that resurrection and creation of something out of nothing are stupendous, fantastic concepts that are truly unbelievable from the perspective of our limited human faculties. To counter these limitations, Isaiah uses hyperbolic symbolism to give us some idea of what it will be like to have eternal life in the second world of God's re-creation (4 Ezra/2 Esd. 7:50). Disabled people are not simply healed; they are endowed with strength and given perfect vision and hearing. Restored mobility of people with disabilities goes beyond walking and running; they can "leap like a deer." The wilderness becomes a place where streams flow, the burning infertile sand turns into pools and lakes of water, and flowers bloom throughout the land. The redeemed can walk safely within this new thing/re-creation, and the ransomed know everlasting joy and gladness.

Who are the redeemed and the ransomed? In reference to Israelite history, they are the people of the Exodus and those who returned from the Babylonian exile. However, they are also those for whom God is doing a new thing. The concepts of ransom and redemption have a significant place in Christian theology. The idea of a ransom is scattered throughout the entire New Testament (Mark 10:45; 1 Pet. 1:18-19; 2 Pet. 2:1; 1 Cor. 7:23; Gal. 3:13; Rev. 5:9). Many of the early Fathers of the Church embraced what came to be known as the "ransom theory of atonement." For instance, Origin (AD 185 to AD 254) was a proponent of the theory that we were slaves to sin, and Jesus purchased /ransomed us at the cost of his own life. Origin said, "Now it was the devil who was holding us, to whom we had been dragged off by our sins. Therefore, he demanded the blood of Christ as the price for us."[45] The idea of paying a ransom to the devil is so unsavory and controversial that it has lost most of its appeal to today's theologians. Nevertheless, the word itself, in its primary meaning of "redeemed, set free, rescued," is appropriate when used to identify those re-created for eternal life in the re-created world.[46]

Friedrich Büchsel unequivocally states,"The redeemed are all men and not just the Jews."[47] The prophets rarely look back and are always looking to the future. For Isaiah, the facts of Israel's history are just that—history, indeed. With the appearance of John and the ministry of Jesus, Israel's national claim on the exclusive favor of Yahweh was denationalized, and God's salvation was extended to all the nations of His creation. Therefore, the identity of the redeemed and the ransomed are not limited to events from Israel's history. This means that we can lift Isaiah chapter 35 from the confines of the past and place it squarely in the middle of life in our own modern setting, where it speaks to the same human dreams and wishes as it did so many years ago.

The re-creation described in Isaiah chapter 35 is not the world of nature that was known before or after the Exodus from Egypt or the return from the Babylonian exile. The peace and perfection depicted in Isaiah 35 could only be known in a world other than the one that was known then or that we know now. Isaiah chapter 35 is the writer's attempt to describe something that is indescribable. Paul also recognized the impossibility of describing God's miracle of re-creation. He said, "What no eye has seen, nor ear heard, nor the heart of man conceived, what God has prepared for those who love him, God has revealed to us through the Spirit" (1 Cor. 2:9-10).

The indescribable, inconceivable world of Isaiah chapter 35 is the world we enter when we die. The Spirit creates in us an awareness that we cannot otherwise apprehend or understand. Awareness such as this is not something that is learned through education and cannot be proved as one might prove a scientific theory. According to Paul, it is an awareness that comes to us as a gift from God: "Now we have received not the spirit of the world, but the spirit which is from God, that we might understand the gifts bestowed on us by God" (1 Cor. 2:12). The confirming activity of the Spirit is also seen in Peter's testimony that Jesus is "the Christ, the Son of the living God." Jesus' response was, "Flesh and blood has not revealed this to you, but my Father who is in heaven" (Matt. 16:17).

This revealed awareness, which is itself indescribable, is the result of a spiritual experience. Rudolf Otto explains this succinctly and with unapologetic clarity. He invites readers of his book, *The Idea of the Holy*, to direct their minds to a moment of deeply felt religious experience. He then says,

> Whoever cannot do this, whoever knows no such moments in his experience, is requested to read no farther; for it is not easy to discuss questions of religious psychology with one who can recollect the emotions of his adolescence, the discomforts of indigestion, or, say, social feelings, but cannot recall any intrinsically religious feelings.[48]

Otto is telling the reader that spiritual awareness cannot be taught. It is awakened in us when we receive it from the Spirit of God. I would caution all of us to not be judgmental about the method the Spirit uses to awaken that awareness in any one of us. To argue about that "process" would be to forget that the sovereign God can and does do anything He wants to do. He told Moses, "I am who I am," also translated as, "I will be what I will be" (Exod. 3:14). And if any of us, in some state of smug satisfaction, thinks that we have a monopoly on how the Spirit is imparted to individuals, we should remember that God said, "For my thoughts are not your thoughts, neither are my ways your ways" (Isa. 55:8). How do we explain that it was Saul, a Pharisee, and persecutor of the church that God called into service on the Damascus Road? It was hatred, not love, that motivated Saul to begin his reign of terror against the Christian community. If we had a vote on the matter, is it likely that we would have elected him to become the great Apostle to the Gentiles? His election can only be explained by accepting the fact that God's ways are not our ways. Also, we have the words of Jesus to the inquisitive Nicodemus, "The wind blows where it wills, and you hear the sound of it, but you do not know whence it comes or whither it goes; so it is with everyone who is born of the Spirit" (John 3:8).

As one who has experienced an awareness of the Spirit, I would speak of my expectations as I contemplate my own death. My expectation is that at the moment of my death, I will receive a re-created body to live in God's second, re-created world. I do not deny that there are many beliefs about whether there is life after death. I will not argue with anyone regarding their personal attitudes and beliefs. My testimony is an unapologetic plagiarism of Paul's testimony to Timothy: "I am not ashamed, for I know whom I have believed, and I am sure that he is able to guard until that day what has been entrusted to me" (2 Tim. 1:12). I believe this because I believe the Word of God. Jesus is the risen Christ. He died so that I might know, as did He, the glorious power of leaving this body of flesh and putting on the unimaginable body of victory that God has prepared for me. I do not know anything about the mechanics and capabilities of the body that awaits me. It is a feature of the "new thing" that God has done and is doing. My faith and the Word of God tell me that the Creator was pleased with what He made at the beginning: "And God saw everything that he had made, and behold, it was very good" (Gen. 1:31). If the beginning was very good, this only heightens the expectancy for our majestic re-creation in a new and wonderful way.

Some might say that my expectation is nothing more than wishful thinking, or just a dream detached from the way things are in the real world. But as Rudolf Otto explained, this is to be expected from anyone who has not experienced a sense of religious awareness. This brings to mind the required participation in one of those group seminars that were much in vogue during my first year of seminary. Students were required to meet in groups and share milestones of the spiritual journey that brought them to seminary for preparation to become ministers. As an introvert, I did not feel comfortable sharing, as this form of self-disclosure was called, personal aspects of my life. However, as people began to speak, the group leader, a professor of pastoral counseling, insisted that participation was required. He emphasized that no one should be concerned about contradictions or judgmental attitudes. Finally, I acquiesced and told the group about something that happened while I was praying for a sick child. I said that I was confident that it was a spiritual experience. The professor immediately took exception and wanted to argue about what I had said. He concluded that during the prayer, I did not breathe normally, thereby denying my brain the oxygen it needed to function adequately. He concluded that my auditory, verbal, and cognitive capabilities became diminished and initiated a bio-neurological dysfunction that I mistakenly identified as a spiritual experience. I considered his analysis to be absurd. I compared him to the Pharisees, who objected to the healing of a blind man. They insisted that Jesus was a sinner and was not from God. The man replied, "Whether he is a sinner, I do not know; one thing I know, that though I was blind, now I see" (John 8:13-33).

I do not know if we will ever fully understand or admit that there is a "knowing" that does not come from formal education. Our Creator has put something in our lives that facilitates a mode of "knowing" that precedes the efforts of structured, formal education. William Faulkner recognizes this "knowing" phenomenon and describes it as "Memory believes before knowing remembers. Believes longer than recollects, longer than knowing even wonders."[49]

Commensurate with our consciousness of life, we are also aware of a sense of eternity. *The Book of Ecclesiastes* tells us that "God has set eternity in the hearts of men" (Eccles. 3:11 NIV). William Wordsworth expresses it this way: "But trailing clouds of glory do we come, from God who is our home."[50] It is a function of human nature that we yearn for something beyond the allotted days of our earthly lives. This is so because the God who made us also put into our hearts and minds a sense of eternity, and a yearning for reunion with those who have gone before us. This yearning is powerful and inextinguishable because God made it so.

We have found solutions and answers to many of our yearnings related to life on this side of eternity. However, we frequently experience yearnings that we soon realize are unreasonable or unattainable. Eventually, we dismiss them and move on to other earthly concerns, but we find it impossible to dismiss the yearning for life after this life. The history of humans, past and present, reveals our constant concern regarding death and the question of what happens to us when we die. More than three thousand years ago, the Egyptians mummified dead bodies in accordance with their belief that the dead would need their bodies for life in the next world. In this century, five thousand years later, when Ted Williams of baseball fame died, he was decapitated, and his head and body were frozen and stored in liquid nitrogen. The intent of this procedure was to preserve his body until science and medicine found a way to restore him to life.

The phrase, "hope springs eternal in the human breast," is not just a fantasy born in the mind of a poet.[51] Everything that we are—birth, youth, education, love of family, vocation, appreciation of all that we perceive through sensory perceptions—yearns and cries out for eternity. When disappointments, failures, dangers, confusions, and uncertainties visit us, the awareness of eternity that God has set in our hearts remains a powerful force. When we are challenged and tormented by life's many frustrations, we can say with the certainty of Paul, "I consider that the sufferings of this present time are not worth comparing with the glory that is to be revealed to us" (Rom. 8:18).

Much of our confusion about what happens when we die lies in our misunderstanding of time and eternity. We quite naturally, but mistakenly, assume that eternity is an extension of time as we know it. The sense of eternity that God put in our hearts refers to something that is timeless and transcends the concept of time as we understand it in this life. God has given us both time and eternity, and while we are alive in this world, we are caught in the tension between the "now" and the "not yet." It is this tension, this "not knowing," that introduces the mystery of death and life after death. Because we "cannot find out what God has done from the beginning to the end" (Eccles. 3:11), we often subscribe to a lifestyle of living life as if there is no tomorrow.

Living in this "time between the times" can be difficult and perplexing, but it would be unbearable without the faith that comes through Jesus Christ. Karl Barth said,

> Like a strange, dark land, God's time lies over against our own time. It is an undiscovered new continent that we cannot enter, excepting that we have left behind us our time, man's time, the time in which our whole terrestrial life runs its course. This time is no more time, it is eternity. And what else shall we say of eternity that we know nothing about it save this: that in everything it differs wholly from that which we know here and now.[52]

The "undiscovered new continent" of which Barth speaks is the re-created world that is described in Isaiah chapter 35. The medium of death is the exit from our time and the entrance into God's eternity. Our physical bodies are not compatible with whatever is involved in living in eternity. We often use the term "shelf-life" in reference to the goods and products we use in our daily lives. We say that an item has a shelf-life of a certain number of years, beyond which time it is no longer safe or capable of performing as it was made to perform. As we age, we become aware of the fact that our bodies also have a shelf-life. The Psalmist says that our shelf-life is seventy years, and maybe eighty years if we are exceptionally strong (Ps. 90:10). Notwithstanding this scriptural truth, in vain, we try to escape the inevitable. Television commercials offer us products to improve our memory, remove our wrinkles, relieve all aches and pains, and repair our bones, nerves, and muscles. Each of these miraculous remedies is offered at the unbelievably low price of nineteen dollars and ninety-five cents per month.

Finally, the scalpels of cosmetic surgeons promise to restore the smooth, teenage beauty of yesteryear to our aging, furrowed facial flesh. The ghastly results of many of these surgeries remind me of a line from Walt Whitman: "Sauntering the pavement or riding the country by-road, lo, such faces!"[53] Sooner or later, a glance into a mirror or an exhausting trip up a flight of stairs drives home the indisputable truth that we cannot stop the ravages of time in this life. Our own personal existence is living and dying proof that flesh and blood become sick and diseased, and they age and decay. These bodies with which we become so familiar, and yes, so in love with, ultimately wear out their welcome in this life, and become unfit for life in God's re-creation.

The writer of Second Enoch offers this unflattering history of human bodies:

> And just as every person has as his nature the darkness of this present life, so also, he has his conception and birth and departure from this life. In the hours in which he was conceived, in that hour also he is born, and in that also he departs.[54]

Second Enoch was probably written between AD 1 and AD 50. It pre-dates our New Testament Gospels and was quite likely known to some of the writers of the canonized books of the New Testament, including Saint Paul. Notwithstanding its early date, it was not included in the New Testament canon because it has no overt references to Jesus as the Christ and is assumed to be the work of a non-Christian Jew. Nevertheless, it is held in high esteem and quoted by many of the early Church Fathers. I appreciate the way the writer sums up our experience of life in this world. Succinctly stated, we are conceived, and at our conception, we are born, (i.e., begin to live). At the moment we begin to live, we also begin to die. Throughout it all, we are confronted with mysteries about which we can know little or nothing at all, and we have as our nature the darkness of this present life.

This is a "bare bones" resume of life—conceived, born, lived, and died. A popular performer sang a song that cataloged events in the life of a girl. The girl remembered watching the whole world go up in flames as her house burned down. She remembered her daddy taking her to the circus, where she saw animals, clowns, and trapeze artists. It was the greatest show on earth. She fell in love with the most wonderful boy in the world, but he went away and broke her heart. She thought she would die, but she did not. When someone suggested that she might be suicidal, she denied it because she thought that even that act would be just another disappointment. Speaking of death, the girl said,

When that final moment comes and I'm

Breathing my last breath, I'll be saying

Is that all there is, is that all there is? to myself

If that's all there is my friends, then let's keep dancing

Let's break out the booze, and have a ball

If that's all there is.[55]

We are familiar with the saying, "old as Methuselah." The Bible says, "All the days of Methuselah were nine hundred and sixty-nine years and he died" (Gen. 5:22). That is it—nothing more—just that he lived a long time and he died. During his nine-and-one-half centuries of life, I wonder if he ever thought, "Is that all there is?"

Paul answers this question for those who believe in Christ: "If for this life only we have hoped in Christ, we are of all men most to be pitied" (1 Cor. 15:19). If Christ's victory does not reach beyond this life, how can He be Lord and Savior? If He has not opened for us the door that provides entry into re-created life beyond the grave, how can hope be anything more than a pipe-dream fantasy? How can faith be anything more than the language of delusion? If we are hopers in this life and have nothing beyond this earthly existence, we should be pitied as one would pity a person who is mentally ill and out of touch with reality. Paul emphatically assures us that these "if" questions have no standing against the power of God in Jesus Christ. The resurrection event has neutralized and reversed the power of sin and death. Paul contradicts all objections with his forceful declaration, "But now, in fact, Christ has been raised from the dead" (1 Cor. 15:20). The "now" to which he refers is not a temporary period; it is a "once and for all time" victory. Isaiah prophesied that God would "swallow up death forever" (Isa. 25:8). Paul declared that prophesy to be fulfilled in Jesus Christ. He said, "Death is swallowed up in victory" (1 Cor. 15:54). The word for "swallowed up" is a participle whose tense reflects a single action that has been totally completed, leaving nothing to be done. It is an act that has achieved a victory that is absolute and everlasting. Death has been swallowed up, gulped down, and annihilated.[56] The good news is that we have a shared future in the once-for-all-time victory. Paul said, "Thanks be to God, who gives us the victory through our Lord Jesus Christ" (1 Cor. 15:57). God gives us the victory and will continue to give us the victory without any possibility of death ever again having any power to reign over us.

The victory has its starting point in the resurrection of Jesus Christ. If you do not, or cannot accept this, you should not expect to understand the life and ministry of Jesus of Nazareth. The entire New Testament is written from the belief that God raised Jesus from the dead. Admittedly, this has been a topic of argument and disbelief since Paul's preaching in the synagogues of Athens and his debates with the Greek philosophers on the hill of the Areopagus (Acts 17:16-24). Resurrection will always be incomprehensible to those who do not believe that through Jesus Christ, the eternal Word of God has broken into time as we know it. In every generation, there will always be those who deem themselves to be too educated, too modern, and too sophisticated to believe something that is, by every objective and empirical measurement, too unbelievable to accept. Paul's word to modern deniers is the same as it was to non-believers two thousand years ago: "For the word of the cross is folly to those who are perishing, but to us who are being saved, it is the power of God. For it is written, 'I will destroy the wisdom of the wise, and the cleverness of the clever I will thwart" (1 Cor. 1:18-19).

Beginning with a few "uneducated and common men" (Acts 4:13), the influence of the life, death, and resurrection of Jesus has swept across the earth and changed the lives of untold millions of people. How is it possible that a message acknowledged to be unbelievable and incomprehensible by leading philosophers and theologians of every age, continues to win the hearts and souls of people all around the world? The story of Blaise Pascal, the brilliant mathematician, physicist, and religious philosopher, shines a light on this phenomenon. Pascal describes his conversion event as happening "from about half past ten at night to about half an hour after midnight while searching the seventeenth chapter of John's Gospel."[57] He was thirty-one years old at the time and was recognized as an expert in the disciplines of mathematics, physics, and philosophy. He referred to the year of his conversion as, "Year of Grace 1654."[58] Pascal recorded his experience on a piece of parchment and sewed it into his coat. Thereafter, he sewed it into every coat he bought and always carried it with him. After his death, the parchment was removed from his coat. It revealed that his testimony consisted of more than twenty phrases, including the following:

> God of Abraham, God of Isaac, God of Jacob, not of philosophers and scholars; he can only be found by the ways that have been taught in the Gospels; total submission to Jesus Christ and to my director; I will not neglect your Word.[59]

This man of great learning discovered that God has a way of imparting truth to us in ways other than through a scientific method and constructions of theories and hypotheses. Pascal said, "The heart has its reasons which reason knows not of; we know this in innumerable ways."[60] In saying this, he was not endorsing irrational behavior. He was confirming that God can communicate with us and impact our behavior and thought processes in ways that transcend the rational, cognitive mediums that we normally use to communicate and interact with others and with our activities in the world. Pascal's observation is an example of Jesus' words to Peter: "But flesh and blood has not revealed this to you, but my Father who is in heaven" (Matt.16:17).

It is unlikely that anyone would be able to read all the books written about resurrection and the possibility of life after death in one lifetime. Both secular and religious disciplines express countless opinions and conclusions on the subject. I embrace the position of F. F. Bruce, a distinguished Professor of Biblical Criticism and Exegesis and a recognized scholar on the life and theology of Saint Paul. In his book, *Paul: Apostle of the Heart Set*

Free, he said that the essential question about death is, "What happens at death?"[61] After all our preaching, testifying, praying, witnessing, evangelizing, and singing, the question is, (to put it in the words of a fast-food motto), "Where's the beef?" From the Christian standpoint, it is impossible to arrive at an acceptable answer without considering what we have received from Paul and Jesus. Both tell us something about what happens at the moment of death. We find answers in Paul's epistles, and in Jesus' response to the dying criminal in Luke 23:43.

We know that Paul responded to Thessalonians regarding the disposition of those among them who had already died. In his first letter to the Corinthians, he addressed the arguments of those who claimed that there was no resurrection of the dead. These letters were written between the years of A.D. 49 to AD 54. In his second letter to the Corinthians (A.D. 55 to AD 56), Paul speaks more specifically about the issue of what happens at the moment of death. Is there a waiting interval of unconsciousness before a "second-coming" (Parousia)? Do the dead remain in a comatose, disembodied state until all the fantastic, cataclysmic events described in most apocalyptic literature have occurred, e.g., *Revelation of John*? Since writing to the Thessalonians and his first letter to the Corinthians, Paul had faced some dangerous situations and at least one close call with death (2 Cor. 1:8-10). He became acutely aware of the probability that he would die or be killed before the anticipated return of the Lord. Confronted with this, he turned his attention to the interim state of the dead in Christ.

We can be sure that as a Jew, Paul would not entertain any thought of being a naked spirit without a body. His confident testimony is, "For we know that if the earthly tent we live in is destroyed, we have a building from God, a house not made with hands, eternal in the heavens" (2 Cor. 5:1). Obviously while living in this "earthly tent," we are not "at home with the Lord" (vs. 8). There is no waiting interval, and Paul is confident that we receive a re-created spiritual body that is identifiable. He maintains the reality of his claim that "if there is a physical body, there is also a spiritual body" (1 Cor. 15:44). He wants his readers to know that death does not destroy the continuance of our personal identity. Contrary to Gnostic teachings, the spirit of man is not incorporated or reabsorbed and lost in a universal "melting pot" of some divine spiritual entity. The particularity of each body is maintained in the composition of a spiritual body. I find it as abhorrent as would Paul to believe that my God-given individuality would be destroyed only to be replaced by absorption into a group "spiritual carpool" existence where all become one and the same.

As Paul considered what happens after death, he could recall his Damascus Road experience. On that occasion, Christ appeared to him in His resurrection body (1 Cor. 15:8). A change had occurred, but there was no doubt that the Jesus who appeared to him was the same Jesus who died on the cross. We cannot comprehend the details of this occurrence. All we can do through human reasoning is acknowledge that it pleased God to raise Jesus from the dead and present Him to Paul with both a spiritual and personal identity. In some incomprehensible way, at the moment of our death, God will give us a "house not made with hands." We can be certain of this because "God has given us the Spirit as a guarantee" (2 Cor. 5:5). The word Paul uses for guarantee is a word used regularly in the ancient Greek business world for earnest money.[62] In our world of real estate, we speak of earnest money as being the amount required as a good-faith demonstration of our serious contractual intent to buy a piece of property. It is the first installment that secures a legal claim on what is being purchased. The deposit of earnest money makes the contract valid. It obliges the contracting party to make further payments and guarantees that the balance of the contract will be paid.

The Holy Spirit is the guarantee, the pledge that God would raise Jesus from the dead and, through Him, would also give us eternal life. Do you believe that there is such a dynamic as eternal life? Do you desire a reunion with your departed loved ones? Do you wonder what it will be like to see for the first time the new creation that Isaiah described in chapter 35? Can you even begin to imagine the ecstasy, amazement, and joy of being in the presence of the One who said, "Because I live, you will live also" (John 14:18)? Why do I ask you to think about these questions? If you have ever thought about these things, you were only able to do so because the Holy Spirit awakened the power of eternal hope in your life. Therefore, you have become a stakeholder in the dynamics of Christ's resurrection. You have the guarantee that you need not look at life and ask, "Is that all there is?" The earnest money has done its job, and the contract has been paid in full.

At the moment of death, nothing remains outstanding. The debt that we have accrued through sin is satisfied. However, praise be to God, that is not the end of the matter! We lose this life in the flesh only to receive eternal life. Paul says, "For the wages of sin is death, but the free gift of God is eternal life in Christ Jesus our Lord" (Rom. 6:23). I reject any claim or argument that there is an interval of sleep or rest between death and being with Christ. At the moment that sin calls for its wages to be paid, the sound of the trumpet of life drowns out the noise of death. It heralds the re-creation of our lives as God intended them to be. Instantly, we learn that the death we feared is the event whereby we enter eternal life with Christ.[63] Walt Whitman's poem, *The Mystic Trumpeter,* seeks to capture some of the victorious pageantry of this event. It appears that he was looking beyond the brokenness and death of this world, and the vulnerable fragility of our flesh and blood. He expresses his poetic vision for many of the characteristics of the re-creation scenes that we find in Isaiah chapter 35. Sensing that the trumpet call of eternity is very real, he wrote,

> Hark, some wild trumpeter, some strange musician,
>
> Hovering unseen in air, vibrates capricious tunes tonight,
>
> I hear the trumpeter, listening alert I catch thy notes.
>
> Now trumpeter for thy close,
>
> Vouchsafe a higher strain than any yet,
>
> O glad exulting culminating song!
>
> A vigor more than earth is in thy notes,
>
> Marches of victory—man disenthral'd—the conqueror at last,
>
> Hymns to the universal God from universal man—all joy!
>
> A reborn race appears—a perfect world; all joy!
>
> Women and men in wisdom innocence and health—all joy!
>
> Riotous laughing, bacchinals filled with joy![64]

The imagery and symbolism of the trumpet announce the advent of God's activity. Saint Clement of Alexandria (AD 153 to AD 217) said, "The trumpet of Christ is His Gospel. He hath blown it and we have heard."[65] And what have we heard? We have heard the Good News that we shall not perish but will have eternal life (John: 3:16). Saint Clement says that the Good News "abides with us till our last breath and is to the whole and perfect spirit of the soul the kind attendant on our ascent to heaven."[66] The symbolic trumpet call began the moment that we first heard the Gospel of Jesus Christ. It cannot be silenced, subdued, or in any way confined or limited in its announcement of new life and re-creation. When the Pharisees asked Jesus to command His disciples to cease and desist from praising God, He said: "I tell you, if these were silent, the very stones would cry out" (Luke 19:40). The sound of the trumpet that calls us to new life reaches across all ages and all places. God's heavenly orchestra is not a one-trumpet band. It is a philharmonic ensemble of voices and instruments that is composed of a multitude too large to number (Rev. 7:9-12). In the moment of our death, not only will we hear that great anthem of victory and re-creation; but we will also join it and live eternally with our Lord and all those who have gone before us.

If Paul's words are convincing, Jesus' words are indisputable. He speaks plainly and clearly to the crucified criminal dying beside him. The criminal's request needs no literary autopsy or search for some esoteric intent or interpretation. A dying man whose remaining hours or minutes of life were beyond his control said, "Jesus, remember me when you come into your kingdom" (Luke 23:42). He did not call him master, rabbi, teacher, or Lord. He called him by the name given to him by an angel who said, "You shall call his name Jesus, for he will save his people from their sins" (Matt. 1:21). How strangely appropriate it is, that a crucified sinner should appeal to the name which means "Jehovah is salvation." We should be careful that we do not miss the miracle that occurs between two condemned humans on a stinking hill of death. A guilty criminal asked Jesus (Jehovah is salvation) to remember him, and Jesus graciously assured him that his request would be granted. The truth of that miracle has been recognized and proclaimed by untold millions in the words of the famous and beloved hymn, *Rock of Ages:*

Nothing in my hand I bring;
Simply to thy cross I cling;

Naked, come to Thee for dress;

Helpless, look to Thee for grace;

Foul, I to the fountain fly:

Wash me, Savior, or I die![67]

Our world family of sinning humanity should never forget that Jesus was and is a friend of sinners. He did not and does not hesitate to accept anyone, under any circumstances, who asks to follow Him. An irredeemably lost criminal, while nailed to a cross, received forgiveness for his sins and eternal life with the Lord.

The miracle becomes more revealing when we apply it to the question, "What happens when we die?" Jesus told the dying criminal, "Truly, I say to you, today you will be with me in Paradise." There have been many questions about Jesus' response. Is Paradise the ultimate heaven, or is it a place of being nearer to God but not fully in His presence? Is it the Garden of Eden where Adam and Eve first communicated with God? Is it the third heaven that Paul said he was carried up to during a mystical experience (2 Cor. 12:2-4)? We need not speculate about answers to any of these questions. The one certainty that we can count on is that at the moment of our death, we will be with Jesus. There is no ambiguity in the exchange between these two crucified men. The criminal said, "When you come, remember me." Jesus did not reply, "When I come, I will remember you." He said, "Today, you will be with me in Paradise." Fulfillment of the request was not postponed until sometime in the future. It was not dependent upon some apocalyptic and dramatic event. Jesus declared the fulfillment of the request as happening today. In the context of Jesus' response, the word today has no theological significance. This means that it has the standard usage of "referring to the span of human activity embracing a day up to evening."[68] In this context, anything said to be happening today, is happening in the present time. It literally means, "This very day Jesus will have the forgiven criminal with him in a place of security and bliss."[69]

The details of that place of security and bliss and the absolute composition of that re-created life are beyond our earthly ability to comprehend. What we know for sure is that Christ is with us in this life, and we will be with Him when this life ends. This assurance is the power and comfort that sustains us when we stand at the grave of a loved one, and when we contemplate our own passing from this life to the re-created life that awaits us. When the thought of death threatens us with fear and grief, it is comforting to think about the Spirit-inspired testimony of Saint Ambrose (AD 340 to AD 397), Bishop of Milan, and one of the first four Doctors (teachers) of the Catholic Church. He said,

> Death then, is a passage for all. One must pass through bravely; it is a passage from corruption to incorruption, from mortality to immortality, from troubles to tranquility. Let not the word death trouble you, but let the benefits of a good passage delight you.... What more can we add about the good of death than the fact it is death that redeemed the world?[70]

Prayer:

Lord, help us to accept Your marvelous grace and open our lives to the fantastic power of Your love. When fear knocks at our door and death interrupts our lives, help us to lift our eyes to the inviting face of Jesus Christ into whose presence we will be welcomed at the very moment of our death. Amen.

CHAPTER TWO
THE NECESSARY PRELUDE

<u>Ecclesiastes 3:1-2</u>: *¹For everything there is a season, and a time for every matter under heaven: ²A time to be born and a time to die.*

I am thankful that I was prompted to think about what happened to me at a graveside service on a cold day in January. My response to that event led me to look critically into the Word of God as recorded in Isaiah chapters 34 and 35. In the spirit of Saint Paul's advice, I was prompted to think about three things: 1) the potential devastation of my faith, 2) an assessment of my expectations, and 3) the re-creation of my understanding of what happens to us at the moment of death. My reflections taught me some things that I had not learned during my formal theological and ministerial education. Standing with three suffering people, I learned that I had been going through the motions of a ritual that was deemed appropriate by a denominational church committee. I saw that the comfort it provided was colder than the winter day on which it was offered.

Those words, "Be strong, fear not! Behold, your God will come and save you," had no meaningful connection to a wife/mother, and two little heart-broken girls. They knew that they were not going to be saved by God or anyone else in that freezing, perplexing, unfathomable moment of time. The weight of their loss made no allowance for any claim that death was the necessary prelude for eternal life. They were entitled to their grief. Neither I nor any other ordained merchant of empty platitudes had the authority to deny them their need to grieve. The grief of those remaining and living in the uncertainty and turmoil of the loss of a loved one is natural and to be expected. In fact, it is more than a need; it is a necessary component for coping with what has been, what now is, and a future yet to be lived.

The words of Ecclesiastes, the Preacher, are set in concrete. For each of us, there was a time to be born and there is a time that we must die. As a result of our disobedience, the end of our earthly existence is irrevocably established. Scripture tells us that "it is appointed for man to die once" (Heb. 9:27). Death is a fixed, non-negotiable event. Given this, it naturally follows that "for as long as people die, there can be no end to mourning and suffering upon earth."[1] The message for those who grieve in the presence of death should not be one that suggests that God will save them from the grief and pain associated with their loss. The cathartic power of prayer, time, and the comfort of the Holy Spirit will sufficiently assuage the suffering caused by grief. Ultimately, we find resolution in Saint Paul's assurance that "we do not grieve as others do who have no hope" (1 Thess. 4:13). The parting words at any graveside experience should be aimed at grasping the Gospel truth that death is the necessary prelude to re-created life in a re-created world with the victorious, resurrected Son of God.

While prayer, time, and the Holy Spirit will eventually soften the pain of grief, we should not be surprised if grief should visit us again. Long after the death of a loved one, we may find that grief re-emerges and becomes a painful memory of our loss. This does not mean that our faith is weak. It is a reminder that we are still living in a body that remains subject to the vulnerabilities of our flesh and blood existence. Perhaps you have experienced a moment like the one that I experienced. I was suddenly and unexpectedly overcome by emotion, accompanied by tears and a memory of my Dad. My wife came into my office and found me sobbing uncontrollably. When she recognized the song that was playing on the radio, she patted me on the back and left the room. She did not say a word, but she knew what was happening. The song was one that my Dad sang every day. I could see him there at the water basin, shaving brush in hand and that big, heavy razor scraping away at his beard as he sang,

There is a song in my heart today,

Something I never had;

Jesus has taken my sins away,

Oh, say, but I'm glad.

Oh, say, but I'm glad, I'm glad,

Oh, say, but I'm glad.

Jesus has come, and my cup's overrun;

Oh, say, but I'm glad.[2]

I was overcome by his memory. My heart and soul ached, and I missed him so much. Momentarily, I thought, "He is dead, and I will never see him again; never again hear his voice." Remembering the words of Jesus' strong rebuke, I said, "Get behind me, Satan! You are a hindrance to me; for you are not on the side of God, but of men" (Matt. 16:23; Mark 8:33). Immediately, memory, expectation, resurrection, and re-creation blended to bring my faith to the surface, and I knew that even though I was sad, my Dad was alive with our Savior. My momentary grief was real, but it was overpowered by the promise of God that there would be a reunion beyond my own death.

Now, when I think about these things, I am not threatened by death. Being created in God's image, I am created for eternity. How dear to God are we human beings? After creating everything else, we became the culminating factor of His great creation. James Weldon Johnson tells the story in beautiful poetry. He writes,

With his head in his hands,

God thought and thought,

Till he thought: I'll make me a man!

Up from the bed of the river

God scooped the clay;

And by the bank of the river

He kneeled him down;

And there the great God Almighty

Who lit the sun and fixed it in the sky.

Who flung the stars to the most far corners of the night,

Who rounded the earth in the middle of his hand;

This Great God,

Like a mammy bending over her baby,

Kneeled down in the dust

Toiling over a lump of clay

Till he shaped it in his own image;

Then into it he blew the breath of life,

And man became a living soul. Amen. Amen.[3]

In the first stage of his creation, our first human parent was the product that an artificer of mud could have made. To begin with, he was nothing more than a lifeless work of art. He could have been formed by a gifted sculptor, an expert potterer, or designed by a clever architect. In any case, he would have been nothing more than a brilliant but lifeless museum piece. But then "God blew into him the breath of life and he became a living soul." We belong to God, not just in the here and now, but also in the full glory of His re-creation. When God blew into us the breath of His own eternal and immortal life, He destined us to be deathless also. Saint Augustine said that God "created us for Himself."[4] We are like God, and He will not let us pass into nothingness. According to the Psalmist, "It is God that made us and we are his" (Ps. 100:13). He has crowned us with glory and honor. He has extended to us the great dignity of being superior to everything else in His creation (Ps. 8).

Does it make any sense that God, who is said to be love Himself, would abandon to eternal nothingness the very creatures that He created for Himself? The Old Testament tells us that God became so disgusted with the behavior of humans that He decided to "blot out man" and "make an end of all flesh" (Gen. 6). He was sorry that He had ever made such creatures as humans, but He could not bring Himself to destroy humanity. He threatened to destroy Israel when they worshiped idols and sinned against their covenantal pledges. When His love proved to be greater than His anger, He showed mercy and spared them (Exod. 32; Deut. 9).

The New Testament shows us a God who has a consuming passion for our salvation. When Jesus was born, humans were no less guilty of rebellion against God than were those citizens of Old Testament times. Nevertheless, God showed His supreme love by permitting the death of His only Son for our salvation. The miracle of the dying Jesus speaking with a dying criminal as both hung nailed to a cross, tells us in graphic detail all that we need to know about God's love for us. First, regarding sin, God's love is unconditional. Unable to use his hands or feet, the criminal could not do anything or go anywhere. He did the only thing that he could do, and according to Saint Paul, that was enough: "If you confess with your lips that Jesus is Lord and believe in your heart that God has raised him from the dead, you will be saved. For man believes with his heart and so is justified, and he confesses with his lips and so is saved" (Rom. 10:9-10). Second, regarding death, God's love is also unconditional. The criminal knew he would die soon, and he asked only to be remembered. Jesus responded with a greater gift than mere remembrance. He freely gave him eternal life to begin that very day at the moment of his death.

The victory that Jesus Christ achieved for us is not easy to accept. This is so because, in our natural way of thinking, we really do believe that "if something sounds too good to be true, it probably is too good to be true." This phrase represents just one of the many defensive cautions we live by in a social and commercial environment that specializes in deceit and greed, and continuously proves the claim that "there is a sucker born every minute." We are constantly reminded that our identities may be stolen, and our personal lives compromised in many ways. Unsurprisingly, our natural way of thinking and our addiction to consumerism almost always comes in conflict with the Gospel concepts of faith, hope, and love. When so many of us are encouraged by societal forces to work hard to be first in everything we do, how can we understand the scripture that says, "But many that are first will be last, and the last first" (Matt. 19:30; Mark 10:31; Luke 13:30)?

In a nation where we call each other names, destroy property, and inflict personal harm on each other in so many ways, how do we respond to a religious admonition that says, "Love your enemies, do good to those that hate you, bless those who curse you, pray for those who abuse you" (Luke 6:27-28; Matt. 5:44)? When we try so hard to be what we want others to think that we are; when we make ourselves and others miserable under the claim that we are "trying to find ourselves," how is it possible to believe Jesus when He says, "He who finds his life will lose it, and he who loses his life for my sake will find it" (Matt. 10:39; Mark 8:34; Luke 9:24; John 12:25)?

It is no small thing to believe in the continuation of life beyond the moment of death. This is why I speak of the deadliness of death. Life as we know it carries the certainty that all of us must die. This knowledge is accompanied by a fear of death that we never completely overcome. Faith is our challenge to that fear. We recognize that the language of faith is more powerful than fear and reaches beyond the language and knowledge of this natural world. The deadliness of death confronts us, but it does not overcome us. Paul includes us in his assessment of what can happen in this life of flesh and blood. He says, "We are afflicted in every way, but not crushed; perplexed, but not driven to despair; persecuted, but not forsaken; struck down, but not destroyed" (2 Cor. 4:8-9). For anyone having faith in Christ, each negative event does not bring disaster, but is countered with a positive outcome: afflicted/not crushed; perplexed/not in despair; struck down/not destroyed.

Our faith calls us to be dependent on God. Living by this faith can seem foolish when measured against the wisdom of the world and the cleverness of our ways of thinking. However, we should not forget that human logic and the reasoning of humankind are frequently found to be unreliable. Lying has become an integral part of our culture. When the claims of this world challenge any part of the Word of God, we can confidently believe that God is trustworthy and dependable. His promises will prevail, and His intentions will be fulfilled. Our watchword must always be, "Let God be true, but every man a liar" (Rom. 3:4).

The world tells us that "seeing is believing." Paul tells us that this commonly accepted aphorism is unacceptable when applied to faith and the activity of the Holy Spirit in our lives. He said, "We look not to the things that are seen but to the things that are unseen; for the things that are seen are temporary, but the things that are unseen are eternal" (2nd Cor. 4:18). The account of Jacob and his dream at Bethel is an example of actual realities that are assumed to be unseen, and yet they impact our lives in fantastic ways (Gen. 28). Jacob was tired and uncertain about the journey that stretched before him. His last interaction with his father had been one of deceit and dishonesty. He was running from a brother who had vowed to kill him. Using a rock for a pillow, he went to sleep in a strange and barren place. I would guess that he did not expect anything would change during his uncomfortable overnight ordeal. He had not considered that the unseen God of his fathers was at work. When he awoke, he said, "Surely the Lord is in this place, and I did not know it. And he was afraid and said, how awesome is this place! This is none other than the house of God, and this is the gate of heaven" (Gen. 28:17-18).

Like Jacob, sometimes we cannot see beyond certain circumstances, and we feel lost, frightened, and hopeless. This certainly can be most true when we are dying ourselves or dying with someone we love. The fact that we, or he, or she, or they were once alive means little or nothing when standing by a grave on the coldest day of the year. The past tense record of a few paragraphs on the obituary page of a local newspaper announces that a certain departed life amounted to a few abbreviated incidents over a certain period. Tomorrow's obituaries will report similar abbreviated incidents about others who departed this life. Obituaries, memorials, eulogies, tributes, testimonies, and the so-called "celebration of life" services are some of those temporary things that are seen. They do not bring us the abiding and victorious comfort that satisfies our yearning for eternity. Who among us is satisfied with ultimately being defined as just another past-tense incident in the adventure of life? We want to believe that God cannot and will not let any of us be nothing more than a brief incident in the architecture of His great creation.

Jacob's experience, in one way or another, is also our experience. Rabbi J. H. Hertz, a former Chief Rabbi of the British Empire, says, "The message to Jacob is the message to all men in all ages."[5] The essence of that message is that God is not far removed from us in our everyday lives. God is not without knowledge and concern for what we do and what happens to us on earth. In his dream, Jacob saw angels going up and down a ladder between heaven and earth. Such action by God's angels is invisible to the natural eye, but we can be sure that this communication is always taking place between heaven and earth.[6] During the dream, the Lord gave Jacob this assurance: "Behold, I am with you and will keep you wherever you go, and will bring you back to this land" (Gen. 28:15). What Jacob saw with his eyes and understood with his natural way of thinking were things and thoughts to which he had become accustomed. They suggested nothing beyond what he routinely took for granted. However, we learned that his life was changed by the unseen and unexpected intervention of God. He said, "Surely the Lord is in this place: and I did not know it" (Gen. 28:16). He marked that place with the stone next to which he had laid his head. He poured oil on it, anointing it as a holy place and staining it so that it would be recognizable when he returned to that land.

The site of Jacob's dream was named Bethel, "the house of God," and it became an important place in the history and theology of Israel. When thinking about Jacob's experience, perhaps we should all ask ourselves if we have experienced a "Bethel" moment in our lives. I personally believe in angels, and I believe that communication is constantly being transmitted between Heaven and Earth. Through the presence and action of the Holy Spirit, we sometimes become aware of an unseen message from eternity itself. It can come to us through any medium that God chooses to use. A song, a friend, a stranger, the beauty of an object, a particular smell or taste; all of these, and countless others, can be used by God to speak to us in a way that only we can understand. We should not dismiss the scripture that tells us that the possibility always exists that we might be interacting with an angel without knowing it (Heb. 13:2).

It is a wonderful gift from God to be able to say of any experience or any moment of time that "Surely the Lord is in this place and I did not know it." Such a moment becomes a reference point for strengthening us for those future times when danger, doubt, failure, loneliness, forsakenness, and Satan and all his demons assault us and challenge our faith. We may be driven back by the tumults of life, but we cannot be driven beyond that reference point that assures us that "the Lord is in this place," even if we do not know it. Cherish your "Bethel" experience, and do not let it slip from your memory. Thank God for it. It will be an anchor that holds in any storm. Do not yield to any force or influence that tells you that your "Bethel" experience is not real. Do not argue with anyone who insists you are irrational or unreasonable. No one else needs to understand your "Bethel" experience. It was given to you, in whatever form it came, by the God who knows you as no one else knows you. It was given to you, and you do not need to try to explain it to anyone under any circumstances. Another person's doubt or denial does not diminish the truth and reality of what God has given to you. God's promise to Jacob was, "I am with you; I will keep you wherever you go, and I will bring you back to this land." In the glory of God's grace, God is with us as we live our earthly lives, and when we die, He will re-create us for life in a re-created world.

Prayer:

Lord, in the natural course of living, we do not question the truth that some things must happen before other things can happen. We accept these necessary preludes because they lead the way to fulfilling our wishes and wants in the world. Waiting for nine months brings us the joy of a newborn child. Working to get licenses, diplomas, and certificates brings us the benefits of employment, professional satisfaction, and the ability to live productive lives. Lord, we confess that we do not understand the mysteries of death. In our anxiety and unknowing, help us to see it as a necessary prelude to eternal life. Remind us that Your Word teaches us that a seed does not come to life unless it dies and becomes more than a seed. Help us to see that our dying is the necessary prelude to our entry into eternal life with You. Amen

CHAPTER THREE
THE PROCESS OF BECOMING

1 John 3:2: *Beloved, we are God's children now; it does not yet appear what we shall be but we know when he appears we shall be like him, for we shall see him as he is.*

Saint Paul tells us that death is the last enemy, and that it will be destroyed (1 Cor. 15:26). Our faith accepts this victorious declaration, but we still experience occasions of fear and anxiety as we contemplate this abyss that separates time and eternity. Inevitably, the time comes when someone we love is no longer with us, or we become aware that we will soon leave our familiar circle of friends and loved ones. It is not a lack of faith that brings the shadow of fear under those circumstances. Our Lord understands and compassionately reminds us, as He reminded His sleeping disciples in the Garden of Gethsemane, "The Spirit indeed is willing, but the flesh is weak" (Matt. 26:41).

In moments of distress, it is difficult to understand that death is not an ending to God's creative activity. It is a necessary singular event in the process of continuing His re-creation. God remains in an active, creative relationship with all of us. Paul says, "If we live, we live to the Lord, and if we die, we die to the Lord; so then, whether we live or whether we die, we are the Lord's" (Rom. 14:8). Life and death do not stand alone as individual, self-contained, autonomous entities. Neither of them has any identity or purpose except as they stand in relationship to each other and to God. Knowledge of this truth encourages me to restructure my vocabulary regarding the business of living and dying.

It has been said that the moment we begin to live in this world is also the moment we begin to die. I prefer to believe that birth is followed by a process of becoming. Perhaps we should not think of ourselves as living or dying. We are always in process, always "becoming." This is true from the moment we are conceived in our mother's womb, and it is true as the last breath leaves our mortal body. For a healthy perspective on life, it is important to think about these two things: 1) On my best or worst day, I am not just living, I am "becoming," and 2) On the day that I am pronounced dead, I am not dying, I am "becoming." Jesus said, "My Father is working still, and I am working" (John 5:17). And what is more, we have been empowered to participate in this creative work: "To all who received him, who believed in his name, he gave power to become children of God" (John 1:12).

The writer of 1st John uses the concept of "becoming" when speaking about life now and life after death. He says, "Beloved, we are God's children now; it does not yet appear what we shall be, but we know that when he appears we shall be like him, for we shall see him as he is" (1 John 3:2). We know what we are in the "now," that is, in the current state of our existence. We are God's children; however, Peter tells us that there was a time when we did not know who we were. He says, "Once you were no people but now you are God's people; once you had not received mercy, but now you have received mercy" (1 Pet. 2:10). Once we were separated, alienated, strangers, hopeless and without God" (Ephesians 2:12). Through

Christ we became God's children, and the process of "becoming" continues to work in our lives. First John tells us that there is a "not yet" that remains to be completed in our growth toward eternal life. It has "not yet" been revealed as to what we shall finally be, but we know that what we are "becoming" will at least resemble the beauty and glory of our resurrected Lord Jesus Christ. We are "becoming" in the sense that we are being metamorphosed.[1] We typically know metamorphosis as that process of "becoming" that occurs during the life stages of a butterfly: egg, caterpillar, chrysalis, and finally a beautiful butterfly.

Through Jesus Christ, this process of "becoming" has already begun in our lives as we progress from the "now" to the "not yet." Paul says, "We are all being changed (metamorphosed) into his likeness from one degree of glory to another" (2 Cor. 3:18). The present tense of the Greek verb tells us that the change is happening now and that it will continue to happen. The use of the passive voice tells us that we are receiving the change and that we are not playing any part in making it happen. The indicative mood of the verb tells us that the verse is a statement of fact that is happening and needs no further verification. The progression of our "becoming" can be compared to the rising of the sun as it shines "brighter and brighter until full day" (Prov. 4:18). It begins as a faint glow on the horizon and continues until it becomes high noon, and the fullness of the day is established. Charles Wesley's hymn presents a marvelous and uplifting description of our metamorphosis, our "becoming,"

> Finish then thy new creation,
>
> Pure and spotless let us be;
>
> Let us see thy great salvation,
>
> Perfectly restored in thee;

Changed from glory into glory,

Till in heaven we take our place,

Till we cast our crowns before Thee,

Lost in wonder, love, and praise.[2]

During the period of being changed, i.e., of "becoming," the writer of First John encourages us to "abide in Jesus." (1 John 2:27). He says that we should abide in him so that we will not be ashamed of him at his coming" (1 John 2:28). The word translated as coming is "Parousia." It is formed and based on another word that has the sense and general meaning of "to be present" and "to have come."[3] Historically, this is the most often understood meaning of the word. To use the word "parousia" as the basis of a doctrine of the "second-coming of Christ in glory to judge the world" requires that the general and regularly established meaning of the word be dismissed in favor of an abstract, special technical use of the word.[4] The problem here is that the "coming" assumes a period of time in the distant future. The cumulative time of that distant future would now be sometime beyond two thousand years that have already elapsed. Over time, the concept of the "second-coming" has been accepted as something that will happen but has not yet happened. It has been systematized as absolutely referring to a future second coming of Christ in glory to judge the world.

While you will not hear this from your local preacher, and certainly not from the "pay for pray and play" television preachers, there are some difficulties in accepting the phrase, "second-coming," in its special technical sense. First, we cannot be certain that Jesus made a clear distinction between His resurrection and His "coming." Who is to say that His resurrection was not His "coming?" Oepke says, "How far Jesus Himself made this distinction, how far he even made a clear distinction between His resurrection and His 'parousia,' it is no longer possible to say with certainty.[5] Second, the term "second-coming" does not occur in the New Testament, nor does it occur in Christian literature until the second century. Justin Martyr (AD 110-165) is the first to use the term.[6] What seems to be missing in the easy acceptance of a "second-coming" located in a distant future is the possibility that Jesus equated His resurrection with His return. C. K. Barrett maintains that "Jesus did not distinguish between his resurrection and Parousia."[7] Wilhelm Michaelis, a distinguished professor of theology, unequivocally writes: "The resurrection does not compete with the Parousia; it is the Parousia."[8]

Suppose we recognize that in its general usage, the word "Parousia" never has the sense of "second coming," and that there exists the strong probability that Jesus equated His resurrection with His return. In that case, we can realistically conclude that the concept of His "Parousia" should be seen in the general sense of "being present," and "to have come." The intent of John's use of Parousia should be understood as "at his presence, and not as "at his coming" (1 John 2:28). John is speaking of an arrival that has already occurred, and not a second-coming. In His resurrection, Christ has already satisfied any notion of an abstract, special, technical translation of the word "Parousia." In fact, in its fullness, the resurrection of Jesus is a transition to an abiding presence which is eternal. Because it embraces all times, it cannot be split into blocks of time and so-called future dispensations.

Jesus spoke about what was happening in the lifetime of His disciples and those who heard Him. When questioned about the Kingdom of God, He spoke of a present reality, saying, "Behold, the kingdom of God is in the midst of you" (Luke 17:21, plural, present tense). It is important to remember what the disciples and others witnessed during the earthly life of Jesus. They witnessed His birth, baptism, ministry, and the Transfiguration (metamorphosis), where Moses and Elijah appeared and talked with Jesus. They saw Him challenge the religious and political powers of their time, and they witnessed His trial, crucifixion, burial, and resurrection. They traveled with Him on the Emmaus Road. They went fishing with Him. They ate breakfast with Him. He stood among them in a locked room and showed them His pierced hands and feet. As they stood in wonder and awe, He invited them to touch Him. I see all these events as representing components of the Parousia, as the word was typically used in the secular vocabulary of the ancient near east through the second century AD. For example, a king's arrival or visit to a city or region was officially announced by the expression, "Behold, thy king cometh unto thee." Adolf Diessemann points out that it would be "incorrect to translate Parousia (comes) as 'coming again.'"[9] At each of the above events involving Jesus, it could be said, "Behold, thy king cometh unto thee." Everything about Him involved kingship and royalty. His claim was a real claim to be king. His entire life was an appeal for a throne to occupy. That throne, however, was not to be found in the royal courts of this world. The throne He wanted was in the hearts of all the peoples of His Father's created world. In everything He did or said, it was appropriate to announce Him not only as a king, but present as the King of Kings and Lord of Lords. It should not come as a surprise that the One who is present, will reveal Himself to us when He receives us at the moment of our death.

    I will not argue with those who insist upon waiting for a final existential, cataclysmic, apocalyptic, sensational event of cosmic proportions under the misinterpreted concept of a second coming. After all, how else could we satisfy and explain our neurotic versions of why our lives and our world are the way they are if we did not have those among us who associated everything they did not like or understand as a symbol of the mark of the beast? Who would we have to expose the evil of bar codes, scanners, smart televisions, and, more recently, the claim that the Covid-19 vaccine is an evil product? Why would we want to forfeit the privilege of being informed that some new global super-villain is the anti-Christ? And no calendar would be complete without recording the date of some modern prophet's prediction for the end of the world.

The early Christians used the word "parousia" for the coming of Jesus in all His manifestations.[10] The person and work of Jesus, as revealed in the New Testament, is multi-faceted and full of movement. It goes well beyond a singular fantastic belief that is based entirely on a block of time when the world will be judged, and people will suddenly be snatched away into the vastness of outer space. This smacks too much of the activity of the Disney creation of the Buzz Lightyear character and his motto of "To infinity and beyond!" Some refer to this singular event as the "rapture." The word "rapture" cannot be found in the New Testament. It made its way into certain religious vocabularies less than two hundred years ago. The Latin Vulgate (late fourth century AD), translated the Greek word "ἁρπάζω/harpazo" as "rapio, rapior." Both have the various meanings of "to snatch, steal, tear something away quickly, to catch up, and other meanings involving force, plundering, and robbery."[11]

The English word "rapture" is a neologism invented in the nineteenth century to refer to the "snatching away of the church into the clouds and into glory." When I served at a church in Chattanooga, Tennessee, I routinely saw bumper stickers that said, "In case of the Rapture, this car will be driverless." The stickers also sported a picture of a "Casper the Ghost" figure floating upwards into the clouds while driverless vehicles crashed into each other and created scenes of death, destruction, and chaos. Other bumper stickers depicted pilots floating away from airplanes in flight while passengers panicked in fear as planes crashed into each other and fell thousands of feet to the earth.

Psychiatric journals are full of reports about the results of "rapture anxiety" on the mental health of those who have been subjected to this variety of fundamentalist religions. Barbara Rosser, a theologian who does not mince words when writing about the so-called rapture, begins her book with this statement: "The rapture is a racket. Whether prescribing a violent script for Israel or survivalism in the United States, this theology distorts God's vision for the world."[12] Throughout the book, she names the many television preachers who make millions of dollars by preaching a doomsday message based on fear and misinterpretation of the Bible. Indeed, it is more than reasonable to label the so-called rapture as a racket. Other reputable scholars have written versions of the same exposures as those highlighted by Rosser.[13]

How does the concept of the rapture figure into what happens to us when we die? The simple answer is, "It doesn't." "Second-coming, rapture dispensationalism makes its claims on the basis and status of Palestinian geography and middle-eastern politics. Any such doctrine is unbelievably short-sighted. The catalyst for the consummation of God's love is reduced to an act of war and a "snatching away" of the humans He created. How much sense does it make to say, "For God so loved the world that He commanded a battle so vicious that the blood at the battle site was five feet deep, and flowed like a river for two-hundred miles?" Revelation 14:20 says, "Blood up to the horse's bridle for a distance of sixteen hundred stadia." Can you imagine a corridor from Washington, DC, to New York City flowing with blood at a depth of five feet or more? Dispensationalism, with its flawed concepts of a second-coming and rapture, is not only a racket and a trap, but also responsible for creating a form of religious fear that leads to spiritual confusion and mental illness.

The author of *The Rapture Trap* asks, "What do the numbers 200, 380, 838, 1000, 1260, 1533, 1844, 1914, and 1988 all have in common?" He answers, "They are all dates when large groups of people thought the world would come to an end. And that is to name only a few."[14] Dispensationalists like to construct elaborate color charts, endless timelines, and graphs to track the progression of scriptures they have mistakenly interpreted. They seem to always be busy correcting their predictions based on new geographic or political evidence. The one thing they must be very thankful for is the Microsoft Power Point Program. False predictions, wrong timelines, and outdated graphs can be explained, updated, and given new future hope with just a few keystrokes.

The only timeline that should matter is the one spoken of by the Psalmist. He wrote, "Teach us to number our days that we may get a heart of wisdom" (Ps. 90:12). He recognized the need for each of us to undertake a serious self-examination. This admonition is repeated in the title of this book, *Think About These Things*. God can and will teach us to get a wise heart if we will yield to Him. To learn to "number our days" is to recognize that we really do have a shelf life. The American poet, Alan Seeger, knew the score when it came to numbering our days. He wrote, "I have a rendezvous with death…. And I, to my pledged word am true, I shall not fail that rendezvous."[15] Rather than engage in the foolishness of trying to calculate exact times, a wise heart will encourage us to realize the certainty of our rendezvous with death, and at the same time to join the Psalmist in singing, "This is the day which the Lord has made; let us rejoice and be glad in it" (Ps. 118:24). A wise heart will teach us to live each day remembering that we have an unknown and limited number of days like the one we currently enjoy. It will teach us to accept ourselves and to take the gift of life seriously. A wise heart will teach us that we should live each day with joy and gratitude for the grace and forgiveness that we have in Jesus Christ, our Lord. A wise heart will teach us that neither our faith, our religion, our government, our cleverness, our goodness, our morality, our health, nor any assumption of safety is any guarantee of protection against our rendezvous with death. It can come at any moment, suddenly, unexpectedly, and in the blink of an eye.

Regardless of the details surrounding the event of death, the wise heart will have learned to have faith in the One who is Lord over both life, death, and life beyond death. In Him, our existence knows no end. Karl Barth says, "The One whom Jesus reveals as the Father is known absolutely on the death of man, at the end of his existence."[16] Whether it be sudden or prolonged, in that moment when life departs our body of flesh and blood, Jesus Christ becomes visibly present and "receives us to himself so that where he is we may be also" (John 14:3). In the end, whatever name anyone applies to this great event, there is no doubt about the eternal life that awaits us when this life is over. A life under the influence of a wise heart will enable us to live every passing day in the knowledge that we are moving toward the resurrected Christ who has come to us and will be visibly present with us at the moment of our death.

Prayer:

Lord, increase our faith. Turn our heads away from those who like to play the guessing games of eternal life. Free us from the foolishness of timelines and schemes that try to predict what you are going to do and when you are going to do it. Teach us to embrace Your presence in every moment of time. Make us joyful people in the knowledge that You have already come to us and that You are with us on this sacred journey to that place You have prepared for us.

Baptize us with the peace that passes understanding and lead us through the valley of the shadow of death and into the unspeakable glory of Your presence. Amen.

CHAPTER FOUR
WHY DOES GOD CARE?

Deuteronomy 32:9-10: *⁹ For the Lord's portion is his people, Jacob his allotted heritage.*

¹⁰ He found him in a desert land, and in the howling waste of the wilderness; he encircled him, he cared for him, he kept him as the apple of his eye.

Zechariah 2:8: *For he who touches you touches the apple of his eye.*

Why does God care whether or not we continue to live after we die? This is not a new question. Our curiosity is but an echo of the question asked by the Psalmist hundreds of years ago. He asked, "What is man that thou art mindful of him, and the son of man that thou dost care for him" (Ps. 8:4)? I would argue that the most obvious reason for His care is one of ownership. The Psalmist said, "Know that the Lord is God! It is he that made us and we are his; We are his people and the sheep of his pasture" (Ps. 100:1-3). The modern protest slogan of "My body, my choice," is one example of a repeat of the prideful demand for absolute autonomy that resulted in expulsion from the Garden of Eden. It is the kind of thinking that either consciously or unconsciously excludes God from the dynamics of living. When we make something for ourselves, we are entitled to claim ownership of what we have made. We know that we have not made ourselves. By virtue of His power to create, God must also be recognized as the owner of what He has created. We owe our existence entirely to God. Paul reminded the Athenians that every living person has his/her beginning in the first man, Adam. Every breath that every human takes belongs to God. His ownership is total, and "in him we live and move and have our being" (Acts 17:24-28).

God's ownership of His creation comes with a self-imposed reciprocal responsibility. He acknowledges this responsibility by affirming that "we are his people and the sheep of his pasture." The love and care He has for us can best be understood in the relationship of a shepherd to his sheep. In Matthew and Luke, Jesus gives us the Parable of the Lost Sheep (Matt. 18:12-14; Luke 15:3-7). In John's Gospel, He tells us that He is the Good Shepherd (John 10:1-27). The life of a shepherd was dangerous. It required constant attention to the flock. A Scottish minister and biblical scholar who traveled frequently and extensively in the rugged terrain of Judea, took notice of the love and courage the shepherd had for his flock. He wrote,

> On some high moor, across which at night the hyenas howl, when you meet him, sleepless, far-sighted, weather-beaten, armed, leaning on his staff, and looking out over his scattered sheep, every one of them on his heart, you understood why the shepherd of Judea sprang to the front in his people's history; why they gave his name to their king, and made him the symbol of Providence; why Christ took him as the type of self-sacrifice.[1]

Jesus tells us that one sheep was just as noticeable to the shepherd as the entire flock. He knew each of them and would go in search of any that might be missing. He protected them from wild beasts and robbers. In the evening, as they passed into the sheepfold, he examined each one and treated any injuries that might have been suffered during the day.

The shepherd claimed ownership in the obvious sense that the sheep were bought and paid for. They were an economic commodity that guaranteed his physical livelihood. However, economics was not the only factor at work in the shepherd's commitment to his flock. Since they produced wool year after year, his sheep were not slaughtered in wholesale lots and sold at a public market. Their primary value was in the wool that was gathered at each shearing and was used for clothing and other essential products. Many of the same sheep remained with the shepherd for many years. He came to recognize them individually, giving them identifying names in the same way we name our pets. The care and protection that he gave them extended beyond economic concerns. They were his sheep and the sheep of his pasture. He understood the responsibilities and the emotional and psychological characteristics of ownership.

Ownership is undeniably one of God's reasons for caring about us. When the members of the church at Corinth were arguing with each other and claiming positions, rights, and privileges for themselves, Paul reminded them of who they were. He said, "You are not your own; you were bought with a price." (1 Cor. 6:19-20). Our ownership is in the hands of God. It was purchased by Jesus Christ, the Son of God. Just as the Good Shepherd goes ahead of the sheep, Jesus has gone ahead of us. Our eternal future is no longer uncertain or unknown. He faced the terror and mystery of death with faith in God, just as we must face it. Calling us His sheep, Jesus said, "I give them eternal life, and they shall never perish, and no one shall snatch them out of my hand" (John 10:28).

Another reason for God's care for us is because He is a jealous God. We are familiar with God's jealousy in His warnings against

Israel's unfaithfulness. We clearly see His jealousy in the demand that He alone must be worshiped. However, just as His jealousy demands faithfulness on our part, it also reveals that He has a stake in our lives. In its everyday Hebrew usage, the concept of jealousy refers primarily to a strong emotion arising from the possibility of losing someone or something. It is strongly associated with the idea of ownership and entitlement.[2] While one side of God's jealousy evokes anger, there is another side that evokes personal concern and active care for us.

We are familiar with the phrase "apple of the eye." What does it mean? Where does if come from? We first hear it in reference to God's rescue of His creation from the *tohu wabohu* of the wilderness: "He found him in a desert land, and in the howling waste of the wilderness; he encircled him, he cared for him, he kept him as the apple of his eye" (Deut. 32:10). The "apple of the eye" is the pupil, the round black area located in the center of the eye and surrounded by the colored iris. God encircled Israel with protection just as the pupil is encircled with protection. The "apple of the eye" refers to anything that is "tenderest and dearest, and therefore guarded with most jealous care."[3] The prophet Zechariah encouraged those who were in Babylonian captivity to return to Zion without fearing that any further harm would come to them. He told them, "For thus said the Lord of hosts, he who touches you touches the apple of his eye" (Zech. 2:8).

The Psalmist prayed that God would keep him "as the apple of the eye" (Ps. 17:8). The value of sight needs no explanation. It connects us to the world around us, bringing colors and shapes into focus. We know from experience that the eye is sensitive and easily irritated. Perhaps that is why the Creator set the eye in a hard, bony socket that provides so much protection. It has eyelashes and eyebrows to catch small particles before they can get into the eye. It has eyelids that can be closed against the wind to keep out flying debris. It has its own flushing system that produces tears to keep the surface well-watered and to wash away irritants. The biblical writers saw the eye as a valuable instrument that required careful preservation. God sees that same value in us. We are valued and important, and He jealously guards us with His care and protection.

God cares for us and our eternal future because we are the reason that everything else was created. The creation stories from Genesis tell us that everything that was made was intended for our sake. The human race was at the center of God's attention as He worked through six days of creation. As He finished each period of work, He declared that it was "good." At the end of the sixth day, after He had made man (male and female), He declared that His completed work was more than good: it was "very good." A thing can be good in and of itself, but if it does not work in harmony with, and as a functional part of the whole with which it is associated, it becomes isolated and of limited use and value. Paul used this picture of the unity of the parts of the body to describe the Church as the body of Christ. A body is healthy and efficient only when each part is functioning as it should (1 Cor. 12:12-31). On the seventh day, God rested in the satisfaction that each part was functioning perfectly and in harmony with the other parts. Creation, in its totality, was serving as intended by the Lord God. Therefore, His work as a completed whole was assessed to be "very good."

God cares for us because, from the beginning, He wanted to meet with us and talk with us. Our first parents "heard the sound of the Lord God walking in the garden in the cool of the day" (Gen. 3:8). This implies that an encounter and conversation with God was not unusual. We know that He had previously spoken to them when He gave them instructions about life in the garden (Gen. 2:15-17). God had prepared everything, and nothing was wanting. We should not be surprised that God wanted to communicate with us. Marcus Dods called God's interaction with the first man and woman "the chiefest act in the history of God."[4] He says,

> Man is dear to God because he is like Him. Vast and glorious as it is, the sun cannot think God's thoughts; can fulfill but cannot intelligently sympathize with God's purpose. Man alone among God's works, can enter into and approve of God's purpose in the world and can intelligently fulfill it. Without man the whole material universe would have been dark and unintelligible, mechanical and apparently without any sufficient purpose…Matter, however beautifully and wonderfully wrought, is but the platform and material in which spirit, intelligence and will, may fulfill themselves and final development. Man is incommensurable with the rest of the universe. He is of a different kind and by his moral nature is more akin to God than to his works.[5]

God cares for us because we are the crowning glory of His creation. Despite our continued disobedience and failures, we are not too insignificant for God to reclaim and re-create us to live forever in a re-created world that awaits us. We should not think it foolish that we have some sense of expectation regarding this re-created world. Saint Augustine spoke of "that great receptacle of memory, with its many and indescribable departments."[6] He spoke of it as a vast chamber that holds things that we have forgotten. Even so, there are times when something we cannot explain comes to the forefront of our consciousness. Although we may not understand its occurrence, we find that we are unable to dismiss it as being unreal or a product of irrational imagination. Augustine's response to this mystery is, "Whence and how did these things enter into my memory? I know not how."[7] Buried deep in the recesses of our primeval memory is the embedded longing for a return to the garden of our creation, which was defined as being "very good." However, our return to that garden is intertwined with the memory of what happened in another garden. We find Jesus in that garden praying and struggling with the fear and dread of a mission given to Him by His Father. It was there that He prayed for the faith and strength to accomplish the will of His Father. In the shadow of the cross, and the approaching unknown darkness of death, He prayed, "My soul is very sorrowful even to death; nevertheless, not as I will, but as thou wilt" (Matt. 26:38-39). It is in what happened in both these gardens that I know that God loves me. The care and concern of both the Father and the Son place my value above any human estimation.

Ultimately, what shall we say and think of death? Some have always found it too frightening to even engage in a conversation about death. Others will immediately terminate any such discussion with a terse, "I don't want to think about it." There is no doubt that we have the capacity to convince ourselves that death will be easier if we refuse to discuss it. This is true of religious people as well as those who claim no faith. I remember reading about an alleged conversation between a Christian and a non-believer. The non-believer asked, "Where do you Christians go when you die?" The Christian replied, "We go to a place of unspeakable bliss, but let's not talk about it. It's too depressing." Saint Augustine said, "Would that we had lived so well in Paradise that in very truth there were now no death! But not only does it now exist, but so grievous a thing is it, that no skill is sufficient either to explain or to escape it."[8] Eighteen hundred years later, his assessment of the human condition is as true today as it was then.

Nevertheless, like Saint Augustine and all those who have gone before us, we claim the promises of our God and our Savior. We already know that we are known as the "apple of God's eye." He is our owner and our keeper, and we know that "He will not slumber nor sleep and that he will keep our living and our dying from this time and for evermore" (Ps. 121). Because there is a re-created world and a re-created life beyond what we now experience, we can faithfully and joyfully embrace the truth that we belong to God, not just in the here-and-now, but also in His great eternal Paradise. The jealous God who created us preserves and provides for what He has made.

David Daube (1909-1999) says that "God is first and foremost a "recoverer."[9] For God, the redemption of His creation is an act of recovery. Daube says, "However desperate the momentary situation, God is the reliable eternal 'recoverer' of his own, the redeemer from everlasting."[10] In the Old Testament, the Exodus event was the great act of recovery, and all other acts of deliverance were extended from the exodus. In the New Testament, God's act of recovery is applied to the person and work of Jesus.[11] From the Book of the Old Covenant, God says, "I have redeemed you; I have called you by name, you are mine" (Isa. 43:1). From the Book of the New Covenant, we learn that "God sent the Son into the world, not to condemn the world, but that the world might be saved through him" (John 3:17).

Both Testaments boldly proclaim that God guarantees that He will recover us from bondage and death. This proclamation begins in the Old Covenant as a promise and concludes in the New Covenant as the fulfillment of every promise made by God. In the Old Testament, we see it coming in a fragmentary and piecemeal fashion through the mediums of prophets, priests, wise men, and singers of the Psalms (Heb. 1:1). In the New Testament we see the fulfillment coming in the "fullness of time" (Gal. 4:4), and completely located and consolidated in Jesus Christ (2 Cor. 1:20;

Heb. 1:2). All the promises of God find their "Yes" and "Amen" in Jesus. He is also the Alpha and Omega, the beginning, and the end (Rev. 22:13). The last word has been spoken. All that remains for each of us is our reception into the presence of Jesus, when we are restored, redeemed, and re-created at the moment of our death. It cannot be otherwise, and as Daube concludes, "God would, in fact he must, 'recover' those who were his property, his children, friends or slaves."[12]

If we are realists, we do not have to be reminded that we live every day of our lives in the certainty that death is coming. However, I do believe that we must be reminded that we also live in the certainty that a re-created life with Jesus Christ also awaits us. We need to be reminded that the God who created us is a gracious God, and that He has been and always will be for us. Facing his own death, Paul said, "If God is on our side, who is against us?" (Rom 8:31, NEB). Our enemies cannot prevail. Paul identified death as the last enemy we will face. That ultimate and final enemy was defeated when Jesus was raised from the dead. The basis of Paul's thanksgiving praise rests in the fact that it is "God who gives us the victory through our Lord Jesus Christ" (1 Corinthians 15:56). This appears to be a simple and straightforward statement, but it tells more than we have typically asked of it. We quickly and clearly see, understand, and accept three things: 1) death is the last enemy; 2) God gives us the victory; and 3) the victory comes through Jesus Christ.

The question that is seldom asked is, "When does God give us the victory over death?" I am not asking about a projected victory that will come at some unknown distant time that will happen concurrently with certain sensational cataclysmic events caused by natural and/or geopolitical forces. I am asking about that "time certain" when victory over death comes to each of us individually.

The answer is both simple and complex. It is simple in the simplicity of the person and work of Jesus. On the other hand, it has accrued an overwhelming complexity under the weight of two thousand years of tradition and the systematizing techniques of human ingenuity and religious partisan preferences.

Take a moment and think on this picture of the Jesus of the New Testament:

> He never thought out a paragraph, never penned a single tractate. He is so simple that the children cry out with joy at His approach, and the very poorest understand Him. Insignificant persons, unknown by name, who had no idea of the value of literal accuracy, handed on His "doctrine" in the homely garb of the popular language. Jesus thought nothing of the theology of His age: He even thanked His Father for having hid his profoundest revelations from the wise and prudent. The lightning of His prophetic scorn descend upon the theological authorities who paid tithe of mint, and anise, and cumin, but omitted mercy and faith. Contemplative theology, the offspring of doubt, was completely outside the sphere of His nature, because He was in daily personal intercourse with the higher world, and the living God was in Him.[13]

He came to us as one of us, and spoke plainly, without any intention of deceiving us or misrepresenting His relationship with us. His guidance was clear and to the point, e.g., "Let what you say be simply 'Yes' or 'No'…" (Matt. 5:37); and "He who has ears to hear, let him hear" (Matt. 11:15). There was no sleight of hand trickery in His healing touch, no bait and switch tactics in what He promised us, and no megalo-maniacal, selfish, narcissistic ambition in His behavior as our Lord. The majestic power of that simplicity is passed onto us through the ecstatic cry of Thomas, the disillusioned doubter, when he exclaimed, "My Lord and my God!" (John 20:28). Jesus blessed him, and then gave us a greater blessing. He said, "Blessed are those who have not seen and yet believe" (John 20:29). He said this after His resurrection, that is, after His victory over death.

The complexity of the "time certain" of the victory is one of our own making. We speak of Jesus as if He were only a person of the future. We are fixed on Him as a Savior who is still to come. In fact, He has come already. Our inability to understand this is the source of much of the confusion regarding what happens to us when we die. Our thinking remains contaminated by our demand for absolute self-rule. The same insistence on complete autonomy that first got us into trouble after we were created, continues to haunt us and plague us in many ways today. Because we cannot see beyond the veil of death with our physical eyes and are unable to understand death according to our own logic and reasoning, we feel compelled to construct explanations that suggest that we have some control over this "tantalizing mystery." Unwilling to accept the promises of God, and unable to manipulate the Word of God to our liking, we have created doctrines, religious denominations, church histories, and theological systems based on our own speculations and preferences.

It does not seem to matter that the words and concepts upon which some end-time schemes are built are not to be found in the Greek New Testament. Words for second-coming, rapture, and various so-called dispensations are not in the New Testament writings. Over a period of years, these words have been employed to support the speculations of individuals and groups. The vocabulary that teaches and preaches the mechanics of these systems has spread dark clouds of fear and misunderstanding over the messages of the New Testament writers. It is a vocabulary largely created from imagination, confusion, misinterpretation, intellectual arrogance, and anti-intellectual ignorance.

Regardless of how passionately end-time systems are represented, they cannot be applied as though they have the accuracy and singular end results of algebraic formulas. The timelines, colored charts, graphs, identity of the antichrist, and the claims of various items being the mark of the beast all have a history of being wrong. It is preposterous to think that the mysteries of God must conform to our logically, mathematically, and scientifically crafted systems. New Testament examples of doing business and exacting justice are not models that our logical thinking is likely to endorse. Consider that a convicted criminal nailed to a tree is forgiven and promised eternal life in Paradise; a profligate son is embraced and receives a banquet in his honor; a white collar robber-baron has dinner with Jesus and changes his philosophy of what it means to be successful; the first will be last, and the last will be first; harlots and cheating tax-collectors will go into the Kingdom of God ahead of some professing religious people, etc. How do you construct a reliably consistent system out of these kinds of contradictions? How do you build a credible system of end-time doctrine and/or theology when it is written, "But of that day and hour no one knows, not even the angels of heaven, nor the Son, but the Father only" (Matt. 24:36; Mark 13:32).

The words of second-coming, rapture, pre-millennial, and post-millennial are not anywhere to be found on the lips of Jesus. The manner and method of the performance of His mission on this earth absolutely defy any attempt at being reduced to an exact system. The coming forth of Jesus from the tomb, and His re-entry into the lives and affairs of human beings fulfilled His promise that He would return. Any concept of a so-called second-coming, in-so-far-as it involves individuals, is that encounter when Jesus comes to us at the moment of our death.

Again, I ask, "When does God give us victory over death?" The "time certain" of this victory is qualified only by the uncertainty of the time of our death. Other than that uncertainty that applies to each of us, there is no validity to the systems humans have developed to solve the mysteries of the end of this world and the continuation of this life. The answers are in the resurrection of Jesus and His promises. There is no trickery, no required password to be applied, no reservation, no equivocation, no riddled mixture of mysterious and confusing words in our Lord's intention for our lives. His words form a promise that is impossible to misunderstand. He clearly and unequivocally says, "Because I live, you will live also" (John 14:19). As I said before, Paul's exclamation of victory proclaims God's intention for all of us: "But thanks be to God, who gives us the victory through our Lord Jesus Christ" (1 Cor. 15:56).

The action of Paul's statement is best understood when read in its literal translation of, "Thanks be to God, ***the one giving to us*** the victory, through our Lord Jesus Christ" (bold italics is the literal translation of the Greek construction). "Giving" translates a Greek participle that is present tense and active voice (διδόντι/didonti). The action of the participle is progressive and is happening continuously. It is also happening simultaneously with that which is being given. The victory being given does not stop at death. It progresses through death and continues into the re-created life that God gives us. Jesus became the "firstfruit" of human resurrection and, as such, became not only the possibility of human resurrection, but the guarantee as well. Because Christ has been raised, our continued existence beyond the moment of our death is assured.

As we contemplate our own rendezvous with death, or as we stand by the grave of a departed loved one, it is very appropriate that we ask, "What happened to Jesus shortly after He was taken from the cross and placed in a tomb?" The Gospels tell us that the first visitors to the tomb were met by heavenly messengers who announced that God had raised Jesus from the dead. Immediately thereafter, Jesus appeared to multiple persons in various places. Without a doubt, a man who had been killed and buried was again appearing among the living. He spoke with them, ate, and drank with them, and confirmed that He possessed the characteristics of any other living human being. These attributes of His re-claimed humanity were manifested before He ascended into heaven. Karl Barth refers to this as "The Homecoming of the Son of Man."[14] Barth says, "It was God who went into the far country, and it is man who returns home. Both took place in the one Jesus Christ."[15] The far country is the wilderness that the world became after humankind's disobedience.

This world, the one we now occupy, is a world of sin and death (Isaiah 34). However, God's love is greater than His disappointment in our failure, and He has refused to condemn His creation to an endless future of sin, desolation, failure, and death. He has made provisions for redemption and everlasting joy (Isaiah 35). This re-creation and victory over death comes through Jesus Christ, who went into the far country as the Son of God and returned home as the Son of Man. Barth says, "He brings with Him the spoils of the divine mercy from that far country."[16] We are the spoils of that divine redemption. We can gladly and thankfully say that the homecoming of Jesus from the far country is our homecoming also.

Jesus' appearances, His coming to us, began on the third day after His death. Why should we doubt that He will appear to us at the moment of our death? That moment of time marks the consummation of His promises: 1) "When I go and prepare a place for you, I will come again and take you to myself, that where I am you may be also" (John 14:3); 2) "Because I live, you will live also" (John 14:19); and 3) "I go away and I will come to you" (John 14:28). Nowhere in the words of our Lord can we find that any individual or any faith group has been given the knowledge or the authority to interpose thousands of years between His presence and the time that we will share with Him the homecoming victory of eternal life. What we can know without contradiction is that we are in the care and keeping of the Lord of glory who has been given rule over everything that has been, now is, or ever will be (John 3:35).

John said that he was in the Spirit on the Lord's day, and the Lord spoke to him and said, "I am the first and the last, and the living one; I died, and behold I am alive for evermore, and I have the keys of death and hades" (Rev. 1:18). The home of death is hades, which is nothing more than the common grave and the realm of the dead. It is the place that Jesus "descended into" during the time between His crucifixion and resurrection. Peter says that "he went and preached to the spirits in prison" (1 Pet. 3:16), and "this is why the Gospel was preached, even to the dead" (1 Pet. 4:6).

The early Church most certainly knew of and believed in this "descent into hades." It first appeared in the Dated Creed of Sirmium in AD 359 and was officially integrated into the Apostles' Creed in AD 750. We can be certain, however, that it was a part of the belief of the early Church before it appeared in writing. J. N. D. Kelly says, "Apart from the possibility of its having been in the minds of New Testament writers, the Descent was explicitly mentioned by St. Ignatius, St. Polycarp, St Irenaeus, Tertullian, and others."[17] The power of God knows no boundaries. There is no space, place, or period of time that does not belong to God. The Father has given this same power and authority to the Son. The resurrected Jesus said to His disciples, "All authority in heaven and on earth has been given to me" (Matt. 28:18). His grace, mercy, and love extend beyond an infinite expanse that our human minds cannot begin to calculate. If, as I believe, there are other dimensions of time and re-created life in domains and environments unknown to us, Jesus Christ reigns there also (Ps. 139:7-12).

There is no time or place, already created or yet to be created, that is not subject to the power and authority of Jesus Christ. He is no stranger to the valley of the shadow of death. He has passed through that valley, and He returns to lead us through it. Having led us through the valley and the wilderness (Isa. 34), He meets us as we pass through the door of death into a re-creation that has bloomed into the beauty and perfection of the original habitat of God's initial creation (Isa. 35). I recall the dying testimony of a saintly lady whose life was nothing less than a history of faith in God and devotion to the Lord Jesus Christ. As she was dying in her own bed at home and surrounded by family, Her eyes gazed off into a corner of the room, and she said, "I see the other side and He is waiting for me. It is a beautiful sight." Then "the silver cord was snapped, the golden bowl was broken, the pitcher was shattered at the spring, the wheel was broken at the well, and the spirit returned to God who gave it" (Eccles. 12:6-7 NEB). With that, she departed into the presence of Jesus, and entered the re-created world of eternal life.

I am aware of the arguments that mock and deny the truth of "death bed" testimonies. A major criticism is that they are anecdotal and unsupported by scientific and factual reliability. I will concede that this criticism may be true when measured by the wisdom of this world. However, the saintly lady referred to above was not speaking under the authority of the facts of history and the wisdom of this world. She was speaking under the authority of the promises of the resurrected Jesus Christ. Anything we say or believe about what happens to us at our death can only be understood by faith. Let the world challenge the reliability of the testimony of a weak, aging saint of God who was essentially voiceless, penniless, and powerless in the world where she served God and thanked Him for her ninety difficult years of life. But let the world also know that Saint Paul said, "But God chose what is foolish in the world to shame the wise, and chose what is weak in the world to shame the strong" (1 Cor. 1:27).

When I recall the dying testimony described above, my mind immediately turns to the martyrdom of Saint Ignatius (AD 30-107). He became a Christian early in his life and was personally acquainted with Saint John the Apostle. He was chosen to serve as Bishop of Antioch and was martyred for his faith during the reign of Emperor Trajan. He was thrown among the lions and other wild beasts and was devoured by them. It was said that "only the harder portions of his holy remains were left, which were conveyed to Antioch and wrapped in linen, as an inestimable treasure left to the holy Church."[18] As he waited to be thrown to the wild beasts, he knew that he would soon be disappearing from this world. Those who knew him said that more than anything else, he was eager to be "manifested before the face of Christ."[19] After his death, his friends said,

> Having ourselves been eyewitnesses of these things, and having spent the whole night in tears within the house, and having entreated the Lord, with bended knees and much prayer, that He would give us weak men full assurance respecting the things which were done, it came to pass, on our falling into a brief slumber, that some of us saw the blessed Ignatius suddenly standing by us and embracing us, while others beheld him again praying for us, and others still saw him dropping with sweat, as if he had just

come from his great labor, and standing by the Lord.[20]

Anecdotal? Probably, if you believe only in the wisdom of this world. For my part, however, I am completely convinced that at the moment of death, both Saint Ignatius and my sainted grandmother were "manifested before the face of Christ."

There is no valid reason to put our concept of time limits on the grace and love of God. Clocks and calendars are instruments of our own creation. They do not restrict, determine, or affect the way God rules His creation. Why should we subscribe to a scenario of life after death that places us in a dark environment where we comatosely wait for a rapture and/or a second-coming that others have conjured up to explain the mind of God? God did not send Jesus into the world the first time simply to advertise a mysteriously projected, fantastic return to earth to give us what He has already given to Jesus.

We foolishly speculate and prophesy about some presumed apocalyptic event that hangs over us like some dark and dangerous cloud. It is treated as an event that will certainly occur at some uncertain time. The distance between the certainty of the event and the uncertainty of its appearance is the element that gives some preachers and all charlatans the license that they need to create messages of fear and control over sincere but unknowing people. They thrive on the old rhyme of, "Yes, no, maybe so, certainly." And they add, "In the meantime, send me some money so that I can continue to perpetuate this fear and make more money."

The "end" is not a rapture, a second-coming, or any other event. The "end" is a person, and that person is Jesus Christ, Savior, and Son of God. He is identified as,

1) The Bread of Life (John 6:35).

2) The Light of the World (John 8:12).

3) The Door (John 10:9).

4) The Good Shepherd (John 10:11-14).

5) The Resurrection and the Life (John 11:25).

6) The Way and the Truth and the Life (John 14:6).

7) The Vine (John 15:1, 5).

If, beyond these identities, a fantastic event is required, what could be more fantastic than the scene witnessed in real-time on what we refer to as Easter morning? During an earthshaking noise, an angel wearing brilliant white clothing opened the tomb and told the two early morning visitors, "He is not here; for He has risen. Come, see the place where the Lord lay" (Matthew 28:1-7).

Have you ever thought about Jesus' promise that He came to give us life more abundantly (John 10:10 KJV)? That promise is not just for the short duration of the time between birth and death. That kind of limited and temporary promise would speak more of cruelty than abundance. He did not intend that we should spend the brief span of this earthly life in an anxious state of waiting for a death that would bring the eternal end of our very being. If that were the case, the question of, "Is that all there is?" would be confirmed and validated as the truth. The content of the more abundant life that Jesus promised is a reference to the superabundance of the blessings of God, the greatest of which is eternal life.

We can live abundantly because we know that this earthly life is a prelude to the unimaginable joy of a re-created life in the beauty of a re-created world. While we are often challenged by situations and events beyond our control, by faith, we rejoice in the victorious truth that "because He lives, we can face tomorrow." The abundant life that lives in our hearts, minds, and souls is more than sufficient to lift us above every fear and failure that can threaten us. It is an overflowing abundance that lifts us above the dark confines of any grave. At the moment of our death, the superabundant life surrounds us with the grace and love of God and transports us into the waiting presence of Jesus Christ.

Having thought about the devastation that death brings, the expectations of faith, and the re-creation of life, what can be said to and with those who stand by the grave of a loved one? We know from experience that God will not come and save anyone left behind in the wilderness of life. They are left to live and cope with even more emotional and physical disturbances that remain in the days ahead. They are entitled to their grief, sorrow, anger, shock, depression, denial, and sense of hopelessness and abandonment. They are entitled to weep and sob until their bodies shake uncontrollably and their eyes become red and swollen. If they require a period of withdrawal and silence, they should not be pressed to act otherwise. The ancient experience of mourning by "rending garments and putting on sackcloth and ashes" is expressed in many ways, but all of them represent therapeutic attempts to come to terms with this living experience of the devastation of death.

Like it or not, death and its collateral results are inescapable. This is the way it is in the wilderness. Literally, everything in our world has been contaminated by the *tohu wabohu*, the chaos, of our disobedience and rebellion against the God who made us. The task of the survivors remaining in the wilderness is to cry with the mourners, to embrace them with the warmth of humanity, to be silent with them when they seek silence, and to refrain from urging them to do what we want them to do. When given an opportunity to speak with them about their loss, we should try to offer the thought that the dead loved one is not experiencing the same misery and loss as those left behind. What was lived and lost in the wilderness (Isa.

34), has become meaningless and has no place in the re-created world (Isa. 35). The grief is ours, and it is for us that we grieve. Those who leave the wilderness do not grieve for those left behind. They are free from every pain of living and aging that they knew and experienced in the wilderness. They now know that the abundant life is not more of the same as it was in the wilderness. It is God's re-creation that conforms to His original intention for the whole of creation. They do not grieve that they have left us behind. They know that we will, in our time, enter the perfection of a re-created life in a re-created world (Isa. 35).

It is ironic that death is the medium through which death is itself defeated and replaced by eternal life. Paul says, "For as by a man came death, by a man has come also the resurrection of the dead" (1 Cor. 15:21). This verse, involving the actions of two men, shapes my expectations about life in the world in which we now live, and the re-created world that awaits us. The first man mentioned is Adam, from whom we all have descended. Death has its origin in that first sin of disobedience, and it continues to manifest itself in us. From this perspective, I do not have any expectations that the human condition will get any better under continued human management. Because we live in the wilderness that has been shaped by our selfishness and resistance to divine guidance, we will inevitably continue to struggle and suffer physically, psychologically, and emotionally. We simply are incapable of taming, eliminating, or reversing the moral, ethical, social, cultural, economic, ethnic, and spiritual chaos that we despise on the one hand, and knowingly perpetuate on the other. With our disobedience and insistence on governing our lives without heeding the Word of God (i.e., grasping at total autonomy), we re-introduce elements of pre-creation chaos into the fabric of everything that touches upon our earthly existence. Martin Luther named the devil as the active principle of this chaos and evil. He said, "We cannot live in tranquility, but must forever live in expectation of new gales from the devil."[21] We applaud the mechanical and technological inventions that have made our lives more comfortable, but we surely recognize the awful results of hate, selfishness, envy, greed, cruelty, and the many other known and unknown human failures that fuel the fires of inhumanity within the human species.

Do we really think that the flaws of human nature are going to go away because of our desire or ability to become better people? Is this the mission and goal of all humans living in this world? Do we believe that if our species can live long enough, we will outlive the power of evil? Do we really believe longevity is the antidote to all that is wrong with the world? Do we believe that the day will come on this side of eternity when we no longer have to ask, "Why can't we all just get along?" I share Martin Luther's assessment of the prospect that longevity will heal the broken condition of human relationships. He said,

> And even if I were to live another hundred years and should succeed by the grace of God not only in allaying the past and present storms and rabbles but also all future ones, I realize that this still would not procure peace for our descendants so long as the devil lives and rules . . . You and I have to die, but after our death he still remains the same as he always has been, unable to desist from his raging.[22]

Perhaps we have reason to subscribe to the belief of the unnamed character in Dostoevsky's novella, *Notes From Underground.* Life had convinced him that humans are incapable of establishing a social utopia in this world. He said,

> Now I ask you: what can be expected of man since he is a being endowed with such strange qualities? Shower upon him every earthly blessing, drown him in a sea of happiness, so that nothing but bubbles of bliss can be seen on the surface; give him economic prosperity, such that he should have nothing else to do but sleep, eat cakes and busy himself with the continuation of his species, and even then out of sheer ingratitude, sheer spite, man would play you some nasty trick.[23]

Underground Man is left unnamed because Dostoevsky knows he represents the nature of all of us, individually and as a corporate body. Each of us can play the role of this unnamed character. Who among us is not subject to both giving and receiving nasty tricks?

We should not expect that our human efforts in the name of religion will move us out of our wilderness existence and into the glory of a harmonious world of our own making. Saint Paul said, "For I do not do the good I want, but the evil I do not want is what I do" (Romans 7:19). With unbridled expectations and romantic enthusiasm, we enlist the vocabulary of religion to announce our social gospel projects, but they, too, are infected by the conflict and distress of sin. Even when we are most involved in the business of our religion, Barth says,

> We belch forth the vapors of sin; we fall into it, rise up again, buffet and torment ourselves night and day; but, since we are confined in this flesh, since we have to bear with us everywhere this stinking sack, we cannot rid ourselves completely of it, or even knock it senseless. We make vigorous attempts to do so, but the old Adam retains his power until he is deposited in the grave.[24]

There is no valid reason to expect that peace and perpetual brotherhood will ever be fully realized in this fallen world. The old Adam, the first of our breed that brought death into the world, retains his place in us through the weakness and corruption of our flesh. As long as we are living in this world, we will be living in a body that will die. To that end, the disobedient, selfish, self-willed nature is active until each one of us is, as Barth says, "deposited in the grave."

My expectations are not located in any hope for historical progress provided by sinful people; by all of us. The nature of life as we know it in historic times will always be subject to the rebellious, perverted forces of our chaotic world. It was precisely this realization that evoked Saint Paul's cry of "Wretched man that I am!" (Rom. 7:24). The idea of a global community living together under the guidance of mutual goodwill and respect is a seductive illusion that ignores the realities of sin and death. Emil Brunner reminds us, "Nowhere does the New Testament promise an earthly state of peace, of social justice, or universal international relationships conforming to the idea of justice and humanity."[25] Our daily lives prove that there are definite limits in our capacity and willingness to grant to others what we militantly claim for ourselves. My only expectation for this world is that it will pass away via the ravages of time, or by some other force of natural or human destruction. As for humanity, we will all die in accordance with the sentence passed by God at the trial and court of our disobedience (Gen. 2:17; 3:19).

The only trustworthy expectation that we have is the one given to us by Jesus Christ, "through whom has come the resurrection of the dead." It is this expectation that gives meaning to my life. I am confident that my eternal destiny is not determined by any present or future event. It is totally determined by a person who has come to me and promised me an abundant life. He will come to me again at the moment of my death, and He will accompany me into that great eternal adventure that God has prepared for me.

After having read these many pages, I encourage you to think about your death and the death of loved ones and friends. In the last sermon he preached before his death, John Donne said, "God will not deliver us from dying, but he will have a care of us in the hour of death, of what kind soever our passage be."[26] Let this be your devotional stimulus for this day, and as you read the remaining "thought offerings" in this book. As you think about these things, let the context of every thought be located in the death and resurrection of Jesus. Recognize Him as the One appointed by God to be the Lord of re-created lives in a re-created world.

As for me, When the summons comes to leave this world, it will be the call that introduces me to the person and presence of Jesus Christ. It makes no difference whether the summons comes through disease, sickness, accident, old age, or by any other of the many disguises worn by death. Regardless of the method or cause of death, the result will be the same. At that moment, it will be the end of the world for me, the death of death itself, and a new life with the Lord in God's re-created version of the primeval Garden of Eden.

The moment of death is God's way of saying, "Amen!" and the content of that "Amen!" is Jesus Christ. As the eyes close and the beat of the heart goes silent, a great rejoicing shout will erupt, but no one remaining in this wilderness of time, history, and sin will hear it. It will be God's high note of victory, soaring through eternity and far beyond the reaches of the brokenness and chaos of this world. As each one passes through the door of death, Jesus Christ welcomes one more prodigal soul, one more sinner, and one more redeemed child of God from the captivity of the wilderness. Through the Victory of Jesus Christ, that which we have feared to be the end of ourselves and our loved ones, has become the beginning, and so shall we always be with the Lord.

Prayer:

Lord, we cannot escape the reality of death. We see it in our world every day, and eventually, we know that we will recognize it in our own future. We try valiantly to escape it, but we know that our efforts cannot prevent or eliminate death. It appears that we live in a kingdom ruled by death. But in Your grace, and because of Your love demonstrated in Jesus Christ, we will prevail over this dreaded enemy. No threat can overpower the blood shed on the cross for us. We are safe, and we are Yours. Amen.

CHAPTER FIVE
SPIRITUAL MYOPIA

Matthew 24:1-2, 13, 35: *[1]Jesus left the temple and was going away, when his disciples came to point out to him the buildings of the temple.*

[2]But he answered them, "You see all these, do you not? Truly, I say to you, there will not be left here one stone upon another, that will not be thrown down."

[13]"But he who endures to the end will be saved."

[35]"Heaven and earth will pass away, but my words will not pass away."

Mark 13:1-2, 31: *[1]And as he came out of the temple, one of his disciples said to him, "Look, Teacher, what wonderful stones and what wonderful buildings!"*

[2]And Jesus said to him, "Do you see these great buildings? There will not be left here one stone upon another, that will not be thrown down.

[13]"But he who endures to the end will be saved."

[31]"Heaven and earth will pass away, but my words will not pass away."

Luke 21:5-6, 19, 23: *⁵And as some spoke of the temple, how it was adorned with noble stones and offerings, he said,*

⁶" As for these things which you see, the days will come when there shall not be left here one stone upon another that will not be thrown down." ¹⁹"By your endurance you will gain your lives."

³³"Heaven and earth will pass away, but my words will not pass away."

I had a friend in junior high school who asked if he could use the notes I had copied from the chalkboard in our history class. It was common knowledge that the teacher's test questions would be taken from what he wrote on the chalkboard. My classmate's parents wanted to know why he had to copy my notes and could not take notes from the board during the class. He told them that he was able to read a book while sitting in his seat but was unable to see the writing on the chalkboard. A trip to the optometrist revealed that he had a condition called myopia. The optometrist explained that, in lay terms, myopia was referred to as nearsightedness or shortsightedness. Myopia exists when light does not focus correctly on the retina. When this happens, objects seen close-up can be seen clearly, but objects further away are blurry and indistinct. A pair of glasses corrected my classmate's condition, and he was able to read from the chalkboard as clearly as he could read a book while sitting at his desk.

Perhaps you have heard someone's views on a particular subject referred to as being "myopic." In such a case, the speaker is using the concept of myopia in a figurative sense. To have a myopic point of view labels a person as being narrow in perspective and oblivious to bigger concerns and potential unintended consequences. While such a person may clearly see the details immediately surrounding a situation, he/she shows no interest in or concern for future probabilities and possibilities.

The scripture passages listed above suggest to me that the disciples were experiencing a form of "spiritual myopia." They very clearly saw what was immediately before them, but they failed to see what Jesus wanted to teach them about their future as his disciples. They were fascinated with the beauty and grandeur of the temple. They seemed to be hypnotized by its detailed construction and its expensive, priceless features.

It is not difficult to understand their reaction as they stood so close to this great man-made marvel. The temple could have compared favorably with any of the so-called "wonders of the world" of its own time. It was constructed of huge blocks of marble and covered with large plates of gold in many areas. Josephus gives this stunning description of the temple in the time of Jesus:

> Now the outward face of the temple in its front wanted nothing that was likely to surprise either men's minds or their eyes, for it was covered all over with plates of gold of great weight, and, at the first rising of the sun, reflected back a very fiery splendor, and made those who forced themselves to look upon it to turn their eyes away, just as they would have done at the sun's own rays. But this temple appeared to strangers, when they were at a distance, like a mountain covered with snow; for as to those parts of it that were not gilt, they were exceeding white.[1]

Jesus' response to the disciples' infatuation with the beautiful building was not what they expected. Rather than joining them in their admiration of this great architectural accomplishment, Jesus told them that the building was destined to be destroyed. In saying this, he was not voicing disapproval of the building itself. He wanted them to understand that the value of the building was not in its own beauty; it was valuable only in-so-far as it facilitated a relationship with God and a commitment to serving the Kingdom of God.

Jesus wanted to make his disciples aware of their spiritual myopia. The glorious temple, for all its beauty, was no more effective in its purpose than was the portable "tent of meeting" that Moses carried with him in the wilderness (Exod. 33:7-11). The purpose of both structures was to unite the people in the obedient worship and service of God. This required, and still requires, looking beyond what we can see up close in the present moment and focusing on God's guidance of our lives into the future.

Jesus knew that our pride in our own accomplishments could create a false sense of security that deadened our trust in God. Considering our perceived cleverness, we are tempted to look only at the work of our own hands and brains and assume that we do not need to recognize God as our Creator and Sustainer. Seeing all that we have built and made for ourselves, we risk ignoring the greater lessons of eternity that are experienced in honoring and glorifying God. Saint Paul reminds us that "the things that are seen are temporary, but the things that are unseen are eternal" (2 Cor. 4:18).

The disciples may have had difficulty in seeing the temple reduced to rubble with not one stone left upon another. Gazing upon the reality of exquisite man-made beauty, it was probably extremely hard to comprehend the predicted destruction of that very beauty. However, we know for a historical fact what they could not know historically in AD 30. Forty years later, the Romans destroyed the temple and much of Jerusalem. A revolt against the Romans erupted in AD 66 which saw rival Jewish factions engaged in a civil war. They were fighting each other while at the same time fighting the Romans. These rival factions foolishly destroyed their own food supplies, and a famine swept through Jerusalem and the adjacent areas. Josephus wrote, "Some persons were driven to that terrible distress as to search the common sewers and dung-hills of cattle, and to eat the dung which they got there."[2] The death toll from war and starvation throughout the siege until the final destruction in AD 70 numbered approximately one million one hundred thousand, with another ninety-seven thousand being carried away into captivity.[3] Josephus' summary of the destruction of the temple and much of Jerusalem reflects the unimaginable suffering of the Jewish people. He said,

> Accordingly the multitude of those that therein perished exceeded all the destructions that either men or God ever brought upon the world; for to speak only of what was publicly known, the Romans slew some of them, some they carried captives, and others they made search for underground, and when they found where they were, they broke up the ground and slew all they met with.[4]

The disciples could not have imagined the scope of the destruction of which Jesus spoke. Nevertheless, his startling words redirected their attention to matters more serious than the beauty of a building made by human hands. They became curious and asked Jesus questions about future events. As Mark tells us in his Gospel, Jesus talked to them about wars, insurrections, earthquakes, famines, plagues, persecutions, and all manner of hatred and evil things. Hearing such a bleak outlook for the future, the disciples must have wondered how anyone could survive under those conditions. Having given this frightening description, Jesus then provided a prescription for survival. In all three Gospels, he says, "He who endures to the end will be saved" (Matt. 24:13, Mark 13:13, Luke 21:19). Then, again in all three Gospels, he told the disciples where they could find the will and the power to exercise the required endurance. He said, "Heaven and earth will pass away, but my words will not pass away" (Matt. 24:35, Mark 13:31, Luke 21:33).

I believe that most of us often suffer from spiritual myopia. We are like the disciples, looking only at some immediate thing or condition without considering that it is our relationship with the Lord Jesus Christ and with other people that defines the fullness of life beyond any immediate moment of victory or defeat, or grief or joy. Sometimes, I become so confused or disappointed that I cannot see beyond the nose on my face. But even then, the Word of God remains as true as always. Jesus said, "In the world you have trouble; but be of good cheer, I have overcome the world" (John 16:33). Some of us have had times of sadness so overpowering that we have felt that life has nothing left for us but endless pain. Jesus said, "I will not leave you desolate; I will come to you" (John 14:18).

Spiritual myopia can make us shortsighted, not seeing the eternal promises of Jesus. It can make us nearsighted so that we trust in our own abilities and fail to have faith in God's love for us. The cure for spiritual myopia is to believe that Jesus meant it when he said, "Heaven and earth will pass away, but my words will not pass away." I need to know that every day of my life. Whether my luck is good or bad, whether I am healthy or sick, whether I am rich or poor, I need to know that I am not alone. I need to know that I am standing on promises that cannot fail because they are established on the words of the One who promises that they will never pass away.

Spiritual myopia can cause us to forget that life is more about relationships than it is about things. What happened to the Jews was more important than what happened to their temple. This should remind us that any life that is worth living is about people and what happens to people. It is about how we live our lives together, and how we let our faith in God lead us and guide us from day to day. The disciple's excitement over the beauty of a building reminds me of how much we, as did they, allow too much of our lives to be governed by things and possessions rather than by our relationships and friendships with each other.

I am reminded of a young sailor whom I counseled when I was a Navy chaplain. Each week, when he met with me, he seemed to be a little more depressed about being in the Navy. Finally, one day, he came into my office with a big smile on his face. I said, "How are things with you today?" He said, "Not too good, but in one week, they will be great!" I said, "Oh, why is that?" He said, "I'm getting out of the Navy, and I am going to buy a Porsche, and then everything will be super okay." I asked, "And how does that significantly change your life?" He quickly replied, "Chaplain, are you crazy? Haven't you ever driven a Porsche?" I wondered how long it would take him to realize that possession of things, even a Porsche, does not in itself bring happiness.

The disciples exclaimed, "Wow! Would you look at that building?" They saw its external splendor, but what they saw was not what Jesus saw. He saw the rot and corruption which was internal, and which would determine the fate of Herod's wicked and corrupt kingdom. He saw the end of Israel's national authority and autonomy. He saw the beginning of a Jewish diaspora that would last for nineteen-hundred years.

It is not the external splendor of things that holds the true beauty, value, and worth of life. Our Lord did not die to save a single building or a single thing. He did not die so that we could erect monuments to our own success and glory. He died so that we might learn to live with each other and to love each other as he has loved us. He died that we might endure and have the strength to not get tired of doing what is right, and to have the faith that his words will never pass away.

As I get older and reflect on occasions of spiritual and relational myopia in my own experiences, there is something that hurts me more than my aches and pains, more than my bodily injuries. The source of that hurt is my memory of the hurt that I have caused other people. Those memories often come at unexpected times and in unexpected ways. Driving to work one day, I suddenly had the memory of a high school reunion I once attended. I remembered seeing a girl, a classmate whose family was poor. She was ostracized, and this led to insecurity and low self-esteem. My family was equally poor, but because I was a gifted athlete, I was spared the ostracism and embarrassment that my classmate suffered. When we first gathered at the reunion, she stood close to me but never said a word. I recalled that I did not recognize her presence. She had done well in life but was very reserved as she moved closer to me. Maybe being back in that environment took her back to school day hurts. Anyway, as I reflect on her presence, I am certain that the scars of her ostracism were still there. She wanted to finally be acknowledged and validated as a classmate. I should have gone to her and said something like, "Gee, you look wonderful, and you have done well for yourself. If you have time, I would like to sit down and talk." I failed to recognize the relational context and importance of the moment. I was too busy looking at the old building with the statue of our mascot raised high above it. I was more interested in the old classrooms, the gymnasium, and the football field. For my classmate, the experience conjured up the years-old pain of insecurity and low self-esteem. Once again, the captain of the football team was ignoring a young girl who was poor. The memory of that reunion moment confirmed that I had been an instrument in the continuation of her pain.

We specialize in our monuments and our external things. It too often escapes us that they will, eventually, be destroyed. Do we spend as much time specializing in people as we do in things? I have been to the Pearl Harbor Memorial, the Washington Monument, the Lincoln Memorial, the Vietnam Wall, and countless other monuments and memorials around the world. These things have their place, and I do not want to minimize their symbolism. However, of first importance, it is essential that we recognize that Jesus taught his disciples to look beyond the external and directed them toward a relationship with God and with each other.

Focusing on our things and our "stuff" has a way of obscuring the joy and beauty that comes from sharing our lives and our experiences with other human beings. Human relationships shared in the name of Jesus Christ will, unlike things, abide forever. I am a former Marine, and I am proud of my Marine Corps heritage. I have been to the Marine Corps Memorial many times and know the story of Marine heroism on the island of Iwo Jima. My wife and I were visiting the parents of some friends a few years ago. I did not know this older gentleman and his wife and was not interested in spending time with them. Besides that, I was looking forward to getting home in time to watch a movie that I had been anticipating all week. We arrived at their home, and everybody went inside except the older man and me. As we sat on the beach and made small talk, I kept wondering how I could end this and get home to watch the movie. Finally, I said, "I must get home. There is an old movie on TV that I want to watch." He said, "What's the title?" I said, "*The Outsider*, starring Tony Curtis." He said, "What's it about?" I said, "It's about Ira Hays, the Indian who helped the Marines raise the flag on Iwo Jima." He sat quietly for a while, and then he said, "O yeah, old Ira was quite a guy." I said, "What do you mean? What are you talking about?" He said, "I was a Marine. Ira was in my platoon. I knew him well. We landed on Iwo Jima together." My reaction to this news was, "Forget the movie! Forget the Iwo Jima Memorial! Here is the real thing in flesh and blood, the human touch!" For the next three hours, I coaxed stories from this incredible old veteran of my beloved Marine Corps. I was exhilarated and felt tremendously blessed by this very personal human relationship. When my new friend suffered a heart attack, he called for me to come and pray for him and with him. When his family faced trouble from within, he asked me to intervene and pray for the family. Later, I received the call that was inevitable. The family informed me that he had died. He had requested that I preside at his funeral, and I was honored to fulfill that request.

The treasure, above all treasures available to us, is the treasure of meaningful human relationships. When we let it happen, God's love is poured into our lives, and it overflows and touches the lives of everyone we meet. If we let it happen, we might find that we have an amazing power to bless each other more than all the things of the world can bless us. The disciples said, "It's a great building!" Jesus said, "It will be torn down and pass away, but my words will never pass away." As we live in this world, the question is not "What is going to happen?" We know that this earth and the things of this earth will be torn down and will pass away. The question for us is always, "What is the state of my relationship with the Lord Jesus Christ and my fellow human beings?" The things we love too much will pass away, and eventually, we will die. We cannot bring back yesterday, and we cannot shape tomorrow so that it always conforms to our wishes and desires. Jesus said, "Therefore do not be anxious about tomorrow, for tomorrow will be anxious for itself. Let the day's own trouble be sufficient for the day" (Matthew 6:34).

Prayer:

Lord, free us from the grips of a spiritual myopia that blinds us to the beauty of the gift of life itself. Help us to see beyond our own self-interests and narrow personal preferences. Teach us that the greatest joys and successes of life are found in our human relationships and in our faith in You. Help us to love one another as you have loved us. Empower us to live so that we might be recognized as your disciples. Amen.

CHAPTER SIX
LEST WE FORGET

Amos 6:1-8: *[1] Woe to those who are at ease in Zion, and to those who feel secure on the mountain of Samaria, the notable men of the first of the nations, to whom the house of Israel come!*

[2] Pass over to Calneh, and see; and thence go to Hamath the great; then go down to Gath of the Philistines. Are they better than these kingdoms? Or is their territory greater than your territory.

[3] O you who put far away the evil day, and bring near the seat of violence?

[4] Woe to those who lie upon beds of ivory, and stretch themselves on their couches, and eat lambs from the flock, and calves from the midst of the stall;

[5] who sing idle songs to the sound of the harp, and like David invent for themselves instruments of music;

[6] who drink wine in bowls, and anoint themselves with the finest oils, but are not grieved over the ruin of Joseph!

[7] Therefore they shall now be the first of those to go into exile, and the revelry of those who stretch themselves shall pass away.

⁸ The Lord God has sworn by himself (says the Lord, the God of hosts): "I abhor the pride of Jacob, and hate his strongholds; and I will deliver up the city and all that is in it."

In the eighth century BCE, independent countries were coming under Assyrian domination. Tilgath-Pileser III demanded tribute from the Israelite leadership, and independence passed out of Israelite control. A sheep farmer named Amos was prompted to leave his farm and serve as a spokesperson for the Lord God of Israel. While the message of Amos was spoken to the nation at large, it was particularly addressed to "the notable men of the first of the nations, to whom the house of Israel come!" (vs, 1).

In assessing the message of Amos, we should not try to superimpose the governmental mechanisms of ancient Israel upon those of our American system of laws and regulations. Israel was governed by theocratic authority without any thought for the separation of church and state. In short, church/religion and state/laws/government were the same entity. Therefore, the warning of the prophet rang with the voice and authority of Yahweh Himself. However, the warnings of the prophet's time do not carry the same national authority for our democratic republic as they did for the theocracy of Israel.

Let us consider that Amos was not a professional prophet, nor was he an extraordinary holy man. He was a farmer living an ordinary secular life within the general population of Israel. He tells us that God "took him" and told him to "go prophesy to my people Israel" (Amos 6:1). At that time, there was no war or public crisis in the land, and the economy was booming. While all was well, Amos saw that the leaders and the well-to-do of the land enjoyed a state of affluence that hardened their hearts against the needs of those who were less fortunate.

His warning was clear and to the point, "Woe to those who are at ease in Zion" (Amos 6:1, RSV), or as in the better translation of the New English Bible, "Shame on you who live at ease in Zion." About 2,800 years after Amos, Rudyard Kipling would voice a similar warning to the great British Empire during the reign of Queen Victoria. The refrain of his poem, "Recessional," is "Lord God of hosts, be with us yet, Lest we forget—lest we forget!"[1] Both the "woe warning" of Amos and the "Lest we forget" of Kipling speak a prophetic message to us today.

How shall Christians living in a secularly governed and administered America hear the warnings today? Should we wait for government action to minister to the poor and oppressed, or should we minister and serve at a local and individual level? America is not ancient Israel, and notwithstanding the common misconception that America is a Christian nation, Old Testament decrees have no compelling authority over our democratic republic system of government. Our secular government does have a system of responding to the needs of its poorer citizens, but it does not function under any divine mandate to meet anyone's needs.

While our Founding Fathers did not write a divine mandate into our governing documents, there can be little doubt that they recognized the wisdom of giving attention to the guiding hand of the God of Abraham, Isaac, and Jacob in the history of Israel. In their quest for a more perfect union, they were not so foolish as to disregard the value of more than three thousand years of biblical tradition. It is reasonable to assume that many of their intentions that did not result in written expression were based on wisdom and knowledge gleaned from the Bible. This does not mean that they intended to create a Judeo-Christian nation. While recognizing religion in general, their motivating intent was to establish the guarantee of freedom of religion. As it happened, the prevailing fact was that Christianity was, and continues to be, the dominant religion in the United States. Holding fast to faith in the God of the Judeo-Christian tradition includes the belief that the breath of life that fuels us is provided by the God who made us.

The absence of a national divine mandate does not excuse those of us committed to Judeo-Christian principles from conducting our lives according to the guidance of those principles. We can, I think, assess our personal lives on an individual scale, just as Amos assessed the life of Israel on a national scale. For instance, acting solely on the authority of God, Amos warned that neglect of the poor would bring disaster to Israel. While our government has no divine mandate to act, we individual Christians live our lives under the authority of God and the charge of our Lord, who said, "Truly, I say to you, as you did it to one of the least of these my brethren, you did it to me" (Matt. 25:40). We are encouraged to function as individuals who are energized by the compassion of Christ. The work of the Kingdom is too compelling to be left in the hands of political hacks who pander to the public and are motivated by partisan pride, and greed.

Israel presumed that it was superior to its neighbors and was entitled to a life of prosperity and ease. Their national love of self-sufficiency and fascination with ever-newer luxuries borrowed from other cultures gave rise to an attitude of indifference within the leadership. As self-indulgence became a routine way of life, the poor and less fortunate members of society were treated cruelly. While the "haves" of the nation indulged their appetites for food, drink, and entertainment, the "have nots" suffered and went unnoticed. Success and accomplishments were taken as a sign of God's favor, and this produced an arrogant assumption that they were exempt from any misfortune. They began to trust more in their own sense of self-importance than in the providence of God. The "woe cry" of

Amos warned them that their confidence in their own security was the confidence of a fool. He accused the government of providing reckless leadership that would lead to defeat and exile to a foreign land. Those who had brought this disaster to the nation "shall now be the first of those to go into exile" (Amos 6:7).

The "woe cry" of Amos can provide preemptive warnings for our personal lives. They caution us to guard against substituting wealth and success for the security that comes from our faith in God. We are reminded that we are never so superior or elite that we are entitled to separate ourselves from the human family. Our Christian mandate requires that we respond to the needs of the poor and oppressed. Regardless of political affiliation, ethnicity, social standing, or gender identity, we are charged to be peacemakers and merciful disciples of our Lord Jesus Christ.

The nation of Israel failed to heed the word of Amos. Consequently, those who had been the most self-sufficient were also the first to lose everything and the first to go into exile. As we take inventory of our lives today, let us place our trust in God more than anything else, remembering that Jesus said, "The last will be first and the first last" (Matt. 20:16). Lest we forget—lest we forget!

Prayer:

Lord, Let us not forget that all that we have is a gift from your bounty. Make us mindful of our daily responsibility to share our gifts, our resources, and our lives with all those who may be less fortunate than ourselves. In Your holy name we pray. Amen.

CHAPTER SEVEN
OUR TIMES ARE IN HIS HANDS

Psalm 31:9-16: *⁹ Be gracious to me, O Lord, for I am in distress; my eye is wasted from grief, my soul and my body also.*

¹⁰ For my life is spent with sorrow, and my years with sighing; my strength fails because of my misery, and my bones waste away.

¹¹ I am the scorn of all my adversaries, a horror to my neighbors, an object of dread to my acquaintances; those who see me in the street flee from me.

¹² I have passed out of mind like one who is dead; I have become like a broken vessel.

¹³ Yea, I hear the whispering of many—terror on every side!—as they scheme together against me, as they plot to take my life.

¹⁴ But I trust in thee, O Lord, I say, "Thou art my God."

¹⁵ My times are in thy hand; deliver me from the hand of my enemies and persecutors!

¹⁶ Let thy face shine on thy servant; save me in thy steadfast love!

If I were a counselor listening to the complaints of someone as they are reflected in Psalm 31, I would suspect that the counselee was demonstrating some form of psychological and emotional pathology. The Psalmist complained that there were people setting traps for him and hunting him as if he were an animal (Ps. 31:4). He believed that everybody was talking about him and that there were plots against him and a conspiracy to kill him (Ps. 31:13). He felt that he had become as useless as a broken glass or cup that could no longer hold water (Ps. 31:12). People avoided him in public, his friends did not want to associate with him, and he had become guilt-ridden and miserable (Ps. 31:10, 11). As I listen to him, I find it noteworthy that he can immediately pivot from his litany of misery and failure to a feeling of hope and assurance (Ps. 31:21).

As a counselor, I would be considering the possibilities (probabilities?) of paranoia, depression, bipolar, and other disorders. However, this Psalm of David is not presented as a face-to-face, real-time event between two people. The context is that of a person looking back over his shoulder and reflecting on life as he has experienced it. He is recalling his state of mind as he dealt with the various conflicts, dangers, and uncertainties of life.

David, although defined as a man after God's own heart, had not been exempt from the shortcomings and temptations that accompany life as a human being. He had his share of family, political, vocational, moral, ethical, and spiritual problems. He spent part of his life as a fugitive, running and hiding from the vengeful jealousy of King Saul. As a man of war, he fought and lived in the rocky terrain and among the caves and hiding places of the rough wilderness. His recounting of these many traumatic experiences does not serve to confirm a diagnosis of severe psychological pathology. His thought process, as we have it in its written form in Psalm 31, seems disjointed and illogical because that is the way past reality comes to us as we pull it back through the filters of our memory. The memories often do not come in chronological order;

in fact, they may come as non-sequiturs that emerge when abruptly stimulated by emotions, moods, and thoughts.

Looking back on the distress, misery, and danger that he had endured, David was able to see the pattern of his life in terms of its completeness. In verse twenty-two he tells us how he responded to his adversity as it happened to him. He refers to his response as "alarm" (RSV, NIV, NEB), "haste;" (KJV), "extreme fear" (Greek), "nervous haste" (Hebrew), and "excitement" (Latin). He realized that he came through it all because while he experienced fear, alarm, and astonishment, he also maintained his reliance on God. Unable to change his circumstances, he found refuge in God. The Christian Church has always sought to understand the suffering and death (passion) of Jesus by associating it with Psalm 31 (also Ps. 22). The Church, looking back, saw that the experience of the Psalmist was a picture of the sacrificial love and mercy of God that was manifested in Jesus Christ.

In any given existential moment, we may find our trust in God to be in the grips of alarm, extreme fear, excitement, or prompting us to act with urgent and unexamined haste. David's fear and alarm challenged his faith, but he managed to "cry to God for help" (Ps. 31:22). Years later, he was able to remember not just the raw pain of suffering and distress, but also remembered that the pain was accompanied by the grace and guidance of God. David wisely accepted the fact that God is the keeper of our lives. He said, "My times are in thy hand" (Ps. 31:15). This reference of "times" does not refer to a period as we measure it (e.g., day, week, month, year). It does not have anything to do with the length of our lives. It means that my fortune, my lot in life, things that happen to me, and that which is assigned to me are in the hands of God. There is a hymn that says, "My times are in Thy hand, Whatever they may be; Pleasing or painful, dark or bright, As best may seem to Thee."[1]

As we age and look back on our own history through the filter of experience, we may recognize that God was with us in our most desperate and alarming moments. We may have thought that we had abandoned or betrayed our faith, but I believe that when we are baptized, we share the testimony of the man who said to Jesus, "I believe; help my unbelief!" (Mark 9:24). What appeared to have been disastrous is revealed to have included the hand of God that we did not or could not have understood at the time. Faith is not always a pleasant stroll down some primrose lane of life. Faith also means claiming our failures, anger, grief, sins, and the worst part of our lives and holding them up to God for healing.

Most of us have known times when we felt like our ability to do anything had been neutralized. We say, "I am at my wits end. I have done everything I know to do." What do you do when you cannot do anything? David said, "Into thy hand I commit my spirit" (Ps. 31:5). The final prayer of Jesus' earthly life was "Father, into thy hands I commit my spirit" (Luke 23:44). The suffering Son of God has become our Redeemer and the example of One whose whole life was lived in dependence on Father God. The misery and mystery of his life has been identified with the pain, suffering, and unfairness that is native to all human life. He has shown us how to respond when evil finds a way through the laws that are designed to protect us. When the human conscience becomes diseased and surrenders to the condition that has been called "man's inhumanity to man," He tells us to commit our spirits to the spirit of love that drove him to a cross through which God has committed Himself to save the world.

In this Psalm of David, we hear the words of our Lord. We see those words in action in the Gospel records of the passion of our Savior: "Father, into your hands I commit my spirit" (Luke 23:44), and "It is finished" (John 19:30). What does it all mean for us? As I have written elsewhere, it means at least this:

Suspended vertically between heaven and earth and horizontally spread-eagled on the cross, heaven spoke to earth and earth spoke to heaven. In that fantastic, glorious exchange between humanity and divinity, we learned that nothing less than love can span the chasm that unites us to and with the God of the universe who created us in His own image.[2]

Prayer:

Lord, sometimes we feel inadequate to face the pressures and demands of life. The weight of our involvement with people, places, and things seems to be more than we can bear. Before we let anger, alarm, fear, or stress get the best of us, help us to pause and have a talk with You. In our most difficult moments, remind us that we can commit our challenges into Your care and keeping with certainty that our times are in Your hands. In Your holy name we pray. Amen.

CHAPTER EIGHT
ACTION VERBS

Psalm 100: *[1] Make a joyful noise to the Lord, all the lands!*

[2] Serve the Lord with gladness! Come into his presence with singing!

[3] Know that the Lord is God! It is he that made us and we are his; we are his people, and the sheep of his pasture.

[4] Enter his gates with thanksgiving, and his courts with praise! Give thanks to him, bless his name!

[5] For the Lord is good; his steadfast love endures forever, and his faithfulness to all generations.

Because of its brevity (only five verses), this Psalm could be mistakenly viewed as having less importance in the life of the cultic worshiping community than those Psalms consisting of many more verses. Recognizing this possibility, Saint Augustine said, "The verses are few, but big with great subjects."[1] Psalm 100 does not ask us to quietly contemplate the beauty or wisdom of its poetry. Each of the first four verses calls the worshiper to actively participate in the event. All the verbs are dynamic action verbs with the force of the imperative mood (command or entreaty); make, serve, come, know, enter, give, and bless.

The call to worship is not limited by the boundaries of the temple walls. In fact, it has no boundaries and is extended to the earth's total population. The Psalmist's vision is that of an integration of all the nations of the world rejoicing before the God of Israel. While the worship of Yahweh originated within the cult of the Israelites, all the nations of the earth were destined to have an equal share of God's blessings (Gen. 12:3; 22:15-18; 26:3-4). This destiny is particularly evident in the Judeo-Christian tradition. Christians are not just "borrowers" of Israelite religion, and we need not, (must not?), see ourselves as marginal servants and second-class children of the God of Israel. In fact, Christians represent the fulfillment of God's creative activity in the life and history of the Israelite cult. Karl Barth recognized this fulfillment and completion in Psalm 100 and called it the "Alpha and Omega of the call of Jesus Christ Himself."[2]

If Barth is correct in that "the call of Christ" commands us from within the Psalm, the action verbs challenge us to "be doers of the word, and not hearers only" (James 1:22). By extension, worship involves more than sitting within the boundaries of the temple/church. It reaches beyond the comfort of the pews and the festivity of the fellowship halls. For my own spiritual orientation, I do not diminish the validity of our corporate gatherings to express our worship of God. However, since I spend most of my time outside of some stated place and time of worship, I find it necessary for me to consider how I worship during those extended times when I am not engaged in some form of corporate worship. How do the action verbs of Psalm 100 motivate me to demonstrate my confession that "the Lord is God, and it is he that has made me, and I am his" (Ps 100:3)?

I am reminded of a certain rainy and dreary day during my seminary years. A student arrived several minutes before class began. He greeted the professor with a pleasant "Good morning, sir!" The professor, who was known to be a sour, curmudgeon sort of person, said, "What is so good about it? I have had enough of this rain and lousy weather." The student said, "This is the day the Lord has made; we should rejoice and be glad in it." The mood and countenance of the professor changed immediately, and he said, "Amen! You are right. Praise the Lord!" Word of his response quickly spread throughout the seminary. Later in the day, he was asked why he was so upbeat and happy. He said, "One of my students blessed me today and reminded me that the Lord is God." One student made a joyful noise to the Lord in a non-liturgical setting, and it spread throughout an entire community of people.

When we enter the sanctuary on Sunday, we take it for granted that we have come to worship the Lord, and that is okay. But I challenge us to think about how the action verbs of Psalm 100 have challenged us to make a joyful noise, to serve, to know the Lord, and to enter His presence when we are not in a scheduled worship service. Do we really understand what it means when we say, "the Lord is good"? When we say that something is good, we mean that it conforms to social, legal, and cultural standards that our society has legislated to be good. However, the Psalmist spoke of the goodness of the Lord in a way that transcends conformity to any of our standards.

The Lord is good because He honors His covenant promises to us. In a world that is always changing due to the conduct and behavior of created humans, the faithfulness of the Lord is the only constant absolute upon which we can depend. When we gather in the sanctuary, we bring memories that are fresh and raw with the trauma of local, national, and international tragedies. Mass shootings, terrorist acts, world catastrophes, viral pandemics, transportation disasters, and violence in our cities have become common events. We may often wonder if we are living in a world that has gone mad. But as a gathered community, we incline our ears to hear the Word of our God. We lift our voices and are reminded that "This is my Father's world, and though the wrong seems oft so strong, God is the ruler yet. The Lord is King; let the heavens ring! God reigns; let the earth be glad!"[3] Whether gathered as a congregation or simply going about our personal everyday business and activities, we serve a dependable God who empowers us with action verbs for the living of these days!

Prayer:

Lord, we thank you for your everlasting mercy and goodness. We ask for the strength and confidence to trust that you are our Great Shepherd and that you will never leave us nor forsake us. Help us to live by those action verbs that bring glory to your Holy Name. Amen.

CHAPTER NINE
NOT WHY? BUT HOW?

Job 1:1-22: *¹There was a man in the land of Uz, whose name was Job; and that man was blameless and upright, one who feared God, and turned away from evil.*

²There was born to him seven sons and three daughters.

³He had seven thousand sheep, three thousand camels, five hundred yoke of oxen, and five hundred she-asses, and very many servants; so that this man was the greatest of all the people of the east.

⁴His sons used to go and hold a feast in the house of each on his day; and they would send and invite their three sisters to eat and drink with them.

⁵And when the days of the feast had run their course, Job would send and sanctify them, and he would rise early in the morning and offer burnt offerings according to the number of them all; for Job said, "It may be that my sons have sinned, and cursed God in their hearts." Thus Job did continually.

⁶Now there was a day when the sons of God came to present themselves before the Lord, and Satan also came among them.

⁷The Lord said to Satan, "Whence have you come?" Satan answered the Lord, "From going to and fro on the earth, and walking up and down on it."

⁸And the Lord said to Satan, "Have you considered my servant Job, that there is none like him on the earth, a blameless and upright man, who fears God and turns away from evil?"

⁹Then Satan answered the Lord, "Does Job fear God for nought?

¹⁰Hast thou not put a hedge about him and his house and all that he has on every side? Thou hast blessed the work of his hands, and his possessions have increased in the land.

¹¹But put forth thy hand now, and touch all that he has, and he will curse thee to thy face."

¹²And the Lord said to Satan, "Behold, all that he has is in your power; only upon himself do not put forth your hand." So Satan went forth from the presence of the Lord.

¹³Now there was a day when his sons and daughters were eating and drinking wine in their eldest brother's house;

¹⁴And there came a messenger to Job, and said, "The oxen were plowing and the asses feeding beside them;

¹⁵and the Sabeans fell upon them and took them, and slew the servants with the edge of the sword; and I alone have escaped to tell you." ¹⁶While he was yet speaking, there came another, and said, "The fire of God fell from heaven and burned up the sheep and the servants, and consumed them; and I alone have escaped to tell you."

¹⁷While he was yet speaking, there came another, and said, "The Chaldeans formed three companies, and made a raid on the camels and took them, and slew the servants with the edge of the sword; and I alone have escaped to tell you,"

[18]While he was yet speaking, there came another, and said, "Your sons and daughters were eating and drinking wine in their eldest brother's house;

[19]and behold, a great wind came across the wilderness, and struck the four corners of the house, and it fell upon the young people, and they are dead; and I alone have escaped to tell you."

[20]Then Job arose, and rent his robe, and shaved his head, and fell upon the ground, and worshiped.

[21]And he said, "Naked I came from my mother's womb, and naked shall I return; the Lord gave, and the Lord has taken away; blessed be the name of the Lord."

[22]In all this Job did not sin or charge God with wrong.

If the message of Job is to make any sense at all, it must be read as a single unit from beginning to end. Relying on cherry-picked verses and catchphrases does violence to the total context and original intent of the writer/writers of the book. Such an approach encourages us to ask the wrong questions and conjure up answers that make no sense as we wrestle with the dilemmas of human existence. Having said this, I hope you are prompted to read the entire *Book of Job*. A reading of all forty-two chapters will introduce you to the real Job and make you aware of those times and places when and where you have personally lived some of the experiences of Job.

During my years of ministry, a common question put to me has been, "Why did God let this happen?" In his book, *When Bad Things Happen to Good People*, Rabbi Harold Kushner says, "Virtually every meaningful conversation I have ever had with people on the subject of God and religion has either started with this question or gotten around to it before long."[1] The question has come to me in the personal form of "Why is this happening to me?" It has also come in the form of concern for others, "Why did this happen to so and so?" Those inclined to pick a fight with religion have often asked, "How can a good God let something like this happen?"

Thirty years of my ministry was spent with young Marines serving in training and combat environments, both of which always held the possibility of danger, injury, and death. To this day, it is painful to hear in my memory the responses of surviving loved ones: "He was only eighteen years old"; "She had joined the Marine Corps and finally found her motivation for living"; "He had such promise and his whole life was before him"; "The military provided the security of family life that he had never known, why was it taken from him?"; "All he wanted to do was serve his country and help people." The underlying question, whether spoken or unspoken, has been, "If there is a God, why has He permitted this to happen?"

I am no more qualified to answer this question today than I was on any of those occasions. I began my seminary education expecting that I would learn the answers to all the great questions that humankind has asked over the years. There have been very few empirical answers to the great, mysterious questions of life and death. The best answer that the learned Saint Paul can give is one that compounds our curiosity when he says, "Behold! I tell you a mystery" (1 Cor. 15:51). A fellow student in one of my New Testament seminary classes once involved the professor in a discussion about God and the existence of evil in the world. He complained that after three years of graduate classes, and many hours of studying theology and biblical languages, that he still did not understand how and why God let evil exist and why bad things happen to good people. When he insisted on an answer, the professor said, "You can't understand it because you are not God." I did not place much value on that answer at that time, but over the years I have come to accept the possibility that it might be the best answer any of us will get on this side of eternity.

But what about Job? In the few verses of 1:1-22 what can we say about him? His background check is impeccable. We are told that he is "blameless and upright, one who feared God and turned away from evil" (Job 1:1). There is no reference to sins committed or failure to conform to the protocols of ritual worship. Not even Yahweh, the perfect and absolute God of all creation, was inclined to bring any charge against him: "Have you considered my servant Job, that there is none like him on the earth?" (Job 1:8).

Job was the kind of person that we would like to have as a friend and the kind of person we would like to be. He was good, successful, honest, wealthy, blessed with a healthy and happy family, had a good reputation, and honored and worshiped God. Unfortunately, the story is so heavenly perfect that it becomes humanly unreal. Following Job's impeccable background check, he began to experience life's common realities. The dynamics of public reputation, economics, family relationships, and health issues plagued him in rapid succession. "When it rains, it pours" became the rule rather than the exception in his life. He had large herds of cattle and many servants to maintain his estate. His great wealth afforded him the luxury of providing for his family. However, things took a turn for the worse. Messengers arrived with news that bandits and fire had killed his cattle and his servants. With the sudden devastation of a modern-day stock market crash, Job's wealth was destroyed, and his estate was bankrupt. Next, he learned that all his children were killed in a storm. Finally, his health began to fail, and his friends and neighbors reported that his misery was a result of sins committed against God.

I want to emphatically declare that not even one of us is exempt from the disturbing realities of life. In America today no family is unaffected by issues resulting from substance abuse, crime, broken relationships, financial difficulties, career problems, or some other painful and stressful condition. Before we jump to conclusions and pass judgment on anyone, before we measure them solely by our values and belief systems, we need to recognize that people, even innocent people, do suffer misfortunes.

We are familiar with the phrase, "he/she got what they deserved." This is what I know about what we deserve. I have seen things happen to people that are far worse than they might have deserved. To name a few, there is employment discrimination, sudden and unexplained sickness, long and painful suffering, cruel and excruciating deaths, paralysis and loss of body mobility, early onset dementia, maltreatment of infants and helpless children, debilitating depression, and the embarrassing agony of not having sufficient resources to provide for a family. What I also know is that these human tragedies do not represent God's punishment for anything they might have done. I maintain unequivocally that these misfortunes do not come from God.

Job was just as much in the dark as we are about these unexplained things that plague us. He does not know why or if God has let these things happen to him. We soon learn that his friends are more than happy to tell him what has caused his problems. They are sure that his sins have brought suffering into his life. They insist that nothing less than repentance will bring relief from his misery and misfortune. All too often, we become like Job's friends and have an urge to straighten people out in their thinking. As you read the rest of the Book of Job, please "beware of Job's friends" in your own life experiences,

In Job, the proper question is not "why?" but "how?" How will we respond to life's adversities? Job expressed his grief and worshiped God (Job 1:21). The life he was given from the moment of his conception and all else that accrued from that time forward was a gift from God. The God who gave it all had the right to reclaim it. Job did not accuse God of injustice or vengeance. He did not argue about the ethical and philosophical inequities of life. While experiencing pain, loss, and misery in his body and soul, Job "blessed the name of the Lord and in all this Job did not sin or charge God with wrong" (Job 1:21-22).

Our lives do not always turn out the way we expect them to turn out. Ours or someone else's carelessness, greed, or irresponsibility can bring turmoil to who we are or what we are trying to do. Our genetic code or a virus or bacteria can condemn us to a handicapped life or even death. Questions that ask "why" may drive our curiosity, but they serve no effective purpose in sustaining our faith. Effective faith cannot be reduced to bumper sticker phrases and magical tokens merchandised by television preachers. Job teaches us that real faith is refined through trusting God in the fires and storms of life. Pain and suffering are common to humankind. We will often misunderstand the condition of friends just as they may misunderstand us. God's silence does not mean that He is absent. Our frustrations, losses, disappointments, and failures do not mean that He has abandoned us. As it was for Job and for Saint Paul, so it is for us: "My grace is sufficient for you, for my power is made perfect in weakness" (2 Cor. 12:9).

Prayer:

Lord, forgive us when we blame You for the pain and difficulties that visit us in life. Help us to understand that we are not being cruelly punished for some unknown transgression. Teach us to rely upon your grace and ask for your help and strength in all of life's experiences. May we never become so defeated that we cannot bless your holy name. Amen

CHAPTER TEN
BUT NOW, A NEW BEGINNING

Isaiah 43:1-7: *¹ But now thus says the Lord, he who created you, O Jacob, he who formed you, O Israel: "Fear not, for I have redeemed you: I have called you by name, you are mine.*

² When you pass through the waters I will be with you; and through the rivers, they shall not overwhelm you; when you walk through fire you shall not be burned, and the flame shall not consume you.

³ For I am the Lord your God, the Holy One of Israel, your Savior. I give Egypt as your ransom, Ethiopia and Seba in exchange for you.

⁴ Because you are precious in my eyes, and honored, and I love you, I give men in return for you, peoples in exchange for your life.

⁵ Fear not, for I am with you; I will bring your offspring from the east, and from the west I will gather you;

⁶ I will say to the north, Give up, and to the south, Do not withhold; bring my sons from afar and my daughters from the end of the earth,

⁷ everyone who is called by my name, whom I created for my glory, whom I formed and made."

Chapter 43 begins with an announcement that things are changing in how God is to be viewed by all the people of His creation. Up to this point, the Word of the Lord, as proclaimed by Isaiah, has been a word of judgment regarding Israel's past and present disobedience. The words "but now" signal a summing up of the past, which had led to this new hour and this new situation. Israel had not been an obedient servant of God, and it was their disobedience that brought them to this "but now" moment of accountability. The people acknowledged their guilt and confirmed the truth of the accusation brought against them by the prophet. They freely confessed that they had "sinned against the Lord and would not walk in his ways and they were not obedient to his law" (Isa. 42:24). The prior focus was on the past actions of Israel. The "but now" action will be focused on the future and on what God will do for Israel going forward.

The "but now" beginning of chapter 43 requires us to return to chapter 42 to learn what preceded and what prompted the "but now" declaration of the prophet. The people of Israel had known the slavery of Egypt and currently were living in exile in Babylon. For at least seventy years they had lived under the foreign policies of a conquering world power. The temple, the central feature of their worship of Yahweh, had been destroyed, and their exposure to the pagan gods of Babylon had eroded their singular commitment to the God of their fathers. As a subdued people living in captivity, they had limited freedom of movement and were forced to conform to the governing policies and cultural mores of their captors. Living under the shadow of misery, fear, and distress, they had forfeited any hope that they could once again enjoy the life that was theirs when they were servants of the God who had brought them out of bondage.

Israel was guilty before God and had no grounds for protest or defense of her infidelity. They had no argument to oppose the accusations of the prophet who identified them as blind servants and deaf messengers (Isa. 42:18-25). Knowledge of their own failures convinced them that they could never again be a servant of the God who had delivered them from so many past difficulties. From their perspective, they realized that they were without hope and deserved to be abandoned by God.

It is at this point that Isaiah introduces Israel to a vision of God that is not bound by the confines of human perception and human reasoning. In contrast to past sin and failure, he proclaims a "but now" moment. He announces an intensive reversal of what appeared to be a hopeless situation. Acknowledgment of guilt and confession of sin fulfilled the precondition for forgiveness and salvation. Isaiah proclaims, "But now thus says the Lord, he who created you, O Israel: Fear not, for I have redeemed you; I have called you by name, you are mine" (Isa. 43:1). This scripture speaks to each individual person just as surely as it was spoken to the Israelite community in exile. The nation was humiliated and disoriented. The world as they had known it had collapsed around them. Given its history of failure, could Israel ever be reinstated as the servant of God? The answer comes in the form of a "but now" contrast of past and present; "but now I have redeemed you." This redemption is extended to all of God's creation. It is for "everyone who is called by my (God's) name, whom I created for my glory, whom I formed and made" (Isa. 43:7).

More than twenty times, Paul begins a sentence or a thought with the words "but now." It was his way of telling us what our lives were like before Jesus Christ and what they had become after his ministry, death, and resurrection. He told the doubting Corinthians, "but now Christ has been raised from the dead" (1 Cor. 15:20). He told the

Ephesians, "For once you were darkness, but now you are light in the Lord" (Eph. 5:8). Peter also proclaimed a great "but now" message of encouragement to the early church. He said, "Once you were no people but now you are God's people; once you had not received mercy but now you have received mercy" (1 Pet. 2:10).

Martin Luther was not without his times of doubt, despair, anxiety, and fear for his own safety. During times of torment, he relied on his own "but now" moment as a source of strength and faith. It is said that he would touch his head and proclaim, "I am baptized!" or he would write with chalk on his desk, "I am baptized."[1] Regardless of what he faced, he knew that his "but now" truth was that as a baptized disciple, nothing could separate him from the redeeming mercy and love of God.

There are times when we might feel displaced and desperate in life. Like Israel, we might lose sight of how we are loved and sustained by God. How many of us have experienced or known someone who has experienced the painful self-questioning of these and similar questions: "What is the use? What is the point of going on? What have I done with my life? How could I have made such a mess of things?" Painful as the questions are, they can be opportunities for us to hear the "but now" message of God's mercy and restoration. Isaiah's message was, "Yes, you were sinful and disobedient, but now God has turned his face to you and reclaimed you with his love." How much more is God's love magnified for us in Christ Jesus? We are a people who are baptized, forgiven, redeemed, and saved. Let us embrace those "but now" moments that remind us that each of us is dear and precious in the sight of the Lord.

Prayer:

Lord, it is so easy to become overwhelmed by the memory of some situation that has the power to produce shame and guilt in our lives. In those times, help us to remember "but now we are baptized, redeemed, and reclaimed by God's mercy and love through Jesus Christ." Amen.

CHAPTER ELEVEN
TO GOD BE THE GLORY

Psalm 115: *[1] Not to us, O Lord, not to us, but to thy name give glory, for the sake of the steadfast love and thy faithfulness!*

[2] Why should the nations say, "Where is their God?"

[3] Our God is in the heavens; he does whatever he pleases.

[4] Their idols are silver and gold, the work of men's hands.

[5] They have mouths but do not speak; eyes, but do not see.

[6] They have ears, but do not hear; noses but do not smell.

[7] They have hands, but do not feel; feet, but do not walk; and they do not make a sound in their throat.

[8] Those who make them are like them; so are all who trust in them.

[9] O Israel, trust in the Lord! He is their help and their shield.

[10] O house of Aaron, put your trust in the Lord! He is their help and their shield.

[11] You who fear the Lord, trust in the Lord! He is their help and their shield.

¹² The Lord has been mindful of us; he will bless us; he will bless the house of Israel; he will bless the house of Aaron;

¹³ he will bless those who fear the Lord, both small and great.

¹⁴ May the Lord give you increase, you and your children!

¹⁵ May you be blessed by the Lord, who made heaven and earth!

¹⁶ The heavens are the Lord's heavens, but the earth he has given to the sons of men. ¹⁷ The dead do not praise the Lord, nor do any that go down into silence. ¹⁸ But we will bless the Lord from this time forth and forevermore praise the Lord!

Psalm 115 may be a hymn that was prepared for public worship or for a particular liturgical event or moment in the life of Israel. It contains the positive elements of praise and gratitude. Conversely, it speaks scornfully of people who have no god and/or those who worship helpless gods that are the products of human hands.

The first and last verses highlight the worship posture of Israel in their relationship with their God. "Not to us, O Lord, not to us, but to thy name give glory, for the sake of thy steadfast love and thy faithfulness!" (Ps. 115:1). The Israelites knew that they could not claim any glory or honor for themselves. Their history was one of complaining, quarreling, and resistance to the guidance of God. They had not been steadfast in their love of God, and they had been unfaithful in their promises to obey the laws set forth by the Lord and His prophets. They knew that the record of their moral and ethical behavior would not serve to magnify the majesty, power, and glory of God. It is God's record of steadfast love and unflagging faithfulness that has provided the blessings and security that have supported them throughout their trials and tribulations. It is not the honor of the Israelite congregation that is at stake in facing the criticisms of the heathen nations. It is as if they are saying, "We know that we have failed but our God has been faithful in keeping his promises to us, and for this He is due all honor and glory."

The irony of this situation is that the glory and honor of God are not realized in the success of Israel but in its perception and confession of its own failure, rebellion, and wretchedness. In full recognition of its unfaithfulness, Israel bowed down in humility before God and confessed its weakness and ingratitude. In the final accounting, the Psalmist's emphasis is not on Israel's failures and shortcomings. Certainly, they are recognized for what they are, but it comes as no surprise that Israel has a great capacity for displaying unfaithfulness. When Moses first interceded for the people, God said, "I have seen this people, and behold, it is a stiff-necked people" (Exod. 32:9; 33:3-5; also, Deut. 9:6-13; 34:9). Israel has not received God's blessings because of its own victories and accomplishments. The Psalmist would have us know that Israel, although imperfect, stubborn, and stiff-necked, maintains the favor of God because of its repentant and humble response to God's faithfulness.

Regardless of success, failure, obedience, or disobedience, Israel's posture before God will always be, "But we will bless the Lord from this time forth and for evermore. Praise the Lord!" (Ps. 115:18). The Old Testament people of God knew that this is the only earthly perspective from which it is possible to deal with the mysteries of this life. We humans are creatures, but we have a permanent living relationship with our Creator (Ps. 115:15, 16). He knows each of us, and He has not forgotten us. Jesus tells us that God knows how many hairs we have on our head and is mindful of every sparrow that falls to the ground (Matt. 10:29-31; Luke 12:6-7). How, then, could He not know those He created and crowned with glory and honor? (Ps. 8).

Fools make fun of the concept of a creator God because they cannot control and master the moving parts of a faith-based life. Their pride blinds them to the futility of evaluating that which is infinite by the limited faculties and standards of the finite mind. The Psalmist recognized our human limitations: "Such knowledge is too wonderful for me; it is high, I cannot attain it" (Ps. 139:6). Many of us share the frustration expressed by the Psalmist. Sometimes, we cannot make any sense of what is happening in our lives and in our world. While we boast of our advancements and our accrued social and psychological knowledge of ourselves, we often ignore that we are created creatures who are dependent upon the care and keeping of our Creator. A genuine humility compels us to accept the fact that we are human and there is no earthly cure for our human condition.

The first question of *The Westminster Shorter Catechism*[1] is, "What is the chief end of man?" The answer given is, "Man's chief end is to glorify God, and to enjoy him forever." The cure for our imperfect earthly humanity is in worshiping the Lord, who maintains us through His heavenly steadfast love and faithfulness.

Our acts of praise and worship are not the frantic primal screams of a temporary coping tactic. Birthed from the womb of our Judeo-Christian history, they proclaim the triumphant witness of the ages that inspires every fiber of our being—physical, spiritual, emotional, intellectual, rational, and irrational—to explode with the energy of Handel's great Hallelujah Chorus, "For the Lord God omnipotent reigneth forever and ever...." It is to this God that the Psalmist urged Israel to offer glory and honor. It is to this God that the writer of Ecclesiastes gave the last word: "The end of the matter; all has been heard. Fear God and keep his commandments; for this is the whole duty of man" (Eccles. 12:13).

Simply put, today is the day the Lord has made for us and given to us. Right now, as you read this, I urge you to rise above everything that is going on in your life and give glory and honor to the Lord, your loving and faithful Creator!

Prayer:

Lord, we know that You have been more mindful of us than we have been of You. Increase our faith and encourage us to give glory and praise to You, especially in those times when we are threatened by fear and doubt. May we find courage in knowing that we are loved by a love that will never let go of us. Amen.

CHAPTER TWELVE
FORGIVEN, LOVED, REDEEMED

Psalm 130: *¹Out of the depths I cry to thee, O Lord!*

²Lord, hear my voice! Let thy ears be attentive to the voice of my supplications!

³If thou, O Lord, shouldst mark iniquities, Lord, who could stand?

⁴But there is forgiveness with thee, that thou mayest be feared.

⁵I wait for the Lord, my soul waits, and in his word I hope;

⁶my soul waits for the Lord more than watchmen for the morning.

⁷O Israel, hope in the Lord! For with the Lord there is steadfast love, and with him is plenteous redemption.

⁸And he will redeem Israel from all his iniquities.

Martin Luther believed that Psalm 130 was one of the four greatest Psalms in the Old Testament (along with Ps. 32, 51, and 143). The Psalm presents us with an understanding of the nature of sin and grace. The writer is concerned with both the mental and physical afflictions that trouble people. Throughout the Psalm, we see a movement from human anguish to an emotional and spiritual assurance of grace and forgiveness.

Although we may be tempted to think that God is not aware of our many situations, the truth still is that the hidden God is present and accessible in every moment of our lives. Walter Chambers Scott, in his great hymn, proclaims, "All praise we would render: O help us to see, 'Tis only the splendor of light hideth thee."[1] In our spiritual short-sightedness, we often confuse the gift that is ours by projecting victory into the future and limiting it to some future time or event. When I was a newly ordained minister, a church member once said to me, "You seem gloomy today. What is the problem?" I replied, "I don't know. I just cannot seem to win the victory." He replied, "It has already been won for you. All you must do is claim it in the name of Jesus Christ!" In retrospect, I realize the spiritual wisdom of that brother in Christ. Too often, we are "pie in the sky in the sweet by and by" people. While it is true that God's promises do own the future, it is also true that His promises are to be realized in every day of this gift of life that He has given us. The power that is available today is no less than the power promised to a consummated future.

The Psalmist cried to the Lord, "Out of the depths." The "depths" spoken of here refer to the mysterious hiddenness and the vastness and greatness of something. For the Psalmist, the "depths" refer to both the mystery of the hiddenness of God and the mystery of the many conditions and circumstances that visit people with daily regularity. Paul says that the "depth" of the riches, wisdom, and knowledge of God is "unsearchable" (Rom. 11:33). He also tells us that we experience our world as a hostile depth wherein we must stand against the "craftiness of the devil" (Eph. 6:11).

In Psalm 130, I hear the cry of one who is both saint and sinner. In fact, I hear your voice and my voice echoing from this distress call that seeks relief and restoration. It is the cry of all those who would be righteous before the Lord God. But let me quickly point out that the righteous person is not someone who has defeated the power of sin by his/her own strength, cleverness, and a toolbox full of personal resources. The righteous person recognizes that the depths of all human living will produce new and challenging difficulties and temptations every day. Tremendous pressures and frequent occasions of distress will appear from the depths of life's uncertainties and threaten us with doubts, fears, and failures. It is in those moments that the truth and power of Psalm 130 should come alive for us.

The hidden God is found to be alive and available precisely today, in this moment of time. Salvation and deliverance from the depth of despair, guilt, shame, failed opportunities, and failed relationships are defined, explained, and understood through the promise of what it means to be a child of God. Our hidden God, who knows the landscape of every depth that can threaten us, is a forgiving God whose love is steadfast, does not keep a record of sins, and is great in its power to provide redemption. Concerning anyone trusting in the hidden power of our hidden God, Karl Barth says,

> He will constantly rise up with wings like an eagle—a pilgrim who is hard pressed but not pressed down, often weary but not exhausted, often distressed but not in despair, often astray but not lost, seeking but also finding, asking but also receiving, and in the last analysis—in the light of his ultimate goal—merry and joyful.[2]

The hidden God who hears our cry from whatever depth of despair that we find ourselves in is our hope, as He was Israel's hope.

When I was a young Marine fresh from the battlefields of Vietnam, I found myself deeply and miserably in the depths of pain and despair. I had returned home thoroughly conditioned by the violence and chaos of months of war. I did not have regard or respect for myself, my family, my neighbors, and certainly not for God. One Saturday morning, on the way to the post office, I was overcome with the very acute awareness that an awful sense of terror and meaninglessness was consuming me. As a Marine, I had lived with complete trust in the protection that came from the might and power of military weapons. I was confident in my physical capability to defend myself. However, on that morning I stood frightened and helpless before my own conscience. I felt overpowered by a sense of my own guilt and brokenness. In that terrible condition, it became clear to me that without God, a person is lost. Out of the depths of my despair, I said, "God, if you don't help me, I will soon be dead or in prison!" I traveled on to the post office, and while there, I bumped into my wife's pastor. Since then, that encounter has made all the difference in my life.

Was my experience just one of those coincidental random events of life? Some would say so. Nevertheless, from that day forward, I have chosen to identify with the Psalmist who cried out to the Lord from the depths of his situation. Like him, I was granted forgiveness, hope, steadfast love, and an abundance of redemption. As Barth stated, during the pilgrimage, I have been hard-pressed, often weary, often distressed, often astray, and constantly seeking and asking. I have been both saint and sinner, but always, in all times and places, I have never doubted that I am a child of God who is forgiven, redeemed, and loved.

Prayer:

Lord, life has taught us that we often face situations that we do not understand. When we feel as though we cannot cope, may we be reminded that Your strength is available to sustain us. Teach us to hope in You so that we might live as victorious disciples who are kept by a love that never leaves us in despair. Whatever the silent opinion of ourselves may be, help us to understand that we are all prodigal sons and daughters who will never know peace until we say "I will arise and come home to my heavenly Father." Give us the courage to come out from behind the places where we hide from You, from loved ones and friends, and from ourselves. Let us hear the liberating Gospel of Jesus Christ that assures us that each of us is much more than the worst or best things we have ever done. We are the sons and daughters of a Father who sees us coming before we get to Him and meets us with compassion and great joy. Amen.

CHAPTER THIRTEEN
MANAGING THE STORMS OF LIFE

Luke 8:22-25: *²² One day he got into a boat with his disciples, and he said to them, "Let us go across to the other side of the lake." So they set out,*

²³ and as they sailed he fell asleep. And a storm of wind came down on the lake, and they were filling with water, and were in danger.

²⁴ And they went and woke him, saying, "Master, Master, We are perishing!" And he awoke and rebuked the wind and the raging waves; and they ceased, and there was a calm.

²⁵ He said to them, "Where is your faith?" And they were afraid, and they marveled, saying to one another, "Who then is this, that he commands even wind and water, and they obey him?"

Exodus 14:10-12: *¹⁰ When Pharaoh drew near, the people of Israel lifted up their eyes, and behold, the Egyptians were marching after them; and they were in great fear. And the people of Israel cried out to the Lord;*

¹¹ And they said to Moses, "Is it because there are no graves in Egypt that you have taken us away to die in the wilderness? What have you done to us, in bringing us out of Egypt?

¹²Is not this what we said to you in Egypt, 'Let us alone and let us serve the Egyptians'? For it would have been better for us to serve the Egyptians than to die in the wilderness."

1 Kings: 17:11-16: *¹¹He called to her and said, "Bring me a morsel of bread in your hand."*

12And she said, "As the Lord your God lives, I have nothing baked, only a handful of meal in a jar, and a little oil in a cruse; and now, I am gathering a couple of sticks, that I may go in and prepare it for myself and my son, that we may eat it, and die."

¹³And Elijah said to her, "Fear not; go and do as you have said; but first make me a little cake of it and bring it to me, and afterward make for yourself and your son.

¹⁴Thus says the Lord God of Israel, 'The jar of meal shall not be spent, and the cruse of oil shall not fail, until the day that the Lord sends rain upon the earth.'"

¹⁵And she went and did as Elijah said; and she, and he, and her household ate for many days.

¹⁶The jar of meal was not spent, neither did the cruse of oil fail, according to the word of the Lord which he spoke by Elijah.

This story of our Lord and His disciples at sea was important in the formation of the faith of the early church. Matthew, Mark, and Luke all wrote about this miracle story. The fear of the disciples on the raging sea is reminiscent of the fear of the Israelites when their escape route from Egypt was blocked by the sea. They were hemmed in by mountains on either side of their march to freedom. Behind them were the hoofbeats of many horses pulling the war chariots of Pharaoh's army. The impassable sea loomed before them. For the Israelites, escape seemed to be impossible.

The disciples found themselves threatened by the raw, uncontrollable power of nature. The mountains and foothills surrounding the Sea of Galilee created a natural wind tunnel that channeled the howling wind onto the surface of the sea. The disciples were being churned about in a whirlwind that turned the water into a cauldron of violent movements. Their boat was filling with water, moving them steadily closer to a certain death by drowning. Both groups, disciples, and Israelites, were confronted by what Longfellow called "the dim, dark sea, so like unto death."[1]

It seems natural for us to quickly surrender to the power of fear when we find ourselves confronted by seemingly unmanageable situations. Whether our surrender is one of panic or quiet resolution to a perceived inevitable disaster, our response is similar to that of the widow of Zarephath. God sent Elijah to her with the intent that the widow would feed him during a prolonged drought in the land. When Elijah told her to bring him a morsel of bread, she replied, "As the Lord your God lives, I have nothing baked, only a handful of meal in a jar, and a little oil in a cruse; and now, I am gathering a couple of sticks, that I may go in and prepare it for myself and my son, that we may eat it and die" (1 Kings 17:8-16). Her hospitable reception of the prophet resulted in an unforeseen reversal of a certain disaster. Because of the widow's obedience, and in spite of her resolute expectation of death, she had enough food to sustain her family throughout the drought. Elijah's faith in God and the widow's obedience overcame the power of fear and despair.

Redemption by the hand of God seems to be the last thing we embrace and trust. Trapped between the sea and the military power of the Egyptians, the Israelites assumed that God had abandoned them. They were afraid and complained to Moses. They accused him of making false promises in order to gain their support and approval of his plan to escape from Egypt. Using the old "I told you so" complaint, they said, "Is not this what we said to you in Egypt, 'Let us alone and let us serve the Egyptians'? For it would have been better for us to serve the Egyptians than to die in the wilderness" (Exod. 17:12).

The disciples accused Jesus of not caring about their welfare. As they feared for their lives, they could not believe that Jesus was asleep. In a state of panic, they woke Jesus and reported that the storm was becoming more powerful, the boat was filling with water, and death seemed certain.

While the plight of the widow of Zarephath has nothing to do with a raging sea, it does reflect the same hopelessness as we see in the Israelites and the disciples. Her life was not threatened by the forces of nature or by a human or animal predator, but she knew that her situation was perilous and without hope. Oil and flour were the necessary ingredients of the bread that sustained life. These life-giving ingredients were an essential gift from God. Having an abundance of oil and flour was a sign of God's blessing on a person's very existence.[2] The widow had only enough for one more small meal, and she had no way to get more. Lacking these essentials, she could assume that God did not bless her. She had no hope of surviving and was certain that death by starvation awaited her and her son.

We will always be wrong when we allow fear to force us to make decisions based on the assumption that God has abandoned us. The Psalmist was unconditionally sure that "God is our refuge and strength, a very present help in trouble" (Ps. 46:1). The same power of God that so often preserved the Israelites is also manifested as the power that God offers through Jesus. The Psalmist reported that "God rebuked the Red Sea, and it became dry; he led them through the deep as through a desert" (Ps. 106:9). In a like manner, Jesus rebuked "the wind and the raging waves; and they ceased and there was a calm" (Luke 8:24). The widow obeyed God's prophet and "the jar of meal was not spent, neither did the cruse of oil fail, according to the word of the Lord which he spoke by Elijah" (1 Kings 17:16). The absence of God, the sleepiness of Jesus, and an empty food pantry did not diminish the power and authority of our God and our Lord Jesus Christ.

Our response to unexpected storms and difficulties of life is not unlike the response of the Israelites, the disciples, and the widow of Zarephath. We often quickly surrender to fear and begin to place blame on persons, places, and things. When fear seizes us, our ability to think clearly is affected, and we feel trapped and alone in what can seem to be an unmanageable situation. In those times, our faith can bring us calm in any storm. This does not mean that the initial impact of surprise and fear should be dismissed as though it did not exist. Any fearful, surprising impact should alert us to the fact that we have unseen resources that will help us endure and overcome when storms threaten us. God is not absent, and Jesus will respond to our despairing cry for help. While our personal resources may be small, as it was with the widow's oil and meal, we can trust that little is much when God is in it. We endure and overcome by knowing that we are participants in the love of God, which casts out fear (1 John 4:18).

This picture of Jesus in a boat during a threatening storm speaks volumes to us about our journey through life. None of us has to be told that life can be difficult. I have heard more than one person say, "I knew I would have bad days, but I didn't know that they could come in bunches like bananas.!" Jesus did not come to us and give His life for us to make life more difficult than it is under everyday circumstances. Churches populated with moral sadists have done more harm to the human spirit than the social forces against which they ranted and raved. A religion of petty rules and requirements governed by an endless list of "don't do this and don't do that" is both exhausting and ridiculous. When asked about the essential requirements of religion and serving God, Jesus said, "Love God and love people" (Matt. 22:34-40; Mark 12:28-34; Luke 10:25-28). My Dad, who was often in disagreement with some of the fanatics in his church, would not quarrel with them. When questioned or taken to task about his beliefs, he would simply quote the prophet Micah: "He has showed you, O man, what is good; and what does the Lord require of you but to do justice, and to love kindness, and to walk humbly with your God?" (Micah 6:6-8). I was with my Dad on the day of his death. He knew that he was not going to live through the night. I asked him to summarize his experience with religion and if he was confident that he had been a disciple of Jesus. He said, "I have tried to do justice, to practice kindness, and to pray humbly to the God who made me."

Jesus is not a micro-manager who encumbers our religious lives with so many rules and regulations that we become miserable in our efforts to be disciples. He does not require that we practice a rigid legalism that has no basis in His teachings. Religious requirements based on someone's personal preferences and traditions are not binding on our faith if they have no standing in Scripture. The religious leaders of Israel were guilty of making religion a burden to carry instead of a joyful experience of lifting the lives of the people. Jesus said that their many rules and regulations were hard to bear and weighed heavy on their shoulders (Matt. 23:4). He said, "Woe to you scribes and Pharisees, hypocrites! For you traverse sea and land to make a single proselyte, and when he becomes a proselyte, you make him twice as much a child of hell as yourselves" (Matt. 23:15).

This storm at sea story is about more than a boat ride across the Sea of Galilee. Much more can be made of it than first meets the eye. We know that fear is normal, nature can be violent and dangerous, and loss of control over circumstances can be frightening. What we may fail to see or understand is the relationship that Jesus was establishing with His disciples. He would always be their master, teacher, and Lord, but He would also be something else that they did not yet understand. He wanted them to understand what it meant to be His friends. John tells us that Jesus said, "No longer do I call you servants, for the servant does not know what his master is doing; but I have called you friends, for all that I have heard from my Father I have made known to you" (John 15:15).

Jesus made it clear that the disciples did not have to forfeit their humanity to be disciples of the Son of God. He was not lord and master after the fashion of prominent people who took pleasure in "lording it over others, and exercising authority over them" (Matt. 20:25). He did not want them to bow and grovel in His presence. They were not worthless underlings without gifts and talents of their own. Jesus wanted them to know that self-respect, dignity, and recognition that they were children of God made them valuable in the eyes of God. As His friends, they were free human beings. He had shared with them all that His Father had revealed to Him. As a friend, He had shared with them the reasons for His actions and the deeper meaning of His mission and ministry. Being treated as friends, they learned how to show the obedience and humility that they saw in Jesus.[3]

We should not overlook the fact that the people in the boat were working-class members of their community. They made their livings by doing work that was essential to the local economy and the lives of everyday people. One of them was a carpenter, and the others were fishermen. The carpenter was traveling with sailors who had worked on boats all their lives. They were familiar with the waters where they plied their trade. They regularly navigated their boat and fished in the waters of the Sea of Galilee.

The work of a carpenter was totally unlike the work of sailors and fishermen. A carpenter could not add anything to assist in the nautical requirements for the voyage to the other side of the sea. Jesus, the carpenter, trusted the skills of the crew and decided to use the crossing time as an opportunity to get some sleep. Without hesitation or concern, he left the navigation of the boat to the sailors.

Because we know the ending of the story, we primarily focus on the power of Jesus to calm the wind and the waves. Our singular focus on this impressive miracle may prevent us from recognizing the wisdom and power inherent in Jesus' trust in His disciples. The carpenter, who was also Master, Teacher, and Lord, made Himself vulnerable by placing His trust in certain fellow "blue collar" workers of His day. His sleeping life was comfortable in trusting them.

It is a wonderfully empowering feeling to learn that someone trusts you. I remember helping my Dad mix concrete when I was a young boy. He explained to me how important it was to get the right mixture of sand, gravel, cement, and water; He emphasized that if the materials were not mixed in the proper proportions, the resulting concrete would be worthless, and money would be wasted. As we worked, he told me that he had to be away for a few minutes. He told me to mix a new batch while he was away. I protested that I was afraid that I would not do it right. He said, "You have watched me do it, and I trust you to do it right." To this very day, I can still feel the pride and empowerment that I experienced when he told me that he trusted me.

When Jesus got into the boat and went to sleep, He demonstrated His trust in the disciples. The very concept of trust involves a projection of the future. Trusting someone involves the risk that trust will be rewarded with either a positive or negative outcome. Will the outcome be betrayal, mistreatment, opposition, or being taken advantage of? Or will it result in respect, success, admiration, and friendship? Trust inevitably involves vulnerability. Jesus was shaping and developing His future fishers of men. He was preparing them for confrontation with difficult people. He was preparing them for resistance by complex and powerful institutions that would take offense to the message of their ministry. He wanted them to understand that their work would not always be pleasant and easy; without exception, they would be reviled, persecuted, lied to, lied about, and accused of all kinds of evil activity (Matt. 5:11).

We might say that establishing trust with the disciples was a stroke of genius on the part of Jesus. He did not ignore the power of respecting their personal expertise as sailors and fishermen. By trusting them with His safety, He affirmed the value and dignity of their abilities. Jesus knew that trust and friendship go hand-in-hand in creating loyal relationships. It can be argued that the commitment resulting from friendship can be more permanent and powerful than commitment based on seniority alone. We see evidence of this in the friendship of Jonathan and David: "The soul of Jonathan was knit to the soul of David, and Jonathan loved him as his own soul" (1 Sam. 18:1). Being both free and friends, the disciples could make decisions about discipleship based on experience and education. That is to say, they were not blindly following Jesus because of His personality, their social inferiority, or some form of coercion. Receiving them as friends, He taught them about what they could expect in the future, and He revealed to them their destiny as His disciples.

The storm at sea became an important teaching event in the life of the disciples. When they saw that their sleeping passenger had control over the power of nature, they were emboldened to trust Him. Perhaps they had not understood the inclusive intent of His statement, "Let us go across to the other side." Whether asleep or awake, He was always in the boat with them.

Going to sleep was not an act of unconcern on His part. It simply meant that a carpenter's skill was not needed to navigate the boat. But when their skill was neutralized by forces beyond their control, the Master was needed. His voice, the voice that once participated in speaking heaven and earth into existence, calmed the wind and the raging waves.

Throughout the storm experience, Jesus was never anything less than master, teacher, and Lord. However, the disciples underwent a change in their thinking as they witnessed His actions. Notwithstanding Jesus' titles and power, they had the opportunity to see His humanity. He was tired and sleepy, just as they were often tired and sleepy. He included Himself in their company and made Himself equally vulnerable to potential threats. He was their Lord, but He was Lord in a way that the world had never known. He became like them and accepted the vulnerability of trust and friendship. They saw that Jesus had proved Himself to be both Lord and friend.[4] They saw that He could be trusted, and this inspired them to reciprocate the trust that He had placed in them. They understood that He would be with them in the work that He was sending them out to do. Jesus, Lord, and friend esteemed these ordinary men who labored for a living to be suitable for leadership positions in the work of God. He was making them stakeholders in the establishment, culmination, and consummation of the Kingdom of God.

Few of us have had to fear for our lives in a storm at sea. However, most of us know about other storms that blow into our lives. They can bring the same doubt and fear that the disciples experienced. They can come suddenly, unannounced, and unforgivingly menacing. Basking in the sunshine of life, we trust our own powers and resources. We are confident that the advances of science, technology, and our own efforts will be sufficient to keep us happily afloat under all circumstances. And then a small microbe, too small to be seen by the natural eye, attacks our body and lays waste to our health. Great fearful words insert themselves into our daily vocabulary, words like cancer, heart attack, stroke, divorce, bankruptcy, loss of job, and a host of other intruders with bad news. Overwhelmed and unable to cope, we wonder if God has abandoned us. We ask, "Why has God let this happen to me?" We shake our heads in despair and unbelief, and we wonder if He even cares about our fear, pain, and hopelessness.

In their distress, the disciples called out to Jesus even though they did not know if He would respond or what His response might be if He did answer them. They found that He was aware of their situation, that He did care for them, and that He was able to provide the relief that they needed.

We may never set foot on a boat or experience a storm at sea, but it is certain that we will be visited by stormy circumstances in life. Eliphaz does not equivocate when he says to Job, "Man is born to trouble as the sparks fly upward" (Job 5:7). In our own time, each of us will have to manage circumstances that will have the same effect on our minds, spirits, and bodies as the wind-driven storm had on the fearful disciples. There is no secret to successful management of difficulties and disasters. Jesus' word to us is the same word that He gave to His disciples two thousand years ago. It has stood the test of time and weathered countless storms of every kind imaginable. As Jesus said then, He says today, "Have faith in me." We will manage the storms and difficulties of life if we remember that the power that split the sea and saved the Israelites, and the power that calmed the stormy Sea of Galilee is the same power that will respond to our cries for help. Our Master, Teacher, Lord, and Friend is in the boat of life with us. He will go with us to the other side, wherever that may be.

Prayer:

Lord, we thank You for trusting us to be workers in Your kingdom. We ask for the will and the strength of commitment to do all that we can do under our own power. We trust that you will provide the power and resources needed when our talents and resources prove to be insufficient for the work that you give us to do. Empower us so that we might never fear that we are alone. If it appears that death, despair, defeat, and failure are winning the day, restore our courage by reminding us that you are in the boat with us. Amen.

CHAPTER FOURTEEN
GOD'S GREAT ABILITY

Ephesians 3:14-21: *¹⁴For this reason I bow my knees before the Father,*

¹⁵from whom every family in heaven and on earth is named,

¹⁶that according to the riches of his glory he may grant you to be strengthened with might through his Spirit in the inner man,

¹⁷and that Christ may dwell in your hearts through faith; that you, being rooted and grounded in love,

¹⁸may have power to comprehend with all the saints what is the breadth and length and height and depth,

¹⁹and to know the love of Christ which surpasses knowledge, that you may be filled with all the fulness of God.

²⁰Now to him who by the power at work within us is able to do far more abundantly than all that we ask or think,

²¹to him be glory in the church and in Christ Jesus to all generations, for ever and ever. Amen.

When our children were young, I served as pastor to rural churches in Virginia and Tennessee. When appointed to one area, we had to travel eighty miles to get medical, dental, vision, and other professional services. This required frequent travel because at least one of the four children was always in need of healthcare that required treatment by a specialist. We tried to use these trips as occasions to shop at the larger grocery store chains and department stores.

The travel route required that we pass through a tunnel on the way to the city. The tunnel was about one mile in length, and the family's challenge was to see who could hold their breath the longest while passing through the tunnel. Our youngest son, the most competitive of the four children, always won the contest. On one particular journey, one of his playmates made the trip with us. He outlasted everyone, and upon discovering that he was the winner, he raised his arms in victory and said, "I am the champion of the world!" Our younger son, not accustomed to coming in second in any contest, refused to congratulate his playmate. He said, "This tunnel isn't anything. God can go around the world as many times as he wants, and he can hold his breath the whole time." Not wanting to acknowledge or discuss his playmate's accomplishment, he silenced the victor by asking, "Can you do that?"

One of the questions I have been most often asked usually begins with, "Chaplain, do you believe that God can do (finish the question with any number of possibilities)?" My immediate response is always, "God can do anything. There is nothing that He cannot do." Hundreds of songs have been written proclaiming the theme that God specializes in things assumed to be impossible. In retrospect, I have wondered how my mother managed a home that was living on the very edge of poverty. I now know that there were times when she did not have much more in her food pantry than did the widow of Zarephath, who fed Elijah during a famine in the land. But I also remember that the family never went hungry. As she made the most of what she had, I can still hear her singing, "It is no secret what God can do."

God can do anything. If you attend a church that values the history of the struggles of the Universal Church, how could you not incorporate this belief into your daily thinking and living? The great creeds that affirm our faith all begin with, "I believe in God the Father Almighty." In the first sentence of the Apostles' Creed and the Nicene Creed, we declare that God can do anything. That is what is meant when we say that He is almighty. "Almighty" is the English translation of the Latin word "omnipotentem" and the Greek word "pantokrator."[1] The Latin word has the meaning "having all power and being all-powerful."[2] The Greek word has the same meaning as the Latin word but also refers to the "absolute reign of God."[3] The Almighty God has no equal. He is the almighty ruler over everyone and everything. Any person or thing named as a rival or competitor is a false god.

Paul prayerfully acknowledges the power of God when he says, "I bow my knees before the Father." He recognizes the absolute reign of God when he says, "from whom every family in heaven and on earth is named" (Eph. 3:14-15). He prays that the Ephesian congregation will receive strength through the Spirit, that Christ will dwell permanently in their hearts, and that their faith will give them a strong foundation built on love and nourished by love. When Christ lives in a person through the power of the Spirit, the "inner man" becomes strong. The ability to reason with discernment and without prejudice is influenced. The conscience becomes sensitive to the manner in which we recognize others as fellow human beings and how we relate to them, as taught by Jesus. Our willpower becomes a force that enables us to not only know what is right but empowers us to do what is right (Eph. 3:16-17).

Paul prays that they will be granted access to and receive the riches of God's glory. These riches are not accessible to the natural mind. They are real, but they are affiliated with the mysteries of what God is doing to re-create and restore us and our habitat to the state He intended when He created the world and all that is in it. If these riches of glory are both real and, at the same time, wrapped in mystery, what can we know about them? Paul says,

> What if God, desiring to show his wrath and to make known his power, has endured with much patience the vessels of wrath made for destruction, in order to make known the riches of his glory for the vessels of mercy, which he has prepared before hand for glory, even us who he has called, not from the Jews only but also from the Gentiles? (Rom. 9:23).

The "riches of glory" are to be deposited in and lived out of "vessels of mercy." We become these vessels of mercy when we realize that God loves us and has sent His Son to be our Savior (John 3:16).

Pause and prayerfully think about what is being said here. You are a vessel of mercy, and you are filled with the riches of God's glory. You know that you are a real person, and you know that, for some reason, you are a changed person. You also know that you do not know all the details of how this change occurred and is still occurring. The picture becomes even more mysterious when you seriously think about the life, suffering, and horrible death of Jesus. You can read the details and study them for the rest of your life, but you cannot fully know why and exactly how God made it all happen. You know that you did not deserve it. You know that there was a time when you could rightly be called a vessel of wrath, but you cannot understand why you should ever be called a vessel of mercy. Karl Barth said,

> Terrible and incomprehensible is the true and hidden significance of all existence! Incomprehensible and beyond all thinking is the emergence of the righteousness of God, as it passes vertically through all human righteousness and unrighteousness.[4]

Life is filled with frightening, baffling, and inconceivable events. The significance of human existence is questionable since we know that we will suffer many things and then one day we will die. We may well be justified in simply saying, "What is the point of this brief, often disappointing journey that ends in death?" How do we square the actions of a righteous God in His acceptance of anything that is unrighteous? The indisputable verdict in the case of God versus humankind is that we are all unrighteous (Isaiah 64:6; Romans 3:10). How can we comprehend that a righteous God would sacrifice His own righteous Son for people who have repeatedly and willingly ignored His laws and commandments?

No reliable focus can be brought to this picture without considering certain "before and after" conditions. Before we become vessels of mercy we are like Saul, the persecutor of Christ, before he became Paul, an apostle of Christ. Resisting the call of the marvelous love of Christ caused him psychological and emotional pain. He could not understand how a convicted criminal who was executed on a cross could be the Messiah of Israel. He was a respected Pharisee, educated in the Law of Moses, and dedicated to the God of Abraham, Isaac, and Jacob. It was incomprehensible that a crucified carpenter could be the Christ. This contest of intellect and tradition versus the call of Christ led to an emotional, physical, and spiritual breakdown as Saul intensified his war against the disciples of Jesus. Finally, lying on the ground blind, exhausted, and helpless, he accepted the futility of his resistance. Jesus told him that his frustration, pain, anger, and blind obedience produced the same painful result as when an animal kicked against the sharp stick that was used to guide it and move it forward. Rebellion and resistance would do nothing but cause him more pain (Acts 9:1-22; 22:4-16; 26:9-18)

After the encounter with Jesus, Saul, a vessel of wrath, became Paul, a vessel of mercy. Things change when we become vessels of mercy. When mercy relieves us of the psychological and emotional burdens we are carrying, when forgiveness heals our conscience, when love neutralizes our anger, and when faith brings hope to our frustrations, we do not care that what has happened is a mystery that transcends and escapes the grasp of our human reason. As vessels of mercy, we begin to see that life is more than the brief span of our earthly existence. The gift of eternity with all its mystery replaces the despair of nothingness and we are confirmed by a faith that assures us that if God is for us, nothing nor anyone can prevail against us. Rather than being uncertain and confused by God's mysteries, we are relieved and grateful to find that there is a place for both mystery and reality in our lives. This does not mean that we become immune to the harsh realities that Barth called "terrible and incomprehensible." The ups and downs of life remain, but we are aware that we have been filled with a mysterious quality of life that is far more satisfying than anything the known world of reality has to offer.

We are humbled because we know that we have not done anything to earn the privilege of being vessels of mercy. When we are anointed to become those vessels, our eyes are opened to a new light in the world as was Saul's after he was blinded and overcome by the Lord. Many of us have painfully learned that God has many ways to subdue us and break the pride that controls us. We have to accept our slice of humble pie and abandon any claims to what we think we deserve. We must disabuse ourselves of any belief that we have earned God's favor. We are not entitled to anything because of any of our accomplishments. We will have to exchange who we think we are for who God wants us to be, and in doing this, we will discover who we really are.

Our pride and arrogance would have us believe that it is possible to bypass the mystery of God's authority and think that we can manage eternity for ourselves. The serpent's voice from the Garden still seductively says today as it did then, "If you disobey God, you will not die. In fact, you will be like God, knowing good and evil" (Gen. 3:4-5). Since then, we have not been able to peacefully manage this spinning, gravity-controlled time capsule in which we live. For now, God still controls the spinning and the gravity, but given enough time and our need to do things our way, we may yet spin our revolving globe off its axis and send it hurtling out of control.

Our selfishness and high opinion of ourselves create what I call Little Jack Horner syndrome. After mixing the ingredients and baking the pie of forgiveness and grace according to our own likes and dislikes, we gleefully applaud ourselves and take credit for the results. You might recall the words of the nursery rhyme: "Little Jack Horner sat in a corner eating a Christmas pie; he stuck in his thumb and pulled out a plum, and said, 'What a good boy am I.'"[5] Jack Horner syndrome disregards the caution of Jesus on at least two counts. First, "Why do you call me good? No one is good but God alone" (Mark 10:18). Second, "When you have done all that is commanded you, say, 'we are unworthy servants; we have only done what was our duty'" (Luke 17:10). As disciples we do not get bonus points, merit badges, or extra credit for doing what the gospel commands us to do.

There is mystery, and there is reality. The reality of this natural world tells us that there is not anything that we cannot have, cannot do, or cannot accomplish if we work hard enough. Some religious people believe that if we pray loudly enough and long enough, we can either force God to do something or we can conjure up the activity of the Holy Spirit. A proper reading of the Bible introduces us to a mystery that proves that formula to be less than true. God's Word tells us that grace, faith, salvation, eternal life, and living by the Spirit does not work that way. Paul says, "For by grace you have been saved through faith, and that is not your own doing, it is the gift of God—not because of works, lest any man should boast." (Eph. 2:8-9). These are mystery words, alive and vital in the vocabulary of the Holy Spirit. The process starts with God reaching down to us before we ever reach up to him. As Barth said, "Incomprehensible and beyond all thinking is the emergence of the righteousness of God, as it passes vertically through all human righteousness and unrighteousness."[6] God's only Son came down to live with us, to suffer and die for us and was resurrected for us so that we would have eternal life.

The mystery that we are unable to solve is more precious than the resounding victory proclaimed by the great Halleluia Chorus. It is the glorious mystical victory of God's love. It defies everything that the world defines as both success and failure. It is good that what we have received as vessels of mercy is hidden in the mystery of God's love. It does not belong to us, and we cannot claim that we have made or produced any part of it. Reality has taught us that anything given by the world can be taken away by the world. Losses by death, unfairness, and just plain bad luck are everyday occurrences in this world. Our Lord tells us that He does not give as the world gives (John 14:27). We are vessels of mercy, and the world cannot take that from us. It is always a gift of God's divine mercy. Regardless of what we did or did not do, how good or bad we have been, or how hard we worked or did not work, we could never have created this gift for ourselves. It comes to us repeatedly by way of God's free grace. Although we know that we are sinners and incapable of not being sinners, this mysterious grace continues to visit us, sustain us, and renew us with the hope of a greater glory yet to come.

As Paul continues his prayer, he knows that there is a certain element of futility in any human attempt to define and describe the love of God and the riches and blessings contained in that love (Eph. 3:18-19). There is a sense in which he is caught on the horns of his own dilemma. He has already admitted that the love of God and the riches of Christ are unsearchable and inexpressible (Eph. 3:8; 2 Cor. 9:15). He is attempting to explain the "mystery hidden for ages in God who created all things" (Eph 3:9). Paul must have felt somewhat of that which Job felt when he said to God, "I have uttered that which I did not understand, things too wonderful for me which I did not know" (Job 42:3). While Paul speaks of the breadth, length, height, and depth of God's love, he does not assign any quantitative or numerical value to these dimensions. T. K. Abbott says, "Some of the ancients sought to find a special meaning in each of the four dimensions."[7] He views these efforts as nothing more than "fanciful attempts" that fail to provide interpretations that can be justified.[8]

John Calvin said that the true meaning of the four dimensions has been "darkened by a variety of interpretations."[9] I believe that he is correct in his conclusion that Paul meant nothing else than the love of Christ in reference to the dimensions. He did not provide a numerical value or a description of what each of the dimensions separately represented because he knew that would be impossible. He knew that he could not avoid contradictory rhetoric in his efforts to introduce them to the great concept of God's love. For instance, he prays that they may have the power to comprehend the dimensions of the love of Christ, and then he immediately says that such love "surpasses knowledge." It is "super-extraordinary in excelling and going beyond knowledge."[10] Paul has created an oxymoronic situation in that it is impossible to comprehend something that is at the same time identified as being incomprehensible. He is trying to use words to explain a mystery for which there are no words to match the picture of the mystery.

I am reminded of a time when I was sitting quietly in a cool, candle-lit worship space in one of the catacombs of Rome. I was the only person in that space, but somehow, I did not think it was a contradiction to assume that I was not alone. I had read that Saint Peter had led worship services in that very space. I felt my spirit quicken within me, and whether real or imagined, I believed very strongly that the Big Fisherman and I were bowing together before the great Lord God. Paul prayed that we should share the love and glory of God "with all the saints" (Eph. 3:18). When we read the scriptures, pray the prayers, and sing the hymns that all the saints before us have read, prayed, and sung we are participating in a mystery with them that does not require cognitive comprehension. In fact, it transcends cognitive comprehension in a "super-extraordinary" way. In reverent awe, our souls and spirits merge with the souls and spirits of angels, archangels, and all the hosts of heaven as we corporately rejoice in the love of God. We share the same questions of why and how we should be so completely forgiven and accepted by the righteous God. With them, we ask:

O Love divine, what hast thou done!

Th' incarnate God hath died for me!

The Father's coeternal Son

Bore all my sins upon the tree!

The Son of God for me hath died:

My Lord, my Love, is crucified.[11]

What can we know about the content of the breadth, length, height, and depth of God's love? We cannot speak of numbers, dimensions, or quantities as we would of a building or a piece of land. Peter said to those who had not seen Christ, "Without having seen him, you rejoice with unspeakable and exalted joy" (1 Pet. 1:8). There is a church in Rome called *The Church of Saint Peter In Chains* (*San Pietro in Vicoli*). It is so named because it houses what are said to be the chains that miraculously fell away from Peter's hands when he was imprisoned in Jerusalem by Herod (Acts 12:1-17). The chains were presented to Pope Leo, (Leo the Great, ca. AD 400-AD 461), by the wife of Emperor Valentinian III (AD 419-AD 455). The *Church of Saint Peter in Chains* was dedicated in AD 442 and was built for the specific purpose of housing the chains which are kept in a lighted glass case (reliquary) under the altar. As I knelt at the altar, I looked at the chains and thought about Peter's imprisonment for being a disciple of Jesus. The chains had been in the church for sixteen hundred years. Still, I knew that Rome was full of relics of questionable authenticity, but it did not seem to matter to me whether or not the chains were those that once shackled the great apostle. I dared to believe that I shared with Peter a mystery so full of glory that there were no words adequate to describe it. Peter simply referred to it as being "unspeakable." The authenticity of an object carried no importance when compared to the life and ministry of one of our Lord's first disciples. It is enough that we can sing and serve with Peter and all the saints and witness to the glory of our salvation:

> Long my imprisoned spirit lay,
>
> Fast bound in sin and nature's night;
>
> Thine eye diffused a quickening ray;
>
> I woke, the dungeon flamed with light;

My chains fell off, my heart was free,

I rose, went forth, and followed thee.[12]

Paul ends his prayer with a doxology that affirms the intention to proclaim God's glory "for ever and ever" (Eph. 3:20-21). We know that His glory includes omnipotence, majesty, splendor, radiance, and much more than we are able to put into words. Paul has made it clear that we are incapable of comprehending the "super-extraordinary love of God in Christ." As he begins his closing doxology, he is aware that he has raised questions concerning contradictions and unsolvable mysteries. I believe that his response to that awareness prompted him to utter one of the most encouraging statements to be found anywhere in the New Testament. He said, "Now to him who by the power at work within us is able to do far more abundantly than all that we ask or think" (Eph. 3:20). He is saying, "Do not let what you are not able to do get the best of you. You are not able to do a lot of things, but God is able to do anything and everything."

Paul uses another "super word" to describe God's ability. He says that God is "super-abundantly" able.[13] It is an extraordinarily strong word that is not limited by the interpretation of "more abundantly," but is best translated as "infinitely more abundantly."[14] God's ability is beyond all measure. Our inability to comprehend the mysteries of God's power does not diminish His ability to do all things.

When faced with problems, pains, and difficulties beyond the reach of our powers, I believe that we are often too quick to think that they are also beyond the reach of God's ability to provide a solution. We see this tendency in the lives of Abraham and Sarah. They both laughed when they were told that Sarah would become pregnant and give birth to a son. It was obvious to them that the messenger had overlooked the fact that Abraham was one hundred years old, and Sarah was ninety years old (Gen. 17:17; 18:12). They had expected a different outcome and were disappointed in the failure of God's promise to them. Nevertheless, they had come to terms with the reality of the failed promise and were willing to accept as a fact that all had been done that could be done. Their attitude was, as we say today, "It is what it is."

As so often is the case with us, the situation was laughable but not funny. When I was a junior officer in the Navy, I once parked in a parking space that had a sign that said, "Reserved for the Command Master Chief." When I returned, the Master Chief was standing behind my car. He saluted and rendered the proper respect required of an enlisted person when addressing an officer. I could tell that he was more than a little agitated. I began explaining why I parked in his space, and he began to laugh. Thinking that to be the end of the matter, I laughed with him. As I got in my car, he saluted me again and said, "Sir, both of us are laughing, but only one of us thinks this is funny." His laughter was not the act of understanding and acceptance that I had assumed it to be. It masked his silent contempt for a junior officer who would be so naïve, arrogant, or stupid to believe he could disregard the restrictions of an official sign.

The laughter of Abraham and Sarah masked a similar silent contempt. They thought to themselves how ridiculous it was for anyone to suggest pregnancy and birth when it was a patently obvious impossibility. The mysterious visitor knew their thoughts and asked, "Why did Sarah laugh?" Not waiting for an answer, he asked, "Is anything too hard for the Lord?" (Gen. 18:13-14). Neither Abraham nor Sarah gave an answer to the question. The answer was in the question itself. If anything was too hard for God, then He could not be God.

Looking back at the history of God's intervention in the lives of Abraham and his ancestors, there was no doubt about the ability of their God to preserve and protect them. Faith in the past was sustained and verified by the memory of known results. It is always easier to validate God in the past-tense than it is in the present-tense. We can read the story of Job and be amazed at the difficulties and sufferings he endured. Because we know the end of the story, we can applaud the power and ability of God to restore Job to physical, familial, and financial health. Looking back over our shoulders, we have no problem validating the past-tense mercy and omnipotence of God. However, when we face problems and sufferings of our own, we find it difficult to apply past-tense faith to present-tense situations. When reminded of past-tense outcomes, we might say, "Yes, if you say so, but how can I know that the same thing can possibly happen to me?" Abraham knew what God had promised, but he did not see any way that a one-hundred-year-old man and a ninety-year-old woman with a life-long history of infertility could produce the child required for the fulfillment of the promise.

In many ways, across the span of our lives, we experience the conflict of past-tense faith versus present-tense faith. Our life situations are not unlike the ones experienced by Abraham and Sarah. Do we associate a sense of present-tense reality with the promises of God for our lives, or do we see reality only in the past-tense sense of God's mercy and ability? Do we simply accept the stories and promises because they have been passed on to us from our childhood? Did God teach us how to say His name, or did our mother teach us how to say God? Think on these things and question yourself as to whether or not they, in fact, occupy the same dynamic in your life as the stories about *Goldilocks and the Three Bears*, *Little Red Riding Hood, Jack and the Beanstalk*, and the other fairy tales that brought, joy, comfort, and entertainment to our very young lives. As adults, we know that the power of a fairy tale to influence us is a past- tense power. We continue to repeat them to our children and grandchildren, but we no longer believe that they are present-tense realities.

We marvel at the stories about an ark, a rainbow, a shepherd boy who killed a giant with a gravel shooter, a baby born in a barn among animals, a dead man restored to life, and many other miraculous stories. Our mothers also taught us many of these biblically based stories. Are they, like mother's fairy tales, relevant only in the past tense, or have we found for ourselves that they retain the truth of God's present-tense power and ability? We profess to believe in a God of unspeakable love for us and unrestricted power over all things. When those great benefits are acknowledged in the past-tense faith of yesterday's sunshine and success, they bring us satisfaction and security. We embrace them without any thought of abandoning the past-tense faith that they represent. However, when present-tense faith is required, we often find ourselves surrendering to distress, hopelessness, worry, anxiety, and all the negative powers that choke the joy of life from our very existence. We may not say that we no longer believe in God; however, in deference to our past-tense faith, we make excuses for Him when we do not receive the answers we expect from our prayers. We blame ourselves so that we can give God a pass, get him "off the hook." The "prayer for sale" preachers tell us that we probably did not pray hard enough or long enough, or that we have not planted enough "seed money" to get God's attention.

Paul knew that we all have limits on what we are able to do. Think now about what he has to say about God's relationship to us when we encounter those impossible crises that are native to all human existence in the wilderness of this world: "Now to him who by the power at work within us is able to do far more abundantly than all that we ask or think" (Eph. 20). God's ability is not limited to the time-sensitive experience of youthful fairy tales. His ability is present-tense ability. The English word "dynamite" derives from the Greek word for "able." It is a word which, in all its forms, speaks of great power.[15] Paul is speaking in the present-tense, active voice when he literally says that God is "being able" to act. He is not just potentially able, and He is never in the process of becoming able. He is always able (present tense) and is eternally and fully actualized to do super-abundantly over and above anything that we ask or even think of asking. John Calvin said that Paul is telling us that "Whatever God can do, he unquestionably will do, if he has promised it. Whatever expectations we form of Divine blessings, the infinite goodness of God will exceed all our wishes."[16]

We use many familiar phrases to describe our feelings when life seems to be backing us into some kind of emotional cul-de-sac. We might say, "I'm at my wit's end," or "I'm at the end of my rope," or "I don't know what more I can do or say." If someone recommends that we should pray, we often respond with the skeptical laughter of Abraham and Sarah. It is easy, even natural, to say, "I am facing a 'done deal' and I can't see any way of reversing my situation." Confronted by obviously impossible odds, we might think that it would be useless to pray. On the contrary, that is the most opportune and necessary time to call out to God in prayer.

When I have recommended prayer, I sometimes have been told, "I am not very good at praying." I reject any assumption that prayer has to have any particular form or use any special words to get God's attention. What are the components of a "good prayer?" The Psalmist said, "A broken and contrite heart, O God, thou wilt not despise" Psalm 51:17). When the weight of the world and the trouble of some unmanageable event renders us helpless and powerless, we can wait before God without saying a word and that too, is praying.

It is a prayer as powerful and as accepted by God as is any lengthy "word salad" uttered by any liturgically costumed person ordained by any faith group. In our silence or in our inability to put what we are feeling into words, Paul says that the Spirit will intercede for us with "sighs too deep for words" (Rom. 8:26).

Paul's entire message and prayer culminate with confidence in the encouraging words, "God is able." He is able, and He cares for us. Think about that and let those words sink into the very core of your being, and let it guide everything that you think about yourself. I believe that most of us, whether as teenagers or senior citizens, have known some moment in life when we wondered if anyone cared about us and what we were experiencing. Regardless of our age, one minute we can be traveling smoothly through life, and the next minute it can seem as if everything is shaking apart and the wheels are coming off. We cannot make any sense of what is happening, the walls of despair are closing in on us, and nobody seems to care. This must have been how the Reverend Frank Graeff felt when he endured a series of disasters leading up to the forty-first year of his life. Feeling alone and overwhelmed, he took everything to the Lord in prayer, and then he wrote this hymn:

Does Jesus care when my heart is pained

Too deeply for mirth or song,

As the burdens press, and the cares distress,

And the way grows weary and long?

Does Jesus care when my way is dark

With a nameless dread and fear?

As the daylight fades into deep night shades,

Does He care enough to be near?

Does Jesus care when I've tried and failed

> To resist some temptation strong;
> When for my deep grief there is no relief,
> Though all my tears flow all the night long?
> Does Jesus care when I've said "goodbye"
> To the dearest on earth to me,
> And my sad heart aches till it nearly breaks—
> Is it aught to Him? Does He see?
> Oh, yes, He cares, I know He cares,
> His heart is touched with my grief;
> When the days are weary, the long nights dreary,
> I know my Savior cares.[17]

I have seen the marvelous power of that care too many times to doubt its authenticity. I have held a thousand trembling hands, heard the agony of grief as it made its way through a thousand stammering lips, felt the thumping of a thousand broken hearts, and shared the tears of people who were struggling to manage the consequences of some devastating storm of life. I have seen prayer and faith bring healing and resolution in incredible ways to the suffering and brokenness of human beings. I rejoice in being able to witness the truth that there are no limits on God's ability to care for people and help them in distress and in circumstances where they do not know which way to turn.

God makes His care known to us according to His will and purpose for addressing whatever has disrupted the harmony of our lives. He is no stranger to sickness, death, grief, sin, failure, disappointment, and anything else that is common to our human vulnerability. When we become impatient, we should remember that God's delay does not indicate the failure of prayer, and His silence does not mean that He is absent. We do not know the future, but God does. We do not know what is best for us, but God does. So, we wait and pray, but it is not an empty, dead-end kind of waiting. It is a waiting filled with the expectation that God will visit us with the Comforter that Jesus asked Him to send to us (John 14:16). We wait with the confidence that God is as near to us as our own breath. He is able to communicate with us through the routine experiences of life. We may think that we are waiting in despair, but behind the scenes of our grief and despair and over against the powers of the dark side of life stands a God who is able. We pray, we watch, we listen, and we wait with expectation. He comes, as Paul says, "in more ways than we can ask or think."

The question put to me so many times now comes full circle, "Chaplain, do you think that God is able to do...?" This brings me to reflect upon the stubborn disappointment of a little blonde-haired, rosy-cheeked boy who lost a "breath-holding" contest. Before going to sleep that night, he said, "Dad, I was right about God, wasn't I"? I assured him that he was 100% right. He went to sleep smiling, content, and convinced that he had won the day.

Is anything too hard for God? Even a cantankerous little child knows that nothing is too hard for God. He is able. He really can go around the world as many times as He wants to while holding His breath all the way!

Prayer:

Now to Him who by the super-extraordinary power and strength at work within us is infinitely more able to super-abundantly do more than we ask or think about, to Him be glory in the church and in Christ Jesus to all generations for ever and ever. Amen.

CHAPTER FIFTEEN
YOU CAN'T GO TO HELL

Luke 9:49-56 (KJV): *⁴⁹And John answered and said, "Master, we saw one casting out devils in thy name; and we forbad him, because he followeth not with us."*

⁵⁰And Jesus said unto him, "Forbid him not; for he that is not against us is for us."

⁵¹And it came to pass, when the time was come that he should be received up, he steadfastly set his face to go to Jerusalem,

⁵²And sent messengers before his face: and they went, and entered into a village of the Samaritans, to make ready for him.

⁵³And they did not receive him, because his face was as though he would go to Jerusalem.

⁵⁴And when his disciples, James and John saw this, they said, "Lord, will thou that we command fire to come down from heaven, and consume them, even as Elias did?"

⁵⁵But he turned, and rebuked them, and said, "Ye know not what manner of spirit ye are of.

⁵⁶For the Son of man is not come to destroy men's lives, but to save them." And they went to another village.

Has anyone ever told you to go to hell? Have you ever told anyone to go to hell? How do we get there if told to go there? How do they get there if we tell them to go there? What do we expect to happen when we tell someone, or someone tells us to go to hell? The phrase has no power as a curse since it has no immediate effect and the one uttering it has no authority to make it happen. If you asked someone why they were unhappy or disappointed and they said, "I told Joe to go to hell and he wouldn't go," what would you think of such an answer as that?

The word "Hell" has become a very versatile word in our everyday speech. To refer to it as a place is the least of all its many uses. Rudyard Kipling, referring to his writing process, paid homage to the versatility and utility of the words what, why, when, how, where, and who. In his poem, *"I Keep Six Honest Serving Men"* he wrote,

I keep six honest serving men

(They taught me all I know);

Their names are What and Why and When

And How and Where and Who.

I send them over land and sea,

I send them east and west;

But after they have worked for me,

I give them all a rest.[1]

Kipling's "six serving men" have provided the formula for constructing invitations and announcements that provide essential information for a planned event. Over the years, we have become accustomed to employing these "six serving men as companions in expressing the versatility of the word "Hell." For instance, it is not unusual that we might hear someone say, **"What** the hell are you doing?"; "**Why** the hell are you doing that?"; "**When** the hell are you coming home?"; "**How** the hell do you expect me to do that?"; "**Where** the hell do you think you are going?"; "**Who** the hell do you think you are?"

What role does hell play in all those sentences? It makes no sense and contributes absolutely nothing to the meaning of the sentence. Remove the word hell and nothing is lost in comprehension of what is being asked. The presence of the word is suggestive of the speaker's frustration, irritation, confusion, anxiety, or disrespect for the person being addressed. Like the concept of Hell itself, the mindless, non-functional use of the word is suggestive of how ignorant we are concerning the human-made traditions that have created a punitive environment defined and described by a place and concept that has come to be known as Hell.

As for being told to go to hell, do not give that a second thought. If you are prone to tell someone to go to hell, just do not do it anymore. It is a meaningless directive, something said by an idiot which, as Macbeth might say, is "full of sound and fury, signifying nothing."[2]

The reality is that nobody really means it when they tell someone to go to Hell. Furthermore, most of the people who say anything about Hell do not believe in Hell.

Why is the title of this chapter, "You Can't Go To Hell"? I have given it that title because you cannot go somewhere that does not exist. You cannot go to Hell because there is no Hell. The expected response to this unequivocal statement usually begins with, "But the Bible says..." What the Bible says and what most of us have been taught are two different issues. This chapter will be rather long and will touch upon several topics before I even begin to direct attention to the Scripture printed at the beginning (Luke 9:49-56). I confess (warn) that what follows will be full of twists and turns after the fashion of the mountain roads where I grew up in the West Virginia hills. As you read, you may get the feeling that my thoughts are meandering, intricate, and confusing. They may appear to be tortuous, excessively lengthy, complex, and removed from the topic of Hell itself.

Again, I confess that I am using a roundabout winding route to get to where I intend to go. Another feature of the mountain roads is what is called a switchback. Mountains that are too steep to travel straight up the slope vertically have roads that take 180-degree turns. They traverse the mountain horizontally without trying to go straight up the slope. When the steep turn is completed, the course of travel is reversed, and the route is "switched back "to the direction from which it had come. Each switchback marks a gradual gain in elevation and the route continues until reaching the top of the mountain.

If you continue to read this chapter, you will find that you are being asked to navigate some switchbacks on the way to the message of Luke 9:49-56. I believe that you will find much to think about in the rigor of the twists, turns, and switchbacks that follow. And may I say that this is as it should be, since the title of this book is *Think About These Things: Ponderings and Promptings*.

The appearance of the word Hell in the English versions of the Old and New Testaments derives from a translation of any one of four Greek and Hebrew words. These words are Sheol, Hades, Gehenna, and Tartarus. The original contextual intent of these words has nothing to do with the concept of a burning lake of fire that becomes a place of everlasting torment for sins committed. Peter Geach, a British philosopher writing from a Roman Catholic perspective said, "We cannot think properly about Hell if we do not start from a right view about God."[3] Similarly, I believe that we cannot expect to arrive at an acceptable understanding of Hell if we are not aware of how the writers used and understood their own words. Writers from various periods of time translated words under the influence of cultural, social, national, international, and religious ideas that informed how they thought, lived, worked, and worshiped.

The Babylonian captivity (586-516 BC) brought Babylonian and Persian influences into the life of Israel. After that, Alexander the Great (356-323 BC) brought the seeds of Hellenistic culture to Palestine. Following this massive infusion of Hellenistic culture, the Romans took control of Palestine (63 BC) and ruled until the fall of the Western Roman Empire (AD 476).

I appreciate Geach's statement that "We cannot think properly about Hell if we do not start from a right view about God." What I find unacceptable is Geach's starting point for introducing his right view about God. He says, "God has no need of us as we need him; no need of us, or of our love."[4] Obviously, God does not need us to sustain His existence. I am willing to provisionally accept Geach's claim that God does not need our love, but I reserve the right to argue about that. However, I am certain that he goes too far in his attempt to "think properly about Hell." He says,

> For God a billion rational creatures are as dust in the balance; if a billion perish, God suffers no loss, who can create what he wills with no effort or cost by merely thinking of it; the perishing of those who break his law is the natural penalty of their folly and can only redound to praise of his eternal justice.[5]

This view speaks to God's ability without giving any consideration to what has been revealed in the person and work of Jesus Christ who said, "I and the Father are one" (John 10:30). His position seems to be based on the modern concept of "built-in obsolescence." For instance, we accept the fact that most items of our making will only be serviceable for a certain period of time. When they become obsolete or non-functional, we find it more cost-effective to buy a new item than to repair one that is old or broken. There is no evidence in the Hebrew Bible or the New Testament that God discards human beings as though we become obsolete or broken and can be easily replaced.

Adam and Eve wasted no time in disappointing the God who created them. The Creator could have discarded them immediately and created two improved or completely different creatures, but He chose to maintain a relationship with them. As the human race multiplied and the population increased, God once again experienced great disappointment in the wickedness of people. Evil had captured the mind and imagination of humankind and God was sorry that He had created such creatures. Once again, He could have discarded His original creation and started over again with a new creation. In fact, His first inclination was to "blot out man whom I have created from the face of the ground" (Genesis 6:7). However, for the sake of one man, He chose to continue the human species. Noah "found favor in the eyes of the Lord" and through him and his family, God continued the human race.

Jeremiah was directed to visit the potter's shop to get a glimpse of how God deals with us. As he watched the potter turn the clay on his wheel, Jeremiah saw that the potter did not always get his product right on his first attempt. Some flaw or imperfection in his craftsmanship was always a possibility. Jeremiah said, "And the vessel he was making of clay was spoiled in the potter's hand, and he reworked it into another vessel, as it seemed good to the potter to do" (Jer. 18:4). The potter was free to discard the product. He had no mandate to repair or retain an imperfect vessel. He had an abundance of clay at his disposal and plenty of water to start the process over again. He could have sold his flawed bowls and vases as seconds or imperfects. When shopping at some pottery store, haven't we all gone immediately to that section that said, "Reduced price on blemished items"? That is the way our world does business, but it is not God's way. The potter that Jeremiah was sent to observe was a craftsman who had a grand design outlined in his artistic imagination. His creative intentions were too powerful to be defeated by flaws and imperfections that might be encountered on the way to perfection. He took the same lump of clay, squeezed, and kneaded it in his hands, placed it back on the wheel, and reshaped and reworked it until it became what he intended it to become.

Any view of God that suggests that God will discard a billion imperfect and flawed human beings, (i.e., sinners), just because He can easily make a billion more is not the view of God that Jesus has given us. The design of our Creator made no allowance for built-in obsolescence. God has never looked at us as though we are throw-away items that can easily be replaced just because He has the power to replace us. His power does not negate or neutralize His love for us. He is always our Heavenly Father and as such His promise to Israel is extended to each of us: "I have loved you with an everlasting love; therefore, I have continued my faithfulness to you" (Jer. 31:3). Jesus Christ has become the guarantee of the Father's continuing love that sees beyond our flaws and failures. His faithfulness gives us cause to shout joyfully with Paul: "If God is for us, who is against us?" (Rom. 8:31).

Thinking properly about Hell and formulating a right view of God requires understanding what Jesus said about both God and us. He had more to say about our value as persons created by God than all the psychology and self-help books that have ever been written. He speaks to our fears and anxieties in four short sentences: "Are not two sparrows sold for a penny? And not one of them will fall to the ground without your Father's will. But even the hair on your head are all numbered. Fear not, therefore; you are of more value than many sparrows" (Matt. 10:29-31). Think about this: the all-powerful, all-knowing, everywhere present Lord God Almighty cares even for sparrows!

Through my kitchen window, I watch the little sparrows and their colorful cousins of other names flying to and from the feeder and hopping around on the ground among the scattered seeds. Not a single sparrow feeding at my window falls to the ground or hops on the ground without God's will. According to Jesus, the monetary value of a sparrow is the cheapest of all other birds, but they are known and cared for by God in the same way as all the larger and more powerful birds. By comparison, Jesus said that one human being is of more value to God than many sparrows, which actually means "than all the sparrows of the world."[6] Every morning as I drink my coffee and watch the birds, I thank God for the amazing grace of His love for us. I begin the day knowing that no matter what happens, good or bad, that I am known by my Creator. I am reassured that when I have fallen to the ground of this earth for the last time, like the little birds taking flight from my feeder, I will take flight into the glorious presence of my God and my Savior.

The Almighty Bird Watcher does not depreciate the value of a tiny sparrow and the Almighty Potter does not discard the bowl or vase that is flawed. He does not discriminate regarding the value of His created children. He labors constantly and lovingly for all of us. Jesus said, "My Father is working still, and I am working" (John 5:17). That loving Creator, in whatever name or way we refer to Him, could never watch a billion souls for which His only Son died experience eternal damnation and punishment. And now, we move to another twisting turn on the way to that non-existent place called Hell.

Speaking of non-existent places, I think it might be helpful to cite an example of how the use of a single word can influence one's understanding of a specific topic or subject. This is a detour that does not readily relate to the topic of Hell per se. Think of it as a switchback that will ultimately be of some help when we turn to an understanding of the words Sheol, Hades, Gehenna, and Tartarus.

Most of us are familiar with the word *Utopia*. A typical definition is "a place of ideal perfection especially in laws, government, and social conditions."[7] In our common usage, utopia is often used to indicate the experience of a feeling of great pleasure, a feeling that everything is very good, or to emphasize that one's environment or current location could not possibly be any better. According to the Urban Thesaurus, the word "utopia" is used as a synonym for more than one hundred thirty-three words and phrases.[8]

The word is probably best known as the title of a book written by Sir Thomas More.[9] He was a lawyer, judge, and Renaissance philosopher who served as Lord High Chancellor of England from October 1529 to May 1532 during the reign of King Henry VIII. His book describes a place where all violence, crime, and human transgressions are removed from society. Making wagers on any game or contest is strictly forbidden. People prefer employment to unemployment, but no one is required to work more than six hours a day. Hospitals are built in every city to care for the sick and injured. Food and medical care are free, and all property is owned by the public. All personal wealth is willingly forfeited to support the state. The total welfare of the family unit is governed and administered by the state.

Thomas More did not believe that the creation of this fantasized, idealized perfect society was possible. Nevertheless, there have been those who have interpreted his tongue-in-cheek fantasy as having the possibility of becoming a reality. What he presented as exaggerated satire has become a reference point and basis for some political and social utopian ideologies. However, we have been unable to establish a single *Utopia* at the basic level of a village or township. Notwithstanding all the realized impossibilities of local utopianism, we now have those voices that tell us that we should abandon our pride in American exceptionalism and pursue global utopianism! How stupid does one have to be to believe that utopian collectivism which has never succeeded at the local level will somehow fare better at the global level?

This reminds me of the churches in the small coalfield town where I grew up. Each church had at least two revivals every year. The preachers were loud, belligerent, aggressive, and urgently proclaimed that if a sinner left a service without being saved and died during the night they would surely go to a devil's hell and burn forever in a lake of fire. Oftentimes, with tears in his eyes and a tremble in his voice, the preacher absolved himself of the sinner's fate. He would announce that he had given the warning, and the blood of the doomed sinner was on his own hands. The message of all the preachers and all the churches was "We will win the world for Jesus!" The truth is that we never won our little town of one thousand souls for Jesus. Nevertheless, we kept paying someone from out of town to come to us twice a year to tell us that we had to win the world for Jesus and warn us that sinners were going to burn in hell.

The beneficiaries of any utopian ideology are the politicians, the opportunists, the religious charlatans, the scammers, the racebaiters, and the confidence thieves that operate in the highest levels of our social structures and the lowest levels of our seedy environments. We are all vulnerable to the utopian promises of those who care nothing about the best interests of people. We need not look beyond our own American political system to see the deceptive lure of these iniquitous, ubiquitous utopian promises that appeal to human greed and selfishness. They are used to gain power over our personal lives and our institutions of labor, education, and government at every level.

The lofty promises of *Utopia* have been as nationally and internationally tempting as were the seductive songs of the evil Sirens who tried to hypnotize Odysseus and his sailors. On the advice of the goddess Circe, Odysseus ordered his men to tie him to the mast of his boat to prevent him from responding to the allures of the Sirens. He ordered his men to put beeswax in their ears to prevent them from hearing the songs that would lead them to wreckage on the nearby rocks and shoals.[10] Their songs were sweet and appealing, but their intentions were evil. Their single purpose was to cause Odysseus to lose control of his boats and his sailors and become victims of Scylla and Charybdis, two ferocious sea monsters.

Western civilization and especially the American way of life, are being threatened by the devastating call of modern Sirens. They are more appealing in form than ugly sea monsters and their seductive messages can be irresistible. The messages of current utopian ideologies are relentless and more numerous than they have ever been. Most of them are little more than attacks against Judeo-Christian morality and the demonization of capitalist ideas. In a research paper, a professor who teaches economics, gender, and transdisciplinary studies recently said that today's economic system looks like an "idea cut from a badly designed science-fiction story."[11] She says that the function of today's economic system is to justify "capitalist patriarchal, colonialist economics that is based on self-interest and exploitation of others."[12]. She sees becoming more inclusive as a corrective to this flawed system. She says that the current flawed capitalist system must be replaced by establishing

"Utopias with fluid, non-binary conceptions of gender."[13] In this scenario, we would establish a Feminine Utopia, a Queer Utopia, a Gender Equality Utopia, an Anti-racist Utopia, an Indigenous Utopia, an Ecologic Utopia, and others as they emerge and are required.[14] It is anyone's guess as to how these individual Utopias would be maintained in a state of perfection under the single umbrella concept of an all-inclusive entity known as *Utopia*. The most likely outcome of an experiment such as this is that each of these self-absorbed utopias would be at each other's throats like mad dogs as their relationships competed for power, position, and resources.

Of course, this idea of multiple *Utopias* is a perfect example of the madness and the impossibility that Sir Thomas More was spoofing in his book. The Sirens, whether ancient or modern, never cease from trying to hypnotize us with the lure of their promises. Odysseus was vulnerable for the short period of time that it took to pass through the strait that separated Sicily from Italy. We are vulnerable all of the time as the Siren songs of social media hypnotize us and seduce our powers to think and reason for ourselves. Our complacency invites us to believe that there can never be another Adolph Hitler or Joseph Stalin.

Submission to utopian ideologies starts in small, relatively inconsequential ways. In 1928, the reasonably achievable political promise to Americans was "a chicken in every pot and a car for every garage." The price of a new Ford was four hundred ninety-five dollars and chickens were thirty cents a pound. These items did not come as government handouts. Each family had to pay for its own car and chicken. But today, ninety-five years later, the utopian political promise is, "You do not have to worry about thirty or forty more zeroes on the national debt. We are offering you happiness and entertainment without effort and wealth without working. We are going to give you the Utopia that you want and deserve."

The steady, relentless march of the promises of Utopian Socialism and Communism is the seductive fruit of today's politics. A statement attributed to Norman Thomas (1884-1968), the Socialist Party's losing candidate for President of the United States on six occasions, reflects the relentless patience of the Socialist ideology. He allegedly said, "The American people will never knowingly adopt Socialism. But, under the name of 'liberalism,' they will adopt every fragment of the socialist program, until one day America will be a socialist nation, without knowing how it happened."[15] Although attributed to Thomas and frequently quoted by politicians, a reference for where and when he might have said this has not been found. Regardless of its origin, this statement reflects the undeterred aspirations of the disciples of Socialism. They refuse to accept the definition of *Utopia* as "no place." They deceptively, mendaciously, and duplicitously restate their ideology in accordance with whatever Siren song is required to undermine Judeo-Christian ethics and morality. Their utopian vision would replace democratic governments with a "one size fits all" program of citizenship that prohibits individual choice and the freedom of personal autonomy.

The apologists of Socialism opportunistically use to their advantage the ambiguity inherent in any attempt to define and describe their utopian ideology. Thomas frequently referred to the confusion associated with the many types of socialist doctrine and practice. He said, "Government ownership, collectivism, and socialism are words used by speakers and writers as if they all mean the same thing."[16] This is a very clever attempt to separate the parts from the whole. It camouflages the reality that while individual words can be given whatever meaning is convenient at any given time, each will always be, in essence, a pure fragment of the same final product which is Socialism.

Those who use the word "utopia" in the sense of goodness and perfection do not understand More's coining of that word to serve as the title of his book. He was a Renaissance scholar educated in both Latin and Greek. He wrote the text of his book in Latin and created the title from the Greek language. He constructed the new word so that it had a double meaning in Greek. Perhaps his intent was to stimulate the imagination of readers who were inclined to believe that the perfection of society could ultimately be achieved through human efforts.

The word is formed from the combination of two Greek words. One word, "topos," means "place." The meaning of the word Thomas More created depends on which Greek word is used to precede "place." One possible suffix is the word "εὐ," which means "well, good, perfection, the ideal."[17] The second possible suffix is the word "οὐ," which means "no, not, the negative of fact and statement."[18] Both these suffixes are pronounced the same in English. When they are transliterated to the English alphabet, both "eu" and "ou" are represented by the single English letter "u." Obviously, some transliterations have the potential to create confusion in translating certain words from one language to another. This is the case with the word coined by More. He intended that the possible double meaning of his new word would be thought-provoking and invite further discussion from his readers. If the word had a history of use, the exact meaning would be obvious. "Good or perfect place" would be written as "Eutopia" and "no place" would be written as "Outopia." As it stands in its English form, "Utopia" remains subject to arguments based on which of the double meanings one prefers.

Based on More's understanding of fallen and flawed human nature as informed by his Roman Catholic background, it is safe to say that he did not believe in such a place as *Utopia*. For him, the meaning was not "perfect place," (Eutopia). It was "no place" (Outopia). Nevertheless, he also knew that there always would be those who dreamed of and aspired to establish such an impossible place on this earth. They would always reject the reading of "no place" in favor of "perfect place." No argument would ever convince them that there would never be a place on this earth that modeled More's Utopia. The wishful thinking and fertile imaginations of many have argued for an entity that can never realistically be more than a literal "no place." The dream of a "perfect place" has been pursued by secular as well as religious forces. The fuel for those efforts has been of a righteous and peaceful nature at times and of the lust for greed and power at other times.

The pursuit of *Utopia* has resulted in the disintegration of entire nations. That may very well be a fate that awaits America today. For some, burning down the country and inciting us to hate each other is imagined to be the blueprint for creating *Utopia* on Earth. Like fools, half of us demand that the other half accept issues such as social welfare, economic development, political stability, personal freedom, and national defense according to exactly the same way one or the other wants it. President Lyndon Johnson, a crude and vulgar professional politician, was right when he said, "Any man who is not willing to take half a loaf in a negotiation, well, that man has never gone to bed hungry." Have we forgotten that even the Lord God Almighty said, "Come now, let us reason together"? (Isa. 1:18).

Do you believe that those systems that promise *Utopia* under the banners of Socialism and Communism have any inclination to engage in any form of compromise or reasonable discussion? Mao Tse-Tung spoke for the world of Communism when he said, "Every

Communist must grasp the truth; 'Political power grows out of the barrel of a gun'."[19] Mao also said, "The seizure of power by armed force, the settlement of the issue by war, is the central task and the highest form of revolution. The Marxist-Leninist principle of revolution holds good universally, for China and for all countries."[20] How do you reason with a system that advocates saying and doing anything it needs to say or do in order to gain power? How do you reason with lies and armed force? What compromise can be made with the Marxist expectation that fifteen to fifty years of civil war will be required to win its supremacy over the world? What compromise can be made with a Mao Tse-Tung mentality that is willing to accept the loss of half of humanity for the sake of creating a world order based on Socialism?[21]

Alexander Solzhenitsyn, the Russian dissident, was thrown into the notorious Lubyanka prison in Moscow and was tortured for criticizing the Soviet government. He was then sent to a Soviet gulag for eight years. He has given us a sobering description of Socialism. He said, "No precise, distinct socialism even exists; instead, there is only a vague, rosy notion of something noble and good, of equality, communal ownership, and justice with the promise that the advent of these things will bring instant euphoria and a social order beyond reproach."[22]

Although Thomas More's word *Utopia* was coined with an intended double meaning, he could not possibly have imagined that it would become a support model for a socialist ideology. His intention was to ridicule the belief that there could ever be a "perfect place" and to show that anyone believing in any such place was actually believing in "no place." Nevertheless, the ideologies that pursue a utopian world have not been deterred by More's argument that there cannot be a *Utopia* on this earth. Solzhenitsyn said, "If one considers human history in its entirety, socialism can boast of a greater longevity and durability, of wider diffusion and control over larger masses of people, than can contemporary Western civilization."[23]

There is no doubt that More's *Utopia* has influenced socialist and communist ideologies over the past five hundred years. How could they not be encouraged by the very ideas of state control of production, abolition of private property, free medical care, free food, free shelter, and a plethora of other welfare benefits? Both Karl Marx and Friedrich Engels were familiar with the message of More's *Utopia*.[24] The degree to which More's book shaped their thought has been debated. The economic conditions during More's time were not the same as they were four hundred years later when Marx and Engels wrote. However, it would be unreasonable to think that a world order on the scale of More's *Utopia* would escape the attention of anyone studying the dynamics of Socialism and Communism. Their recognition of utopian principles involved much more than a casual socio-economic interest and mere idle curiosity. At the very least, what they gleaned from *Utopia* became a necessary fragment of their ultimate concept of Socialism and Communism.

Vladimir Lenin (1870-1924), founder of the Russian Communist Party and first head of the Soviet State, made a public display of his belief that *Utopia* had influenced the thinking of Marx and Engels. In nineteen eighteen he included the name of Thomas More along with the names of Marx and Engels on a monument in Moscow. Lenin began his dedication speech with these words: "We are unveiling a monument to the leaders of the world workers revolution, to Marx and Engels."[25] He listed More's name below the names of Marx and Engels because he saw him as a revolutionary socialist thinker whose *Utopia* represented the ideal communistic democracy. Lenin recognized him as one of the most influential thinkers "who promoted the liberation of humankind from oppression, arbitrariness and exploitation."[26]

I have taken this detour to *Utopia* (no place), to show how the interpretation and understanding of a single word can be a major determining factor in a decision to believe one way or another. The mission of the detour could not have been completed without elaborating on some of the social, cultural, and economic stops along the way. Perhaps you disagreed with some, or all of the politics reflected in the detour. If so, that is perfectly okay. There was no intent to change anyone's mind about anything. The fondest expectation would be that you were stimulated to "think about these things."

The mission was to show how a word could mean "good place" in one form and "no place" in another form. In coining a word with a double meaning, More wanted to raise the consciousness of his readers. Given his religious beliefs about human nature, he knew that humans would not be willing to sacrifice their personal liberty for the ideals required to establish *Utopia* as a perfect place. He knew and expected that it would be obvious that his *Utopia* was a "no place." However, history has shown us that facts and reality are not necessarily effective obstacles in deterring humans from believing what we want to believe. This seems to be especially applicable to those who argue from the viewpoint of utopian ideologies. Shafarevitch says, "The basic driving force of socialist ideology is subconscious and emotional. Reason and rational discussion of facts have always played only a subordinate role in it."[27]

Everywhere Socialism has been tried, it has failed. Human beings will not accept the reduction of human personality to the level of simply being a cog in a state-controlled system. We are inclined to cherish those things that are the source of courage and spiritual strength. Religion, culture, family, and private ownership of property are essential to the nourishment of personalities that give us our individual identities. Nevertheless, the irrational impossible search for a "perfect place" continues.

A misunderstanding of More's coined word has resulted in making him a champion of an ideology that he did not believe in or support in any way. This misunderstanding has gained momentum and provides some of the fuel that motivates Socialist and Communist ideologies today. Karl Kautsky, an important Marxist theoretician, and scholar, identified More as "The father of Utopian Socialism which was rightly named after his *Utopia*."[28] His final assessment is a perfect example of how a misunderstanding of a single word can perpetuate belief in an idea or concept that has no merit. He concludes, "Although *Utopia* is more than four hundred years old, the ideals of More are not vanquished, but still lie before striving mankind."[29] And now we turn onto the road from *Utopia* to *Hell*; or more accurately, from one *No Place* to another *No Place*.

Most English dictionaries define Hell as the place where people go after death to be punished for the things they have done during their life on earth. The punishment is everlasting and is administered in a fiery environment. It is a place of eternal misery and torment. Jonathan Edwards' famous sermon, *"Sinners in the Hands of an Angry God,"* is representative of the dictionary definition of Hell.[30] He told his congregation that God held them over the pit of hell, much as one holds a spider, or some loathsome insect over the fire."[31] He portrayed Hell as

> A great furnace of wrath, a wide and bottomless pit, full of the fire of wrath that you are held over in the hand of the God, whose wrath is provoked and incensed against you; as against many of the damned in hell. You hang by a slender thread, with the flames

of divine wrath flashing about it, and ready every moment to singe it, and burn it asunder.³²

He preached this sermon at Enfield, Massachusetts in 1741. Many of his sermons presented the God of the Old Testament as a fierce and angry God who consigned sinners to Hell. It is difficult to argue against the intensity and energy of Edwards' preaching style. However, critics have not shown much praise and approval of his views on eternal damnation and eternal punishment in Hell.

The criticism of Edwards' connection between the God of the Old Testament and a fiery Hell is completely justified. Nowhere in the Old Testament do we find a place of eternal punishment. In fact, the Old Testament does not speak of a place called Hell. The Hebrew word that is wrongly translated as Hell is "Sheol." Not a single one of its sixty-six appearances in the Hebrew Scriptures has any connection to a fiery place of eternal punishment.

According to the worldview of the ancient Israelites, "Sheol lies beneath the subterranean ocean upon which the earth disk floats."³³ They believed that a huge hollow space that resembled a pit existed below the ocean. The image is like that of a frisbee floating on the surface of a swimming pool. Beneath the lining on the bottom of the pool, the dry earth continues untouched by the water in the pool. Continuing the swimming pool analogy, the space beneath the lining is the equivalent of the space the Israelites referred to as Sheol. The path to Sheol passes through very deep water. The dead travel through that watery grave and enter Sheol, a dark land of shadows.

The writings of the Hebrews from the Egyptian Exile to the Babylonian Captivity (ca. 1450-586 BC) do not provide us with a specific doctrine, creed, or set of beliefs concerning the destination and fate of the dead. Instead, what we find is "a mass of antique conceptions regarding the life beyond the grave which the Israelites shared with other peoples, and which had been handed down from time immemorial."[34] These "antique conceptions" represent the traditional folklore that existed within the community of the ancient Near Eastern cultures to which the Israelites were exposed. T. H. Gaster says that the Old Testament ideas about the fate of the dead are based on "earlier traditions taken from Mesopotamian folklore."[35]

It is not surprising that the Old Testament writers would not be inclined to establish a formal explanation of the exact nature of the post-mortem journey's end. No person had returned to offer an eye-witness account; therefore, they could not speak with authority on this subject. They believed that "The secret things belong to the Lord our God; but the things that are revealed belong to us and to our children for ever, that we may do all the words of this law" (Deut. 29:29). There are limits to what human beings can know and the future belongs to God. To speculate or guess about this great mystery would be an infringement on the exclusive prerogative of Yahweh. Certain things are to be left in the hands of God. We must live according to what has been revealed to us and have faith in God, the master of all mysteries.

The Old Testament does tell us that some of the writers found it strange that God did not give them more specific information about the fate and destination of the dead. Isaiah expresses his curiosity when he says to God, "For Sheol cannot thank thee, death cannot praise thee; those who go down to the pit cannot hope for thy faithfulness" (Isa. 38:18). The Psalmist says, "For in death there is no remembrance of thee; in Sheol who can give thee praise?" (Ps. 6:5). Are these writers trying to prompt God to provide more information on the mystery of death? It appears that they were uncomfortable with the lack of reassuring details about the nature of life in the hereafter.

Whatever the ancients may have thought of existence in the underworld of life after death it is certain that they did not view Sheol as an eternal place of punishment. John Gray speaks for the majority of credible scholars when he says, "Sheol is the shadowy insubstantial underworld, the destination of all, good and bad without discrimination."[36] There is no doubt that the Israelites believed that all humans descend to Sheol when life is over. While it was seen as a gloomy place of shadows, it was never seen as a place of punishment or reward. The last word on Sheol is that it is not a synonym for a place of punishment in the flames of everlasting fire.

Hades has the same meaning in the New Testament as does Sheol in the Old Testament. It is the land of the underworld where all go when they die. The word occurs ten times in the New Testament Greek manuscripts that were used in compiling the "Textus Receptus" or "received text" that became the standard Greek text of the New Testament.[37] This standard Greek text "lies at the basis of the King James Version and of all of the principle Protestant translations in the languages of Europe to 1881."[38] Acceptance of the received text is one thing, but the accuracy of the translators who converted the Greek text into other languages is also of paramount importance. The most recognized English translations were Tyndale (1534), Coverdale (1535), Matthew Bible (1537), The Great Bible (1539), Geneva Bible (1560), Bishop's Bible (1568), Douai Rheims (1609), and King James (1611). Of the ten occurrences of Hades (Ἥδησ/ἅδησ) in the New Testament, eight are translated as Hell, (Matt. 11:23, 16:18; Lk. 10:15, 16:23; Acts 2:27, 31; Rev. 1:18, 6:8, 20:13-14). In the other two occurrences (Acts 2:27, 31), the Geneva Bible translates Hades as "grave."

The Greek word Gehenna (Γέενα/γέενα) is a transliteration of the Hebrew "ge-hinnom" which means "Valley of Hinnom." As with the word Hades, it is improperly translated as Hell in the King James Version and other English versions of that period, (Matt. 5:22, 29, 30; Matt. 10:28; Matt. 18:9; Matt. 23:15; Matt. 23:33; Mark 9:45, 47; Luke 12:5; and James 3:6.) The Valley of Hinnom was a deep gorge located on the southern boundary of Jerusalem. It became known as a place of evil and of abomination. It was there that children were burned as a sacrificial offering to pagan gods. King Ahaz and King Manasseh both erected altars for Baal and each sacrificed a son (2 Kgs. 16:3, 21:6). Jeremiah called the place the Valley of Slaughter (Jer. 7:30-33).

The cultic site in Gehinnom where the actual burning of sacrificial offerings took place was called Topheth. Jeremiah said,

> For the sons of Judah have done evil in my sight, says the Lord; they have set their abominations in the house which is called by my name, to defile it. And they have built the high places of Topheth, which is in the valley of the son of Hinnom to burn their sons and daughters in the fire (Jer. 7:30-32).

Topheth represented a site of absolute terror and horror. Some scholars have said that it has its origin in the Hebrew word "topet" which means "place of fire".[39] Others, including Martin Luther, have said that "topet" is based on the root word "toph" which means "drum".[40] Both of these explanations conform to the context out of which the name of this cultic site emerged. Jeremiah clearly indicates that it was "a place of fire." The association of drums and percussion instruments with Topheth is based on "ancient Jewish tradition that there were many drummers and musicians who drowned out the screams of the young consigned to the flames, so that the parents of these wretched children would not perceive the terror."[41]

Topheth, in the valley of Gehinnom, was a gruesome and horrible place where some Israelites joined pagans in the worship of idols and false gods. The people had forsaken God and Jeremiah knew that they faced a disastrous future of their own making. Because of their infidelity and their participation in the abominations committed in Topheth, Jeremiah told the rulers and the people that Jerusalem would experience the terrible wrath of God. To impress upon them the serious intent of God, he painted a dark picture for Jerusalem's future. He said that the valley where they burned children and filled the place with innocent blood would become more disastrous and deadly for them than it was for the victims of their apostasy. From the time of Moses, the price of disobedience was spelled out in the curses listed in the twenty-eighth chapter of Deuteronomy. They had been warned that the Lord would bring on them and their offspring "extraordinary afflictions, afflictions severe and lasting, and sicknesses grieving and lasting" (Deut. 28:59).

The calamities that await them will become so great and terrible that the Valley of Hennom will become known as the Valley of Slaughter (Jer. 19:6). Gehinnom will become a graveyard just outside the walls of Jerusalem. They will bury the dead there until there is no more space to bury anyone. When that happens, bodies will be thrown out on the ground and left exposed. They will become food to the birds of the air and to the beasts of the earth" (Jer. 19:8). Jerusalem will become a city of horror. When it is put under siege, "parents will eat their children, and everyone will eat the flesh of his neighbor" (Jer. 19:9). In 586 BC Jerusalem was captured by the Babylonians. The temple was destroyed, and the city was burned. The afflictions listed in Deuteronomy became a reality in the siege that preceded the fall of the city.

The Book of Lamentations records the misery, suffering, and degradation that resulted from Israel's disobedience. The dirge commemorating the destruction of the dead city begins like this: "How lonely sits that city that was full of people! How like a widow has she become, she that was great among the nations! She that was a princess among the cities has become a vassal" (Lam. 1:1). The young and old lie dead in the streets, slaughtered without mercy. The children beg for food, but no one gives them anything. The situation becomes so bad that they resort to cannibalism. Women begin to boil their own children for food. Skin becomes shriveled upon the bones of starving victims. They have to pay for the water they drink, and they are ruled by strangers who have taken ownership of their homes. The stark, humiliating truth cannot be ignored. The writer of the dirge says, "For these things I weep; my eyes flow with tears; for a comforter is far from me, one to revive my courage; my children are desolate, for the enemy has prevailed" (Lam. 1:16).

King Josiah, the sixteenth king of Judah (reigned 640 BC-609 BC), instituted reforms throughout the land. He tore down the altars of false gods that had been erected and called for a united return to the worship of Yahweh (2 Kgs. 23). He declared the Valley of Hinnom to be a place of abomination. Being defiled and unclean, it became a place where the city of Jerusalem burned its trash and garbage. Jeremiah called it the "valley of dead bodies and ashes" (Jer. 31:40). It is not surprising that Gehinnom retained its abominable reputation. Based on the Talmud and other early Jewish writings, Adolphe Neubauer found that the valley was known as a "garbage dump" as well as the site of child sacrifices.[42] Joachim Jeremias says that Gehinnom, in the time of Jesus, was "the place for rubbish, carrion and all kinds of refuse."[43] Of course, it was that kind of place! Jerusalem was a city with a population of twenty-five thousand to ninety-five thousand people. Moreover, with the influx of pilgrims and visitors during Passover and other feast days, the number could grow "to far more in excess of the normal population."[44] As with any city, there had to be a specified place for the disposal of household trash, commercial and industrial refuse, and rotting animal flesh.

The Jerusalem site had been selected by events occurring hundreds of years before the time of Jesus. A precedent for the disposal of animal and human remains was geographically predetermined. Repetition had established the routine for what was best for the cleanliness and public health of the city. As a result, Gehinnom was accepted as the site of the city dump. When the Romans placed Jerusalem under siege in AD 70, thousands of Jews died from starvation. When there was no more room to bury the dead according to traditional customs, they resorted to how they had managed such crises in the past. Josephus says that when they could no longer endure the stench of dead bodies, "they had them cast down from the walls into the valleys beneath."[45] When Titus, the Roman General, "saw the valley full of dead bodies, and the thick putrefaction running about them, he gave a groan; and such was the sad case of the city."[46] (Josephus, Wars, 5.12.3-4.413).

When Jesus preached and taught throughout Palestine, most people knew the history and reputation of Gehinnom. It was remembered as a common burial ground for the dead. That would include the disposal of unknowns, criminals, and the enemies of Israel during various periods of warfare. It was also common knowledge that the bones and remains of animal sacrifices from the temple and other dead animal remains were dumped in the valley outside the walls of the city. Common sense tells us that protection from disease and pestilence would require burning this awful mess of filth. Once set on fire, chemical reactions produce flammable gases that prolong a hot, smoldering effect long after the visible blazes have disappeared. The daily addition of garbage supplies a steady source of fuel that sustains the smoking, smoldering effects of the dump. Jesus and the people He lived with saw and used the Jerusalem garbage dump on a regular basis. It is this filthy geographical location that Jesus referred to when He said, "Where their worm does not die, and the fire is not quenched" (Mark 9:48).

There is no mystery as to how the Valley of Hinnom passed through Hebrew, Aramaic, and Greek translations and finally became anglicized as Gehenna. The question to be asked is, "How did the word Gehenna come to represent more than the words from which it was translated?" In the twelve times that it appears in the Greek New Testament, how did it come to be translated as Hell in our English versions? The word Hell never appears on the lips and tongue of the Hebrew, Aramaic, and probably Greek-speaking Jesus of Nazareth.

When Jesus spoke of Gehenna, He was speaking literally of a real place that existed in real time and had a definite geographical location. The word Hell used in our English versions is based on the myths and legends of our human failures and the power of our own guilt and shame. Regardless of how many times we sing "Jesus loves me, this I know, for the Bible tells me so," my experience has been that we have never graduated from the Old Testament law of retaliation: "If any harm follows, then you shall give life for life, eye for eye, tooth for tooth, hand for hand, foot for foot, burn for burn, wound for wound, stripe for stripe" (Exod. 21:23-24).

We may not like to admit it, but our behavior suggests that we love that temporary surge of satisfaction that comes with "getting even." We see it and feel it in the way we drive our cars, the way we vote for our public leaders, the way we spend our money, the way we relate to people who do not meet our standards, and many other ways that are known only to each of us. It is much easier to "get high on getting even" than it is to practice the law of love that we have received from Saint Paul: "Love does not insist on its own way; it is not irritable or resentful; it does not rejoice at wrong, but rejoices in the right. Love bears all things, believes all things, endures all things" (1 Cor. 13:5-7).

Love calls us to live in the present. The retaliatory, vindictive concept of Hell calls us to live in the past memories of our failures and inadequacies. It encourages us to bury our spirits in the dark places of shame and guilt. Israel projected the memories of all the horrible things that happened in Gehinnom into the future. The memories of the past became synonymous with an actual location, and they were unable to separate the events from the location. Under the influence of religions of revenge and fear, we have done the same thing, and in doing so we have created our own mythical place that never existed and never will exist. We have named it Hell and armed it with all our fears and all of the emotional and psychological torments that churn up the acids of shame and guilt that cripple us. Misunderstood memories can do that to a person.

I fondly recall my visits with a one-hundred-year-old lady who was a member of a church I served in southwest Virginia. She was born in eighteen hundred and sixty-nine, four years after the end of the Civil War. I enjoyed sitting on the porch of her old homestead and listening to her stories. The first time I visited I commented on the beauty of the farmland and how pleasant the place was. She rocked in her chair a few times, and then she pointed to the hillside and said, "We used to keep a lot of cattle over there. And we had smokehouses where we kept our hams and other food." After a lengthy period of silence, she said, "My mother told me that when the Yankees came through the valley they stole the hams, drove off our cattle, tore down our fences, and burned the outhouses." Over the next three years of my ministry there, she told me that story each time I visited. On many occasions, all she talked about was the time when the Yankees came through and destroyed their farm. As I became familiar with the area, I learned that everybody referred to that section of the valley as "The place where the Yankees came through and stole food and burned buildings." That beautiful farmland was not referred to for its beauty and its present potential as a farm. It was captured in the local memory as the place where the Yankees desecrated the land.

The Valley of Hinnom/Gehinnom/Gehenna was remembered as that evil place where terrible sins were committed and where garbage was dumped and burned. It was not seen as a section of real estate with value as a place to build, farm, and raise cattle. From generation-to-generation Gehinnom/Gehenna was remembered as a place associated with fire, death, and the stench of rotting animal and human flesh. Any mention of Gehenna stimulated the power of memory to produce the image and odor of smoldering, decomposing garbage, and trash.

The fourth word mistranslated as Hell is the word Tartarus. It appears only one time in the New Testament (1 Pet. 2:4). The English version of the text says, "God did not spare the angels when they sinned, but cast them into hell and committed them to pits of nether gloom." The Greek texts used to compile the early English versions say, "cast them into Tartarus," not "into hell." I will avoid the many problems associated with the meaning of this verse. The assumptions of 2 Peter 2:4 and Jude 5-7 regarding "fallen angels" are based entirely on the apocryphal Book of Enoch. Enoch connects the fallen angels to the story of the Nephilim in Genesis 6:1-4.[47] He blames the punishment of the angels on their experiences of sexual intercourse with earthly women. J. H. Hertz, former Rabbi of the British Empire said, "There is, however, no trace in Genesis of fallen angels or rebellious angels; and the idea of intermarriage of angels and human beings is altogether foreign to Hebrew thought."[48] Many of the early Fathers condemned the accounts of Enoch and labeled them as repulsive. Saint Augustine advised that these stories be omitted as unfound fables. He said, "They contain so many false statements, that they have no canonical authority."[49]

We can only speculate as to why the writer of Second Peter used the word Tartarus instead of the more commonly used Hades or Gehenna. One suggested explanation is that the Hellenization of Israel introduced the stories of Greek mythology to Jewish society. Jerome Neyrey believes that the use of Tartarus "suggests a plausible audience of Jew and Gentile, as well as an author familiar with and eager to employ pagan stories which reinforce the Bible."[50]

Again, we can only speculate as to why the English translators replaced Tartarus with Hell. Perhaps they did not appreciate relying on pagan myths to reinforce the truth of the Bible. Tartarus was identified as a gloomy, shadowy place where super-heroes known as Titans were imprisoned when they disobeyed, or otherwise offended the gods. Greek mythology was grounded in audacious stories about these creatures. We do know that the Apostles warned their churches about the heretical character of myths. Paul urged Timothy to tell certain members of the congregation "not to occupy themselves with myths" (1 Tim. 1:4). Peter made it known that mythology played no part in his teaching and preaching. He said, "For we did not follow cleverly devised myths when we made known to you the power and coming of our Lord Jesus Christ, but we were eyewitnesses of his majesty" (2 Pet. 1:16).

We also know that some early Fathers opposed the association of any pagan mythologies with any part of the Judeo-Christian Scriptures. Saint Clement of Alexandria (AD 153-217) insisted that he had no tolerance for the invented fables of Greek mythology. Origin (AD 185- 254) strongly objected to associating any of the myths with the accounts recorded in the Bible. He said that, unlike the people in the Hebrew and Christian scriptures, the fictitious gods of the Greek myths "never had a real, substantial existence" and were without any historical connection to the message of the Bible.[51]

It is doubtful that sixteenth and seventeenth-century Christian leaders would see any benefit in endorsing any aspect of a mythology that recognized multiple gods. When Jesus was questioned about the commandment that was above all commandments, He said, "The first is this, 'Hear O Israel: the Lord our God, the Lord is one'" (Mark 12:28-29). The many Olympian gods of mythology could be imprisoned, lured into illicit relationships with multiple human and divine persons, capriciously launch thunderbolts and lightning strikes, and initiate other natural disasters. How could the reformers of the Protestant Reformation give credence to satyrs and centaurs, half-beast, and half-man creatures? It could be argued that to validate Tartarus as a place not previously established in canonical Christian literature would give a measure of standing to a pagan idea that could proliferate in scope and content. This would confuse the biblical proclamation that Jesus alone is "Before all things, and in him all things hold together" (Col. 1:17).

In the final analysis, we cannot know for sure why the writer used a specific word in some contexts. Neither can we know with certainty why the translators replaced one word with another word. An intent to use pagan stories to reinforce the Bible may have been acceptable when Second Peter was written (ca. AD 95-110). However, fifteen hundred years later, Church scholars and leaders may have seen things differently. At the height of the Protestant Reformation, can you imagine Luther, Calvin, Knox, and Zwingli, with their very lives as collateral, deferring to Greek mythology to prove the truth of what they affirmed to be the Word of God?

Perhaps they rightfully saw that an instance of blending scripture with pagan tradition had outlived its intent to influence a pluralistic audience. Even so, the word Hell fares no better than the word it replaces. It simply reads a sixteenth-century ideology and doctrinal assumption back into the Greek text. Pause for a moment and think about this question: "What is it about our human sickness that compels us to confirm the existence of a non-existent "no place" that we call Hell?

For any who absolutely must have a more terrible picture of Hell than the one represented in the English versions of the New Testament, I can recommend a book that contains the "mother of all" descriptions of Hell. Accordingly, I refer you to the *Koran* and the Koranic traditions known as *Hadiths*. The images of Hell as recorded in these documents are full of unimaginable horrors. An initial reaction to some forms of torture employed in the Koranic Hell forces one to wonder what kind of mind could even conceive of such punishments. Some of them are unbelievably disgusting. For example, an unbeliever who refuses to feed an indigent person will be chained, thrown in the fire, and given no food "except the foul pus from the washing of wounds, which none do eat but those who sin."[52]

My comments are not intended to deal extensively with Islamic doctrine and practice. My Christian biases would surely surface during any attempt to do so. This does not mean that I do not doubt the validity of the *Koran* itself. At the very least, I do not view the *Koran* as conveying the same theology as the Hebrew scriptures and the Christian New Testament. I have heard some folks say, "The *Koran* is the same as our *Bible*." My answer is always, "No, it is not." The *Bible* is a collection of documents that testify to the sovereignty of God, while also speaking to the reality of our human weaknesses and God's response to those weaknesses through the love, compassion, sacrificially redeeming death, and resurrection of Jesus Christ. I believe that Philip Schaff's assessment of the *Koran* is completely accurate. He says, "Whatever is true in the Koran is borrowed from the Bible; what is original is false or frivolous."[53] I also share his evaluation of Islam. Based on his extensive research he says, "Islam is a compound or mosaic of preexisting elements, a rude attempt to combine heathenism, Judaism and Christianity, which Mohammad found in Arabia, but in a very imperfect form."[54]

There were Jews who settled in the Arabian Peninsula many years before the birth of Mohammad. In the northern part of Arabia, a number of localities had been populated largely by Arabic-speaking Jews for centuries.[55] The Jewish population increased when many Jews fled to Arabia following the destruction of Jerusalem in AD 70. Later, the Christian Church gained enormous power when the Emperor Constantine (AD 280-337) legalized Christianity. With increased authority and imperial support, the Christian Church was empowered to exercise authority in adjudicating matters of political and doctrinal ecclesiastical issues. Many of those who held the doctrines proclaimed to be heretical by orthodox standards sought refuge in the Arabian Peninsula. There can be no doubt that there was considerable Christian influence in Arabia prior to the advent of Islam.

Mohammad was forty years old when he began his career as a prophet in AD 610. Before that, he earned his living as a merchant. When he was a boy, he worked as an attendant on caravans where he came in contact with the Talmudic fables of Rabbinic Judaism and the unorthodox theologies of Christian heretics. At age twenty-five he married Chadijah, a forty-year-old rich widow who had hired him to help with her late husband's trading business. He took charge of her business and made many trading journeys with her commercial caravans. While doing business in Syria and other locations he met many anti-Christian Jews who were influenced by the post-AD 70 teachings of Rabbinic Judaism. He heard the imperfect and inaccurate stories of Christians who had been expelled from orthodox Christianity and belonged to heretical sects. Being unable to read or write, he listened to these stories that he had heard many times throughout his travels. These word-of-mouth stories told by unreliable sources provided his education regarding Jewish and Christian writings and traditions.

The *Koran* refers to Hell in a variety of ways, all of them referring to a place of fiery punishment. Jahannam is a specific Koranic name for Hell. It corresponds to the biblical words Gehinnom and Gehenna. Jahannam has seven stages which are separated from each other by a five-hundred years' journey. Each of the stages has seventy thousand different kinds of torment that can be inflicted on those consigned to any of the seven stages. The sixth stage of Jahannam is reserved for Jews and Christians.

Punishment is a common theme in many of the one-hundred-fourteen Suras (chapters) in the *Koran*. I have counted references to hell and fire in ninety-two of the Suras. The following are representative of the ninety-two that mention punishment:

Sura 4:56 – As often as their skins are roasted through, we shall exchange them for fresh skins.

Sura 18:29 – Any who ask for relief from the fire will be granted water like melted brass, that will scald their faces.

Sura 22:19-21 – Over their heads will be poured out boiling water. With it will be what is within their bodies as well as their skins. In addition there will be maces of iron to punish them.

Sura 40:71-72 – They shall be dragged along in the boiling fetid fluid, then in the fire they shall be burned.

Sura 54:48 – They shall be dragged through the fire on their faces.

The constant threats of punishment and vivid descriptions of Islamic Hell in the *Koran* are repeated in more repugnant and exaggerated descriptions in the Islamic *Hadiths*. They are a collection of the sayings of Mohammad that were passed on by his close companions and by others who verified that they had received their information from someone who said that he knew that it had originated with Mohammad. A verified line of transmission would take the following shape: Mohammad told me, or I heard him say so-and-so; I told Joe that I heard Mohammad say so-and-so; Joe told Bill that I told him that I heard Mohammad say so-and-so; Bill told Mary that Joe told him that I heard Mohammad say so-and-so; Mary told Jane that Bill told her that Joe told him that I told Joe that I heard Mohammad say so-and-so. Voila! There we have it. Authenticity is confirmed. Truth is assumed to be validated by traditions passed on through this allegedly infallible line of transmission that confirms that what is being reported really did come from the mouth of Mohammad.

Mohammad knows exactly how the fire of Gehennan was created. He said: "The fire was stoked for a thousand years till it became red. Then it was stoked for a thousand years till it became white. Then it was stoked for a thousand years till it became black, so that it is black as the darkest night."[56] Some eye-witness companions said that Mohammad told them about the awful creatures that inhabited Hell. Gabriel said to him,

> In Gehenna are pits in which are snakes the size of camels' necks, and scorpions the size of black mules. The Damned are driven towards these serpents who seize them by the lips and skin them from the hair of their heads to the nails of their toes and fingers, and

the only way they can escape from them is by rushing into the Fire.⁵⁷

Mohammad said that Gabriel took him to the gates of the descending circles of Hell. He was curious as to how the gates opened and asked Gabriel if they were like the gates that are used on earth. Gabriel told him that the gates of Hell were attended to by the angels of punishment who torment the sinners in Hell (Sura 96:18). These angels, called Zabaniya, meet the sinners with fetters and chains. Mohammad said,

> The chain is inserted in the man's mouth and brought out his rectum. His left hand is fettered to his neck and his right hand is thrust through his heart and pulled out between his shoulders, where it is fastened with chains. Moreover, every human will be chained to a satan. He will be dragged on his face while angels beat him with iron cudgels.⁵⁸

Another story that originated with a companion of Mohammad explains how an unbeliever is treated while en route from this world to the next one. First, angels with black faces join him. Next, the Angel of Death arrives and says to him, "O thou pernicious soul, come forth to Allah's discontent and wrath."⁵⁹ Mohammad then tells his listeners that the Angel of Death "drags the man's soul like the dragging of an iron spit through moist wool, tearing the veins and the sinews."⁶⁰

During his visit with Gabriel, Mohammad learned that some punishments are easier than others. Informed through the authentic line of transmission, a companion says that the prophet said to them,

> The weakest punishment a man has in the Fire is that of his feet, which are put into two sandals of fire, which cause his brains to boil like a copper cauldron,

make his ears and molar teeth glow like live coals, and his entrails melt and flow out at his feet. He will think that he is the most tormented of the Damned, but really his is the weakest punishment.[61]

Is it possible that the ones who dispensed these terrible punishments might be inclined to occasionally show some mercy? It is reasonable to think that the hideous sights and sounds of torture could provoke an attitude of pity in a tormentor and persuade him to diminish the intensity of the method of punishment. Mohammad had the answer to this potential problem involving leniency of punishment. Again, through the authentic line of transmission, Mohammad was reported to have said that those who punished an unbeliever would be "deaf and dumb and blind and cannot hear his voice so as to be touched with mercy, nor can they see him so as to pity him."[62] While these sadistic angels of punishment beat their victims with hooked rods of iron and subjected them to the flames of Hell, they could see no evil, hear no evil, or speak no evil. This was not an act of mercy to protect the emotional sensitivities and mental health of the tormentors. It was designed to ensure the production of maximum pain and punishment.

When we consider the environment in which Mohammad put together the hodge-podge collection of mostly plagiarized and fantasized sayings that had been carved and scratched onto coconut shells, animal bones, and palm leaves, we should not be surprised that the result was a book that reflected incredible brutality and violence. The Arabian peninsula is located between the Persian Gulf, the Indian Ocean, and the Red Sea. We usually think of the Peninsula as a place of sandy, wind-blown deserts. However, it also has rocky coasts, barren hills, plains, valleys, and some rich pastureland. At the time of Mohammad, nomadic tribes and caravan traders moved throughout the land. The inhabitants were fierce, brave, and independent people who were skilled in both offensive and defensive warfare. Gibbon said that they were a people "whom it is dangerous to provoke and fruitless to attack."[63]

Over hundreds of years, the Arabs had cultivated a way of life that placed a strong emphasis on vengeance and revenge. The spirit of "an eye for an eye" took precedence over any recognition of pity or forgiveness. It was accepted among the Arabs that the requirement to exact revenge was an undeniable right. There were no exceptions, and it was extended to all individuals, families, and tribes. There was no statute of limitations on the time to satisfy this right. A grudge could be retained for many years and acted upon at the convenience and pleasure of those who had been insulted or wronged. No insult was too obsolete to be avenged. Honor, more than the injury itself, was the driving force of the necessity for revenge. The powerful obsession to satisfy honor and justice was a deadly factor in the quarreling environment of the Arabs of the Arabian Peninsula.

We can reasonably assume that during his many years as a successful merchant and trader, Mohammad developed the skill of assessing customers and business rivals. His experience as a salesman had taught him the value of the business principles of "the customer is always right," and "give them what they want." In his book, *Psychology of Mohammad*, Dr. Massoud Ansari says that even though Mohammad was ignorant, "He possessed a preposterously exaggerated ego, and a native cunning, and intelligence."[64] Without mincing words, the historian Henry Sheldon says that Mohammad was "devoted to fraud and trickery."[65]

In terms of human relations, Mohammad knew how to "read people" and was an expert at marketing himself and his product. He spoke with authority, confidence, and a sense of urgency. He understood the culture and the social mores of the Arab community.

He instinctively knew that the illiterate and tradition-bound nomads would not respond to any religion that did not conform to their harsh, inflexible, and non-negotiable understanding of the necessity of imposing punishment for offenses committed. If retribution were required in this world, surely it would also be required in the next world. Gibbon says, "The rewards and punishments of a future life were painted by the images most congenial to an ignorant and carnal generation."[66]

Mohammad projected into the afterlife the extremes of violence and merciless brutality already known to the inhabitants of the Arabian Peninsula. The grotesque and absurd scenes of Hell portrayed in the *Koran* validated their belief in the legitimacy of revenge and punishment for offenses committed. The shrewd Mohammad convinced them that he was the prophet of Allah and to disobey him was to disobey Allah and make them vulnerable to the horrible litany of punishments found in the *Koran* and the *Hadiths*. He ensured his own unquestionable authority by claiming that Allah had said, "And if any believe not in Allah and his messenger, we have prepared, for those who reject Allah, a blazing fire!" (Sura 48:13). As has always been the case with religions in general and charlatans in particular, fear trumped the love of God and became a tool to control people and to protect self-appointed megalomaniacal authority figures from rejection.

While Mohammad and Islam are obsessed with the idea of Hell and its unthinkable punishments, it is interesting to note that Saint Paul was not the least bit interested in the doctrine of Hell. Neither the Greek texts nor their English translations contain the word Hell in Paul's writings. He preached, established churches, lived, wrote, and was killed before any of the Gospels were written and distributed, but he is silent regarding the doctrine of Hell. His total focus is on the redeeming power of the cross of Christ and the victory of His resurrection.

In Matthew, Mark, and Luke, Jesus uses the word Gehenna eleven times. Referring to those eleven instances, Hans Kung says, "Certainly Jesus too spoke of Hell, as people generally spoke of it at that time: in the language and imagery of his time."[67] When placed alongside Jesus' teachings regarding forgiveness, eternal life, love, and mercy, it is obvious that He had no direct interest in sending human beings to an eternity of punishment. As a teacher, He was an expert in using hypothetical constructions and hyperbole to emphasize the urgency and seriousness of embracing the principles of the Kingdom of God. He used the image of the Jerusalem garbage pit to portray the wretched state of life that exists for those who shut themselves out of fellowship with God.

Think about this question: Why is it that we show not only a willingness but a certain satisfaction in welcoming the idea of Hell? How could we wish the horrible stories of unbelievable methods of punishment on any human being? The Christian Church has been guilty of participating in the claim that the righteous saints in heaven will find delight in the horrible pains of sinners in Hell. Saint Thomas Aquinas, the great teacher of the Catholic Church, taught that the "blessed in heaven will see the suffering of the damned. They will show them no pity and will rejoice in the punishment of the wicked."[68]

Think about that statement made by Aquinas, known as the "Angelic Doctor" of the Catholic Church. What hymn should we stand and sing after hearing this good news? How about, *"When we all get to heaven, what a day of rejoicing that will be!"* But wait, I see something moving in that blazing inferno just across the clouds. It's Mom and Dad! They did not make it and I do not feel much like rejoicing.

Pope Gregory the Great said, "For as just men do rejoice and be glad at the retribution of eternal justice, so necessary it is that the wicked at the same justice should be greatly tormented."[69] The fourth great doctor of the Catholic Church has spoken. Perhaps we should stand and sing, *"When the roll is called up yonder, I'll be there."* But wait, when the roll was called, I did not hear the names of my children. They missed roll call, and now I see them over there in the flames of Hell. Under those circumstances, one might agree with Ivan in Dostoevsky's *The Brothers Karamazov*. In so many words, Ivan said that some prices might be too high to pay for entrance into heaven. He said,

> And so I hasten to give back my entrance ticket, and if I am an honest man I am bound to give it back as soon as possible. And that I am doing. It's not God that I don't accept, only I most respectfully return Him the ticket.[70]

Think about this: When the roll is called up yonder, is there anything that might make you give back your entrance ticket?

I think that our willingness to believe in the absurdly monstrous concept of Hell represents a surrender to the instincts of our vengeful and cruel primeval experiences. I agree with Nicolas Berdyaev's claim that "The Christian mind has not yet been emancipated from the residuum of a retaliatory and penal eschatology."[71] While claiming to be disciples of Jesus Christ, we have confused His message of the Father who loves, forgives, and re-creates with our own image of a God who behaves and acts as we do. I am in no way suggesting that we should not establish governments, laws, and methods of punishing anyone who violates those laws. We have it on the authority of the two great pillars of the Church, both Peter and Paul, that government is established to preserve peace and prevent crime. Saint Paul says, "Let every person be subject to the governing authorities," and "he who resists will incur judgment/punishment" (Rom. 13). Peter says, "Be subject for the Lord's sake to every human institution, whether it be to the emperor as supreme, or to governor's as sent by him to punish those who do wrong and to praise those who do right" (1 Pet. 2:13-14). Without laws and law enforcement, we would find ourselves living in chaos. To use a Wild West analogy, without law and order, we might find ourselves living like characters in a Dodge City television episode of *Gunsmoke*. Some might say that we are already at that point in America today.

In his letters to proconsuls and magistrates, Saint Augustine expresses his recognition that laws are essential in the defense of society. Making use of judges and laws can provoke a healthy fear that becomes a deterrence to criminal activity. He advises that the criminal "ought to be punished with a severity corresponding to the enormity of the crime."[72] He is generally opposed to capital punishment but concedes that "If there were no other means established to curb the malice of the wicked, extreme necessity might perhaps urge that such men be put to death."[73]

Saint Augustine understands Paul's insistence that the officials of secular governments have a valid authority to legislate laws, maintain law and order, and judge the punishment of lawbreakers. The appointed authorities "do not bear the sword in vain," and they are granted the power "to execute wrath on the wrongdoer" (Rom. 13:4). Both Paul and Augustine are talking about laws and punishments that pertain to the actions and behaviors of life in this imperfect world.

In the flesh, we are finite creatures living in a world that is subject to the limitations of our knowledge, wisdom, and physical capabilities. We are all affected by the lawlessness of our fallen nature and each of us is capable of transgressing one or more of the laws of society at any given time. A line written in 165 BC by Terence has given me much to think about after first having read it many years ago. In his play, *The Self-Tormentor*, Terence has one of his characters say, "I am a human, and I think nothing human is alien to me."[74] Because I am a human being, I am capable of committing any act that has been committed by another human being. Having learned this, I now bring this awareness to any judgment I make regarding human behavior and our criminal justice system. Our human nature is not pure. In all of us, the good and the bad are all scrambled up together. Our condition reminds me of an old saying that has been worth memorizing: "There is so much good in the worst of us, and so much bad in the best of us, that it ill behooves any of us to find fault with the rest of us."[75] Both of these competing contradictory forces are resident in our human nature. In an obvious state of exasperation, Saint Paul said, "I do not do the good I want, but the evil I do not want is what I do" (Rom. 7:19)

Our human nature will always express itself in this world in ways that require civilized society to protect us from each other. This involves maintaining order by imposing punishments for breaches and violations of governmentally sanctioned laws. Saint Augustine writes about the dual nature of life in our human environment. He says, "Two cities have been formed by two loves: the earthly by the love of self, even to the contempt of God; the heavenly by the love of God, even to the contempt of self."[76] The earthly city is "filled with lawsuits civil and criminal, and is never free from the fear, if sometimes from the actual outbreaks, of disturbing and bloody insurrections and civil wars."[77] The laws of the earthly city are "judgments which men pronounce on men, and which are necessary for communities, whatever outward peace they enjoy."[78]

Martin Luther, probably inspired by Saint Augustine's *City of God*, writes about two kingdoms. The first is the Kingdom of God and the second is the kingdom of the world. He says, "In the kingdom of the world, we must first establish secular law and the sword, that no one may doubt that it is in the world by God's will and ordinance."[79] Being a Christian does not disqualify or exempt a person from the obligation of serving to preserve law and order. In the service of law and order, the Christian is actually serving others by protecting those who need protection and limiting the crimes of the wicked. He said,

> Therefore, should you see that there is a lack of hangmen, beadles, judges, lords, or princes, and find that you are qualified, you should offer your services and seek the place, that necessary government may by no means be despised and become inefficient or perish. For the world cannot and dare not dispense with it.[80]

Punishments necessary for government in the earthly city (Augustine), or the kingdom of the world (Luther), are restricted to the domain of this world. There will be no need for punishment in the heavenly city or the Kingdom of God. Luther said, "Worldly government has laws which extend no farther than life and property and what is external upon earth. For over the soul, God can and will let no one rule but Himself."[81] Saint Augustine emphasized that we must not superimpose the need for punishment in this world onto an assumed need for punishment in God's re-created world. He said, "A matter of interest for a province is not the same thing as a matter of interest for the Church. The government of the former should be carried out with severity; the forbearance of the latter should be carried out with mercy."[82]

Do we really believe that it is the will of God that some of us will die and go to a place we call Hell? Who among us is qualified to speak of the will of God? Few things are subject to more abuse than the interpretation of the will of God. In the hands of human beings, it is like a child's playdough/putty. It is always shaped, molded, and formed to correspond to our own opinions and desires. Before the medieval Crusaders went forward to kill thousands of Muslims and Jews, their battle cry was, "God wills it!" Of course, the Muslim armies had their own cheerleading chant of what they considered to be the will of Allah. We still hear it today echoing above every Islamic terrorist attack: "Allahu Akbar," (Allah is the greatest). One historian of the era of the Crusades has said, "High ideals were besmirched by cruelty and greed, enterprise and endurance by a blind and narrow self-righteousness; and the Holy War itself was nothing more than a long act of intolerance in the name of God, which is a sin against the Holy Ghost."[83]

I cringe when I hear any human being talking about the will of God. Such talk is usually based on one's own presumptuous understanding of a given situation. It is used as a defense mechanism to justify personal behavior and to endorse political and governmental decisions according to what we support and want to happen. The will of God too easily becomes synonymous with our own distorted views as expressed in our speech, conduct, and behavior. I have found it unwise to identify human future projections as the will of God. There is just too much of "me, you, and us" involved in such projections. We do not always know what is best for us, but God does. We do not know the future, but God does. The best we can do is to move forward in faith, and then at some time in the future, we can look back over our shoulders and try to understand why and how things happened as they did.

The fear of eternal damnation in a burning place of horror has given religion more leverage and power over people than the power of love. The primitive Christian Church, using secret symbols to identify its connection to the resurrected Lord, knew about love, sacrifice, and commitment. Driven to the catacombs of Rome to worship, they maintained a faith that lived through persecution and embraced hope in an environment of hopelessness. But the day arrived when the Church came into its own environment of secular power. Power over people, places, and things intoxicates the human personality like nothing else. The Church, no longer subject to the restrictions of public worship in the Roman Empire, and no longer subject to the abuses of public humiliation by non-Christians, fell in love with its new public standing.

Suddenly, the Roman Eagle became more influential than the Christian Dove. I compare the change to that of a hard-working person who has finally been able to take a vacation to a warm, sunny beach and found it to be more soothing, refreshing, relaxing, and peaceful than anything ever experienced. After a few days of rest and recuperation he says, "I could get accustomed to living like this!" The Church, having tasted the thrill of power, exchanged love for power and the control that comes with it. However, the ecclesiastical authorities soon learned that people are not easy to govern. Well aware that the power of the Roman Eagle was sustained by the threat of punishment, the Church perceived that it needed a similar structure to maintain its ecclesiastical authority. It was not difficult to arrive at the conclusion that punishment was far more effective in attaining its objectives than was the message of love. Over the years, this opting for power over love created an ecclesiastical institution that was coopted by kings and nations to serve the interests of secular wealth and power at the expense of the spiritual and physical well-being of the masses of the people.

What purpose did the creation of this ghastly realm called Hell serve? Think about this: If you can sell people the awful concept of Hell, it will be even easier to sell them a "get out of Hell permit" (indulgence) for a certain sum of money. How else was Leo the Tenth going to be able to pay for building the great Saint Peter's Cathedral to leave as his legacy? It is reported that Pope Leo said, "It has served us well, this myth of Christ." While no credible authority has verified this, the Church can say with certainty, "It has served us well, this myth of Hell!" A realistic reading of Church History reveals that nobody plays the real-life game of *Monopoly* better than the Church. And the Church has always been in the real estate business.

Since the Protestant Reformation that began in the sixteenth century, organized and independent Protestant denominations have proliferated. Each has brought its own emphasis on Hell and its fiery punishment. While Protestantism has not sold indulgences the same way that Pope Leo sold them, it has benefited financially and numerically from the power of fear to influence and control people. The raging fire of eternal damnation has been used as an instrument of religious and moral terrorism. I use the word terrorism because the fear of Hell as taught by many churches can cause psychological damage. Exposure to that kind of terrifying fear at an early age can cause emotional scarring that impacts a person throughout a lifetime. I have known people who were unable to relax and enjoy the gift of life in this world because they were always worried about where they were going when they died.

The television evangelists and the high-pressure revival preachers seem to be today's self-proclaimed experts on Heaven and Hell. They especially like to emphasize the torments of Hell. If they can frighten you enough to contact them by phone or internet, they assure you that "prayer warriors" will be standing by to help you.

The contact and the prayers are free, but you can be assured that your personal information will go into a database. Shortly after that, you will be contacted and encouraged to send money for water from the Jordan River, anointed prayer cloths, vials of special anointing oil from the Holy Land, and a card certifying you as a prayer partner in a ministry that is trying to save the world for Jesus. As experts, they will share with you their vivid descriptions of the Hell you are being saved from, profiles of people who are going to Hell, and what kinds of punishment they will receive. They know about such things as the kind of furniture that will be used in Heaven and the temperature of Hell at any given time. They distort the love of God in Christ Jesus by creating the terror of Hell in the minds of human beings. I agree with Berdyaev who says, "There is no Hell. It is a phantasmagoric, illusory, and non-existential sphere."[84]

We know that life on this earth is short. It is much shorter for some than for others. Furthermore, if time as we know it and live it, and if the eternal future which we have not yet experienced represents two separate dimensions of experience, how can there be any fairness or justice in using eternal torments to punish wrongs committed in finite time? Time and eternity cannot be judged by the same standard. There is no common standard of measurement to compare these distinctly separate dimensions. As we might say today, "It is like comparing apples to oranges." Considering this, is the concept of Hell rational or irrational? Think about this question and answer it for yourself. As for me, there is something repulsive and tyrannical in the idea of eternal torment as punishment for something that happened in a short moment of life. A sobering appraisal of the concept of eternal punishment reminds us that eternal means forever. Unending punishment for failures, sins, or mistakes experienced in these seventy or fewer years of life is a nightmarish perversion that distorts the mission of God as implemented through the life and death of His Son.

If the doctrine of Hell is thought to represent the failure of humanity, it cannot stop with its condemnation of God's creatures alone. More than the failure of finite humanity, the concept of Hell represents the failure of God. His great act of Creation becomes a failure and victory belongs to the serpent "who was more subtle than any other wild creature that the Lord God had made" (Gen. 3:1). Can there be a rival king and kingdom to the Kingdom of God? A kingdom of Hell would be an awful place, but it would still be a rival kingdom. While it would be inferior, it would still be akin to our aphorism of "In the kingdom of the blind, the one-eyed man is king."

The Old Testament repeatedly tells us that "God is a jealous God" (Exod. 20:5, 34:14; Deut. 4:24, 5:9, 6:15; Josh. 24:19). There is no possibility for the existence of any kind of kingdom to rival the Kingdom Of God. Paul explains it this way: "When all things are subjected to him, then the Son himself will also be subjected to him who put all things under him, that God may be everything to everyone" (1 Cor. 15:28). The final standing of God will be uncontested. All struggles involved in the re-creation of the world and humankind will have been completed. No rival kingdom, whether good or evil, will exist. There is no room or place for a kingdom of Hell in an eternity where God maintains total sovereignty.

The conception of a place called Hell has nothing to do with the message of Jesus Christ. It was never seriously touched upon by the Lord of mercy and love; however, it does have the human touch of revenge all over it. We have conflated what we have found to be necessary in our fallen world with what we imagine will be structured into the domain of the afterlife. In a sense, we have become victims of our own imaginations. Conditioned to get revenge and dedicated to the ancient laws of retaliation, we really are ignorant about the length, depth, and breadth of God's grace. Whereas we go to extremes to condemn each other, God goes to extremes to save us and forgive us. Paul referred to this as the "unsearchable and unknowable ways of God" (Rom. 11:33), and the "love of Christ that surpasses knowledge" (Eph. 3:18-19).

The extremes to which our vengeful nature can carry us are reflected in a story told about a soldier who was arrested for playing cards during a worship service. It is anecdotal and may not be true or reliable, but it has been passed on in various versions over the past two hundred and fifty years. When taken before the judge, the soldier said that he could justify the use of his cards in church since they served as his "Bible, Almanack, and Prayer Book." The judge said, "If you cannot justify this strange scandalous behavior, I will cause you, without delay to be severely punished."[85] By the time the story became a song in the United States, if the soldier was found guilty the sentence was no longer that he would be "severely punished." The judge said, "I shall punish you more than any man has ever been punished!" Think about how much the sentence increased in severity over the span of many years. For playing cards in church, the soldier would be punished more than any murderer, rapist, serial killer, or any other crime known to humankind. This story is representative of how myths grow and how far the human mind can go in exaggerating any concept of retaliatory punishment.

There is no mystery as to how we have established the concept of everlasting punishment in a mythical place called Hell. I seriously doubt that anyone with an awareness of the human capacity to sin not just once, but multiple times, has had any say in the creation of this monstrous idea of hellfire and brimstone. People who demonstrate a strong self-righteous nature seem to have a need to vigorously hold onto the idea of Hell. Thinking themselves to be above the shortcomings and failures of other people, they have to believe that those who do not meet their standards cannot possibly be entitled to the benefits of God's grace. They fit the profile of the elder son in Jesus' story of the Prodigal Son (Luke 15:11-32). Erich Fromm says that people who think like this "believe themselves to be godlike, superior, and entitled to condemn or forgive."[86]

The unacceptable element in this kind of thinking lies in the unchallenged assumption that justice and punishment in the eternal Kingdom of God will be consistent with the methods of justice and punishment in the kingdom of the world. It is one thing to use the power of secular authority to punish someone for violating civil and criminal laws. This kind of judicial activity is legally imposed according to life in the kingdom of the world. Those decisions are made within the limitations of human judgment and are based on evidence and ethical values recognized and enforced by the state. It is quite another thing to migrate this system of judging and justice to the realm of the Kingdom of God. It amounts to an infringement on the sovereignty of God. Few things can be more distorted and misguided than the arrogance of any person, institution, or religious doctrine that presumes to speak for God when human consequences are in the balance.

Decisions about anyone's eternal fate are not safe in human hands. Jeremiah said, "The heart is deceitful above all things, and desperately corrupt, who can understand it" (Jer. 17:9). We are not competent to decide what will be the population and demographics of eternity. Erich Fromm echoes the warning of Jeremiah. He notes that the opportunity and authority to render moral judgments changes the character and moral sensibility of many people. He says,

> Their attitude often contains a good deal of sadism and destructiveness. There is perhaps no phenomenon which contains so much destructive

feeling as "moral indignation," which permits envy or hate to be acted out under the guise of virtue. The "indignant" person has for once the satisfaction of despising and treating a creature as "inferior," coupled with the feeling of his own superiority and righteousness.[87]

In our imperfect world, many of our fellow human beings who conform to this psychological profile are sitting in places of authority and judgment. It does not require a stretch of the imagination to suspect that some of those same characteristics live in each of us and tempt us from time to time. Turning the other cheek is not always easy. An injury or insult done to us, a spouse, a child, or a friend can trigger the "get even" response. It is not unusual that any one of us might take great delight in contributing to the failure or ill fortune of an old enemy or adversary. Each one of us is an imperfect person living in a world that is one hundred percent populated by other imperfect people. It is ridiculous to think that we are honest enough or competent enough to speak for God regarding the eternal judgment of others who are just like us.

Pascal was even more critical of the human condition than was Jeremiah. He said, "We are only falsehood, duplicity, contradiction. We both conceal and disguise ourselves from ourselves."[88] If there is some truth to his evaluation, and I believe there is, how dare we even remotely presume to speak for God. I have some friends and colleagues who have the various impressive titles of Reverend, Reverend Doctor, Reverend Father, Very Reverend, Right Reverend, and Most Reverend. That is a lot of "Reverend power," but I would not want any one of them to be my eternal judge.

I am just a generic Methodist Reverend, but I would not want myself to be my own eternal judge. My past report card is not exactly what I remember it to have been. Most of the bad stuff has fallen out and been swept under some rug somewhere. I am sure that what I recall and what really was are not the same things. When I need sympathy, my selective memory presents me as the victim of someone's unfair treatment. I peevishly take on the role of the unsuccessful prize fighter who famously said, "I could 'a been a contender!" When I am full of myself and want applause and congratulations, I can readily recite a list of my accomplishments. However, authentic confession demands an acknowledgement that my fantasy thinking is often as meaningful to me as my rational thinking. I have a long list of things I want to do, but what it shows and what the record shows are not the same. No human being is qualified to be the judge of another human being's entire life. Not in this world and certainly not in the next life. God alone knows the true physical and emotional disposition of any person at any given time.

The writer of Proverbs said, "All the ways of a man are pure in his own eyes, but the Lord weighs the spirit" (Prov. 16:2). The first part of this verse is an acknowledgement of our self-congratulatory nature. It serves as a warning that we tend to think too highly of ourselves. This is a vanity that supports Pascal's claim that we "both conceal and disguise ourselves from ourselves." What we or others think of us will have no impact on our eternal destiny. In this verse from Proverbs, our attention should be upon the word "but." It is a conjunction that introduces the probability that either a contradiction, an exception, or an objection will follow. Karl Barth calls this "The Great But," and says that it means that there is "still something that is overlooked and forgotten, still something to be taken into consideration, there is still another possibility at hand."[89] Our human ideas of justice, reward, and punishment become of no consequence when we cross the boundary that separates the kingdom of the world from the Kingdom of God.

We live in a world where we can manipulate all manner of personal factors and present ourselves with a high degree of cosmetic perfection. We are schooled in the mechanics of body language and the tactics of how to win friends and influence people. But what really counts in terms of eternity, is the truth that "the Lord weighs the spirit." God is an eyewitness to our real selves that Pascal says are often "concealed, disguised, desperately arrogant, and deceitful above all things." The bad news is that we are all susceptible and vulnerable to the power of these undesirable character flaws. The good news that outweighs the bad news is that God sees our acts, thoughts, and intentions in their true contexts. Our imperfect human nature often incites us to say and do things that we do not mean. We are given to impulsive outbursts and careless reactions. Who among us has not been told or heard someone say something like the following: *I hate you! I wish you were dead! I wish that I were dead! I never want to see you again!* The accounts of our impulsive behavior and careless reactions would fill many pages and if read back to us at some future time, would cause us grief and regret beyond understanding.

At an individual and personal level, our ideas about justice, judgment, and punishment are not nailed down fast and hard in our minds and consciences. They bump into and collide with other experiences of anger, fear, guilt, shame, grief, and remorse. They slosh around in a potpourri of knowing and not knowing. They are linked to powerful human emotions that incite confusion and indecision. One day we are sure of something, and the next day we are not so sure. We condemn people, places, and things that are not to our liking, but we are experts at making excuses for those people, places, and things that we like.

The awakening of our moral consciousness presents us with difficult situations. There is no escaping the tension that is produced by the arguments of our moral conscience. After Cain killed his brother, God asked him, "Where is Abel your brother?" Cains's answer was, "I do not know; am I my brother's keeper?" (Gen. 4:9-10). I have often wondered how Abel, the victim, would answer if God should ask him, "Where is Cain your brother?" Would an acceptable answer be, "He is in Hell where he belongs!" The question, "Am I my brother's keeper?" works both ways. Cain hid his moral conscience behind an evasive answer that did not exonerate him. We do not know what Abel would have said about the brother who murdered him. Perhaps any satisfactory answer to that hypothetical situation will have to be found in the moral conscience of each of us. It appears that God did not give the parents any say, influence, or authority in judging the behavior of either of their sons. Neither has God given any human being permission or authority to speak for Him regarding the eternal fate of anyone created in His image.

There are those who speak of the Great White Throne of Judgment as though this poetic symbol and others like it are convincing arguments for a solemn ceremony of eternal judgment. They convert images from the literature and vocabulary of Jewish apocalypticism into a literal timebound reality. In fact, there is a judgment, but it has already taken place. It occurred in the trial, death, and resurrection of Jesus. John's Gospel says, "The Father judges no one, but has given all judgment to the Son" (John 5:22). The judgment is an act that does not wait for a court scene before some poetically mythical Great White Throne. When we step out of this life through the door of death, we will already have been judged by Jesus Christ.

Jesus is the sole judge of our eternal destiny, and His coming to live among us is the refutation of any place called Hell except the literal burning garbage dump outside the walls of ancient Jerusalem.

Belief in damnation and eternal punishment is unbelief in the power of Jesus Christ and the legitimacy of His appointment by God to serve as the ultimate judge of all things. The Gospels tell us that Jesus was committed to bringing glory to the Father. He completed the work that the Father had sent Him to do. In bringing God's love to humankind, Jesus could say, "I glorified thee on earth having accomplished the work which thou gavest me to do" (John 17:4). There is no doubt that the objective of His ministry was to teach the world to glorify God (Matt. 5:16). This fact alone should give us a reason to wonder how millions of people suffering forever in a lake of fire can bring any glory to God. The love of God as expressed in Jesus, was unwilling to accept the loss of one sheep out of the fold of one hundred. The loss of one coin out of a purse of ten was unacceptable. A reckless and undeserving son who dishonored his father and wasted his inheritance on irresponsible living was worth reclaiming and was welcomed back into the father's home. The loss of even one of us to some place of eternal damnation would be a contradiction to everything that Jesus teaches us about the Father's love.

God's judgment bears no resemblance whatsoever to what we have learned and practiced in this world. His love is all-triumphant and will not accept failure or rejection. It knows nothing of the human necessity to exact vengeance and punishment on each other. If we are to come to some peaceful understanding of what God has prepared for our eternal future, we must divorce all associations of His justice from our human systems and concepts of justice. The lexicon of criminal justice is a product of this world. Jesus, the God-approved Alpha and Omega Judge, has shown us the boundary and extent of the power and application of criminal law and human justice.

Two criminals were crucified with Jesus. All three had been tried in court, found guilty, and sentenced to death. That was as far as criminal justice could go. The power of human punishment could not extend beyond arrest, prosecution, conviction, sentencing, and execution. The guilt of the criminals was not in question. Speaking for both felons, one of the criminals said, "We are receiving the due reward of our deeds" Luke 23:41). Jesus did not tell the criminal that his punishment on the cross was just the beginning of his punishment for crimes committed during his brief life in this world. He did not say, "Just you wait! There is more far worse than this that is yet to come." He said, "Today you will be with me in paradise." Think carefully about this. The man was a criminal when they nailed him to his cross. He did not become less than a criminal when he died on his cross. He remained a criminal, but death did not make him a candidate for more punishment beyond death. In fact, the Great Judge, Jesus Christ, granted him access to Paradise. To the criminal justice system of the world, he was just another dead thug who got what he deserved. Good riddance! But could it be that the Eternal Judge knew more about this man's journey in the world than the world knew or cared about?

When we have a medical problem involving the heart, we go to a cardiologist, a specialist who studies and treats heart diseases. Saint Peter called God a "cardio-knower," (καρδιογνώστης). In a sermon to the Jews of Jerusalem, he preached about "God who knows the heart" (Acts 15: 7-11). Does it matter that God knows the heart, both yours and mine? I remember an occasion when a preacher in the town where I first served was saying every bad thing possible about a man whose family attended my United Methodist Church. He painted the man as a drunkard and a scandalous character. The preacher was, in all of his water-baptized self-righteousness, speaking for God. Our lay leader, one of the wisest men I have ever known, was with me and he finally spoke up and said, "Preacher, you do not know what you are talking about. I have known him all of his life, and you do not know how hard it is for him to be as good as he is right now." That was fifty-four years ago, and I have never forgotten it.

Think about these questions. Does Jesus know and does He care? Does He know the state of the mind and heart before the crime was committed? Does He know the circumstances that were there before alcoholism or substance abuse addiction took control of a troubled life and mind that ended in incarceration? Does He know the details that led to the destruction of countless human relationships? Does He know when physical, emotional, or psychological pain becomes so severe that a person thinks it is better to be dead than alive? Yes, He knows, and He cares.

He knows because He became like us. He is no stranger to the temptations and hardships that accompany life in this world. He cares because He is the embodiment of the love of God. He has no interest in this myth of a diabolical eternity that we have created. Over against an argument for Hell, I place Jesus' own words: "I did not come to judge the world but to save the world" (John 12:47).

This chapter began with a reading of Luke 9:49-56 (KJV). And now the beginning has become the end, the last word on everything else that has been written. The scripture selection as printed is from the King James Version (KJV) of the New Testament. I departed from the Revised Standard Version (RSV) because of its omission of parts of verses 54 and 55 and its entire omission of verse 56. I see no compelling reason to believe that the longer version (KJV) does not represent the original text.[90]

Luke tells us about two encounters that the disciples interpret as disrespect for Jesus. They met a man who was using Jesus' name to cast out devils. When he could not produce a "Disciple of Jesus" union card, they told him that he was not allowed to do ministry in Jesus' name. They became angry and demanded that he discontinue his ministry. Jesus did not share their indignation. He told them to leave the man alone and very pragmatically concluded that "he that is not against us is for us." We might say that Jesus saw him as a "force multiplier" instead of an opponent.

Later, on the journey to Jerusalem, Jesus sent messengers into a Samaritan town to tell them to get ready for his visit. The Samaritans, acting on the ancient differences between Samaritans and Jews, made no preparations for Jesus' visit. They did not give him the hospitable reception that the disciples anticipated. James and John responded as we might expect the "sons of thunder" to respond. They were angry and wanted to imitate the action of Elijah who called down fire from heaven and killed 102 soldiers (2 Kings 1:9-12). They were still emotionally under the influence of the old habits of responding to personal insults and injuries in the same manner as they had received them. In time, their Teacher, would show them a better way, and by His example, they would learn to serve God in that way.

There is a lesson here that we often overlook. Baptism and acceptance of Jesus as Savior do not immediately equip us with every correct answer to every problem that accompanies the complex world of human relations. The "new way" that we accept, is still being carried in a memory bank of conditioned responses that we have learned relative to certain stimuli. This presents us with a conflict that Jesus described as, "The spirit indeed is willing, but the flesh is weak" (Matt. 26:41). Those powerful conditioned responses do not just go away like leaves that fall off because the season has changed. Jesus had to teach the "sons of thunder" that their impulsive, unchecked anger was not an acceptable characteristic of his disciples. We do ourselves and the Gospel a great disservice when we stop listening to and learning from Jesus. With or without college degrees, we are all kindergarten students in God's classrooms of life. While Paul was making his defense before King Agrippa, the Proconsul Festus shouted, "Paul, you are mad; your great learning is turning you mad" (Acts 26:24). Paul was a theological genius if ever there was one, and yet he tells us that our knowledge is imperfect and what we do know appears as something that is a riddle reflected in a badly polished mirror (1 Cor. 9-12). He would never remotely suggest that we are saved by education. However, our history, individual and corporate, suggests that most of the time we function under the warning of, "You know not what manner of spirit you are of." We must continue to learn as we ask our Lord to teach us that "faith, hope, love abide, these three; but the greatest of these is love" (1 Cor. 13:13).

In terms of the history of Israel, I have no doubt that Elijah was a great prophet. I would never question the authenticity of his commitment to God. However, I do think it is interesting to consider some of his personal characteristics. It is possible that we might identify with some aspects of his behavior. From my perspective, Elijah's action was a clear example of "killing the messenger." King Ahaziah commanded the soldiers to take Elijah into custody and they were acting on those orders. We are told that the angel of the Lord directed Elijah to "Arise, go up to meet the messengers of the king of Samaria, and say to them, 'Is it because there is no God in Israel that you are going to inquire of Baalzebub, the god of Ekron?' Now therefore, thus says the Lord, 'You shall not come down from the bed to which you have gone, but you shall surely die'" (2 Kings 1:3-4). There is no indication that the Lord directed Elijah to kill anyone while fulfilling this mission ordered by God.

Why did Elijah kill the soldiers who were only doing their duty? Did he need to prove his authority? Was he the kind of person who needed to get in the face of anyone who opposed him? Was throwing fireballs the only way he knew to overcome adversaries? Was this the only way he was able to make his point or to express the superiority of his view? What was the point of the annihilation of 102 people? In those killings, we see the ego of Elijah responding to a challenge to his position as a "man of God." His response was not unlike ours when we justified our response to a threat, challenge, or insult by saying, "I guess I showed them who they were messing with!" Elijah did what he did for the same reason we often do what we do. He killed the soldiers because he could. James tells us that "Elijah was a man of like nature as ourselves" (James 5:17).

Is it possible that we might see some of our own character flaws in the person of Elijah? Walter Bruggemann calls Elijah "an untamed, unresponsive character."[91] Gerhard von Rad described him as "unapproachable, unpredictable, feared, and even hated, but always someone to be reckoned with."[92] Honesty compels me to own a couple of those characteristics. A reading of First and Second Kings depicts Elijah as intolerant, constantly on the move, preferring to work alone, and thinking of himself as the only prophet left to do God's work. King Ahab called him "the troubler of Israel" (1 Kings 18:17). Ahab does not call him a troubler just because of some of his actions. He is saying that Elijah is a troublemaker by his very nature. He has not caused trouble simply by the commission of a particular action. He possesses the attributes and character flaws that make him a perpetual and indiscriminate troublemaker. He is what we would call "a born troublemaker."

In the showdown with the prophets of Baal on Mount Carmel, Elijah resorted to taunting them as they hopped and danced around the cultic altar, screaming, and cutting themselves until the blood gushed out of their wounds. The taunting was unnecessary and contributed nothing to the outcome of the contest. God had chosen Elijah to be a prophet of Israel. Prayer and obedience were all that was required of him to be the instrument through which God would demonstrate His power and superiority as the only true God. Elijah's theatrical and self-aggrandizing additions to the contest were products of his own character traits. The taunting was an act of malicious and excessive behavior.

There is nothing complimentary of human behavior in the word that identifies Elijah as a taunter. At a minimum, it defines someone who is acting arrogantly.[93] It is not unusual for someone who resorts to taunting to be a big-talker and a braggart. On Freud's couch, Elijah might be diagnosed with symptoms of covert narcissism, perfectionism, insecurity, and depression.

When Jesus rebuked James and John, he was not criticizing Elijah. He was telling them that they would have to change their way of thinking about both the law and the prophets. They were living in a new time—a time when the old was being fulfilled through Jesus Christ. Isaiah had said, "Remember not the former things, nor consider the things of old. Behold, I am doing a new thing; now it springs forth, do you not perceive it?" (Isaiah 43:18-19). There had not been a prophetic voice in Israel for four hundred years. The last word was from Malachi. He wrote that God would send Elijah to prepare the new way, and that the "sun of righteousness shall rise, with healing in its wings" (Malachi 4). Indeed, the role of the return of Elijah had been fulfilled in the person and ministry of John the Baptist. Surprisingly, the fireball-throwing hero of the Old Testament deferred to Jesus, saying, "He is mightier than I" (Matt. 3:11; Mark 1:7; Luke 3:15; John 1:30). His medium of baptism would not be common water. It would be the fire of the Holy Spirit. Archbishop Rabanus Maurus (AD 780-856) contrasted the baptism of John with the baptism of Jesus like this: "It is as though John had said, I am mighty to invite repentance, He to forgive sins; I to preach the kingdom of heaven, He to bestow it; I to baptize with water, He with the Spirit."[94]

Jesus wanted His disciples to understand that a new dispensation of the Holy Spirit was replacing the ancient ways of hatred, violence, vengeance, and revenge. If they were to be His disciples, they would have to conduct themselves and perform their ministry according to Jesus' formula of, "You have heard that it was said to the men of old... But I say to you..." (Matt. 5:21-48). Jesus was not devaluing the knowledge of God that previous generations had lived by. However, time and the self-interests of the leaders of Israel had complicated and unduly burdened the lives of the people. Serving God had become a burden instead of a means to the abundant life that God wanted them to have. Jesus said, "Woe to you, scribes and Pharisees, hypocrites! Because you shut the kingdom of heaven against men; for you neither enter yourselves, nor allow those to enter who would go in" (Matt. 23:13).

Jesus spoke plainly and with authority. He called the corrupt ecclesiastical and justice systems to give an account of themselves. His message pre-dated the popular protest songs of our own time. He made it clear to His disciples that "The Times They Are A-Changing." The writer of Hebrews said, "In many and various ways God spoke of old to our Fathers by the prophets; but in these last days he has spoken to us by a Son" (Hebrews 1:1-2). The Son reflects the glory of God and bears the very stamp of his nature (Hebrews 11:1-3). Under the old system, there was a margin of error that could be exploited. Earthquakes, storms, visions, dreams, confusing commandments, exhortations, threats, oracles, and stories about the adventures of larger-than-life characters could all be challenged and discredited. However, when God sent His Son to walk among us, we were given a clear picture and definite understanding of God's relationship to us. In Jesus, we see that God's glory is not found in destroying people and consigning them to a place of torment and eternal misery. His glory is located in love and sacrifice.

When the disciples wanted to imitate Elijah, Jesus told them that they did not know the nature of the spirit that motivated them. It is noteworthy that they did not want to simply frighten the Samaritans who ignored Jesus. Like Elijah, they wanted to utterly destroy them. They were motivated by the same flawed attitude and violent impulsivity that Elijah demonstrated. He acted beyond the boundaries of the mission God had given him. Jesus wanted them to know that any model of behavior that would take pleasure in the death of those who provoked them was an unacceptable spirit and attitude for those who followed Him. The disciples would be expected to imitate Jesus, not Elijah.

And now, finally, without saying a word about Hell, Jesus tells us why we cannot go to any place called Hell, real or imagined. He says, "For the Son of man is not come to destroy men's lives, but to save them" (Luke 9:56). I do not find any equivocation or reservation in Jesus' mission statement. He does not acknowledge the possibility of failure and He does not specify any conditions required for His total success. We do not hear the scathing and condemnatory words of the fireball throwers. We hear the determined voice of the Son of God proclaiming that He will complete His mission and fulfill the will of His Father.

What He did not say on that occasion is important for us to consider. He did not tell them that there might come a time when they would need to destroy certain people. Neither did He pass any judgment, good or bad, on Elijah's behavior. The truth is that there was no harmony between Elijah's action and the existential context of the ministry of the disciples. The old tradition had to stand for itself and the new call to the service of God had to yield to the "But I say unto you" proclamation of Jesus Christ. The teaching and preaching of Jesus brought a new paradigm to the relationship of divinity to humanity.

We have yet to fully understand the method, motivation, and mission of God in sending Jesus to the world. In terms of what we know of Jesus, we may think that we are swimming in the Jordan River and drinking deeply from Jacob's Well. In reality, we are merely wading in the morning dew and wetting our lips with what we can catch from the thin, misty spray of a mountain waterfall. Even though we are baptized, catechized, confirmed, ordained, consecrated, and otherwise marked for service in some religious institution, we have yet to grasp the action of God Almighty in Jesus Christ. The love of God will not be fenced in by what we think should be the governing principle of judging any human situation. God's response to Moses' questions is the same today as it was then: "I am who I am" or, "I will be who I will be" (Exod. 3:14).

God, in Jesus Christ, has made it known that He will save us and that He will not destroy us. We have no say in the matter. We may find it impossible to believe that our fellow human beings who have committed horrendous crimes will not be punished for eternity in an unspeakably awful place. In relation to that belief, think about this: first, what do we know about the mind of the One who said, "I will be who I will be"; second, we humans, not God, created this awful place to satisfy our primitive need for revenge; and three, what do we know about eternity?

We may, of course, believe what we want to believe. In any case, God will not be influenced by the protests of our finite minds. We should remember that Jesus' assessment of James and John applies to each of us as well: "You know not what manner of spirit you are of." God's plans will not be frustrated or defeated because of our sins and failures, no matter how great or how horrible they might have been. It has been said that necessity is the mother of invention. Necessity has forced us to invent penal systems that protect us from each other. In an attempt to make punishments conform to the degree of harm involved in a violation of law, we judge violations through words like misdemeanor and felony. We speak of life sentences, corporal and capital punishment, monetary fines, suspended sentences, and parole and probation. Our name for the disruption of human harmony is crime, but God's name for it is sin.

Sin is the common identifying factor of all of humanity. Paul tells us that "There is no distinction; since all have sinned and fall short of the glory of God" (Rom. 3:22-23). With God, there are no misdemeanors, felonies, or plea bargains. There is only sin, and God's word says, "The person who sins, he shall die" (Ezekiel 18:20). We measure the magnitude of crimes and violations through the lens of the legal systems of our own creation. We afford lawyers, judges, and juries the power to decide how egregious our violations might be. The laws governing the administration of the United States Federal Penal Code are contained in more than six thousand sections of guidance. Think about that, and then think about this: "You shall not bear false witness against your neighbor," and "You shall not covet anything that is your neighbor's," are both written on the same tablet of stone as "You shall not kill." In the eyes of God, sin is sin and there is no provision for extenuating circumstances; no explanation that one sin is greater than another. The one and only remedy for all sin is the death and resurrection of Jesus Christ for the sin of the entire world. Jesus has made it clear that none will be destroyed, and all will be saved. Our evaluation of the degrees of inhumanity that we inflict on each other during our short life spans has no impact on life in the next dimension that God has prepared for us. God's verdict does not require volumes of explanation and amplification: "The person who sins, he shall die." However, that very death, so feared and misunderstood, purges us of our sins committed on this side of eternity.

It is impossible to read the Gospel of Luke and not recognize that God wants to be with us. He eats with sinners, tax collectors, and outcasts. He lives among people with disabilities, the people with leprosy, the deaf, the poor, and the blind. He shows favor to Samaritans and Roman centurions. The phrase, "person of questionable character," means nothing to Him. The life of Jesus shouts out the message that God intends to have communion with all of us. The boundaries that we have created through our religious and legal systems cannot restrict or prohibit the power of the One who said, "I will be who I will be." Jesus Christ, the One who is "God with us," has accompanied us through the thick and thin of life's journey. His mighty power silences the voice of any religion that would call for eternal vengeance and punishment to be poured out on His Father's creatures and creation.

We have no viable personal argument against our own condemnation of ourselves. Are we guilty? Yes, each one of us is guilty before the righteousness of God. On our own merits, we are unable to win a not-guilty verdict. Fortunately, we do not have to plead a case that we cannot possibly win. God has sent us an advocate (1 John 2:1) of whom we say with great thanksgiving and joy, "Surely he has borne our griefs and carried our sorrows" (Isa. 53:4). Is there any punishment left that He has not accepted and endured on our behalf during His three years of ministry on this earth? Think about these words: despised, rejected, sorrowful, grieved, ostracized, stricken, smitten, afflicted, wounded, bruised, chastised, oppressed, judged, and killed.

Now, look at the man as defined and described by those words. What do you see? From beginning to end, in all of that pain and ugliness, John the Baptizer saw a portrait of victory. Knowing what had to be done and what had to happen he said, "Behold, the lamb of God who takes away the sin of the world!" (John 1:29). That Lamb is ours and we are His. However, in terms of ownership and belonging, we know that the Lamb has been far more loyal to us than we have been to Him. It reminds me of the father who said to his child, "I love you when you are good." The child replied, "I love you all the time, Daddy." God loves us all the time and He will never stop loving us. His kind of love does not keep a record of wrongs. This alone is enough to end this foolish myth of Hell. To let it influence the life that God has given us is to travel on a road to "no place." No such place will ever be populated by the creation of those of whom it is said, "Then the Lord God formed man of dust from the ground, and breathed into his nostrils the breath of life; and man became a living soul" (Gen. 2:7).

The history of the God of Abraham, Isaac, and Jacob is not an account of failure, surrender, or the destruction of His great Creation. It is a story of victory and preservation. In Jesus Christ, we hear the voice and see the majestic grace of our Creator who will never give us up to any power other than His love: "For the Son of Man is not come to destroy men's lives but to save them."

Prayer:

Lord, our thinking and living are often affected by the power of guilt, shame, cultural myths, crazy preachers, and ignorant teachers. Sometimes we do not know what to believe and what not to believe. When we find ourselves in the grip of conflict and uncertainty, help us to look to Jesus, "the author and finisher of our faith." Remind us that You love us, and in the assurance of that love we are kept now and forevermore. Amen.

CONCLUSION

I will be the first to admit that I have embraced, with some sense of certainty, issues that are clearly argumentative. For instance, those persons who have become enthralled with the word "rapture" will always find it difficult to give up the drama and sensationalism that has accrued to the word. A word, by the way, which does not appear in the Greek New Testament. The favorite and much used phrase of a pastor in the small town where I first served as a student pastor was, "When the little church is raptured." The phrase itself was a "dog whistle," reminding the coal miners and mountain people that there would be a day when common, hard-working, honest folks would be set free from the oppression of the rich and powerful. It was a phrase of endearment that assured them that they would be set free from their lowly economic and social status in the hierarchy of elitism.

The church they attended was referred to as the "little church," a diminutive structure housing a diminutive group of like-minded people. It was not a symbol of the great Church Universal. It was simply the "little church," a self-deprecating cluster of personalities lacking a healthy sense of individual and corporate self-worth. With their social, cultural, economic, and intellectual insecurities, they took refuge in and found validation through a coming rapture event that promised to elevate them above those persons and things that made them victims.

The bellicose rapture vocabulary of the end times is intoxicating. It ignores the Gospel Manifesto of "For God so loved the world" and boisterously and gleefully replaces it with a manifesto of vengeance that proclaims, "And now you sinners will get what you deserve." For the rapture crowd, it is not enough to quietly and humbly accept the fact that God's love for His creatures and creation has prevailed. Apparently, the pain and gruesome horrors of crucifixion are not shocking enough to emphasize the love of God. The still, small voice that says, "I love you," must be drowned out by the overwhelming cacophony of lightning, thunder, earthquakes, floods, cosmic excitations, and the death of millions before any concept of the end of time (eschatology) can have any credibility. Some people like and need that sort of drama. Perhaps they subscribe to the masochistic motto of "No pain, no gain." Others do not need this drama, and I cannot find any evidence that God requires it. Dispensational maps, charts, and timeline constructions are all part of the rapture vocabulary regarding the return of Christ and the end of time. They represent schemes that have been turned into carnival events by the ingenuity of men, some of whom have been honest seekers but many others who are nothing more than charlatans and opportunistic deceivers.

My basic belief is that each person's death represents the end of the world for that person. It is a quiet, previously decided affair. There are no Fourth of July fireworks or retirement speeches. Our eyes are closed in death, and time, as we have known it, no longer exists for us. With a new spiritual vision, we look into the face of Jesus Christ and are immediately welcomed by a power of love that could never have been known in the dimension of time as we measure it. From that meeting forward, we live in the re-created dimension of God's making.

I can only speculate that it will be like the breaking of a new morning. However, it must be said that our earthly brains, as wonderful and powerful as they are, do not have the imaginative or intellectual capacity to comprehend what awaits us in the presence of Jesus Christ. A fundamentalist preacher once asked me what I thought Heaven would be like. I told him that I really did not know the answer to that question. We had played in a golf tournament that day and were enjoying the food and fellowship following the tournament. He was relentlessly determined to get me to comment on his question about Heaven. He said, "I know you have earned a few degrees in the field of biblical studies, and I really do want to know your thoughts about Heaven." He quoted some scriptures and recited some of the doctrinal requirements of his faith denomination. He looked around, taking in the party atmosphere of eating, drinking, and talking about the day's tournament, and said to me, "Well, tell me this. Do you believe there will be cold beer, hot dogs, and golf in Heaven?" I said, "I certainly hope so." With that, he walked away and would never again ride with me in the same cart at any golfing event.

There is a standard response about Hell in the mountain area where I grew up. If you said, "There ain't no Hell," someone would immediately say, "The hell there ain't!" The existence of Hell was an indisputable given. It was the powerful leverage that the evangelists used during their revival campaigns. If you got saved according to their formula of salvation, you were okay, but if you did not, you were headed for a devil's Hell. There was always a warning that an introduction to Hell might come sooner than you expected. Coal mining and timbering (cutting down trees and moving them to a sawmill) were dangerous jobs. The only insurance against going to Hell was to get saved.

I have written at length about these subjects because I believe it is worthwhile for all of us to think about these things. Most of what we have learned about creation, death, resurrection, the end of the world, and Heaven and Hell has come to us through our preachers and Sunday School teachers. I think it is accurate to say that, in most cases, they turned apocalyptic and mythological symbols into empirical absolutes and superimposed their own emotional interpretations of these mysterious topics. Being the "only show in town," they were accepted as authorities on all things religious. (Think about this: Have you ever compared the licensing and credentialling requirements of preachers and Sunday school teachers to those of doctors, nurses, lawyers, engineers, social workers, public school teachers, and real estate brokers? For further thought, consider that even your local electricians, plumbers, and building contractors have to be certified for building code compliances.)

Rather than thinking of God as a Supreme Being who rewards some and punishes others, I believe that we should think about God as a Father who has created us and will bring us to the full perfection of His original creative intention for us. Think about the joy and satisfaction experienced by humans who have brought their inventions, dreams, and accomplishments to full fruition. Can we not believe that God, as the Great Creator, will not rest until He has brought each of us into the fullness of our created potential? That is who God is. He is not the administrator of a system of rewards and punishments.

The story of Rabia of Basra, an Arab Sufi saint, offers an example of what I want us to think about. She was born in Basra, Iraq, in the eighth century AD. She was known for walking through the streets, carrying a bucket of water in one hand and a flaming torch in the other. When she was asked what she hoped to accomplish through this gesture, she said: "I want to put out the fires of Hell and burn down the rewards of Heaven. They block the way to God. I do not want to worship from fear of punishment or for the promise of reward, but simply for the love of God."[1] Unfortunately, our religious culture has too often taught us to view God as an Automated Teller Machine (ATM) that blesses us when we push the right buttons. We often use prayers and good behavior as though they were coins or tokens for a vending machine. We put them in the proper slot, select what we want, and receive it on demand. Our reward and punishment culture has indoctrinated us to believe that God's love is founded on the same principles. That is what Rabia of Basra meant when she said that the fires of Hell and the rewards of Heaven have "blocked the way to God."

The first sentence of the 277 chapters of Saint Augustine's *Confessions* says, "Great art thou, O Lord, and greatly to be praised."[2] Everything else that he writes is subsumed under that observation and declaration of faith. The saints and the religious mystics and seers teach us that we should love God for who He is and what He is, and not for reward or to escape punishment for our behavior. To love God for who He is means that we understand that He seeks maintenance between Himself and His creation. His intent for our future is not one of damnation but one of redemption. From the beginning to the end, in spite of all the crimes, infirmities, and perversions that are defined in our medical, psychological, criminal, and social vocabularies, God is committed to restoring and maintaining eternal fellowship with us.

God's reference point is always seen as both Word and Deed, e.g., "God so loved that He gave." His motivation is never one that says, "If you do this or that, I will give you my love." That is the way we usually conduct our business and establish our relationships, but our ways are not God's ways. We may consider mercy as a factor in our decision-making, but we do it selectively. We show mercy when we choose and when it is in our own best interests to be merciful. We can give mercy, and we can take it back as it pleases us. However, God's mercy, goodness, and love endure forever (Psalm 136).

We often say to someone who is caught up in their own sense of self-importance, "You need to get over yourself." We need to get over ourselves in our thinking about who God loves and does not love. When it comes to mercy, the best we can do is to accept it and be silent. What can be said against any of us applies to all of us. There is no degree of righteousness that counts any more for one of us than it does for all of us. The prophet Isaiah excluded no one when he said, "We have all become like one who is unclean, and all our righteous deeds are like a polluted garment" (Isa. 64:6). Think on this: If there is no hope for even a single one of us sinners, there is no hope for any of us. Why is this so? It is so because "The Son of Man came not to destroy our lives but to save them."

Prayer:

Lord, we are easily blinded by anger, vengeance, pride, and all the other emotions that have accrued to our imperfect thinking. We confess that our hurt feelings and our selfish wants and wishes too often separate us from thinking positively about Your love. We fail to ponder over the great gift of life, and the even greater gift of eternal life that awaits us. May the angels You send to us prompt us to remember Your mercy, grace, forgiveness, peace, and love. Heal our minds of the fear of death and everlasting punishment. Help us to accept the fullness of Your eternal love that will never forsake us. We pray this in the victorious name of Your Son, Jesus Christ, our Lord and Savior. Amen.

ENDNOTES

Preface

[1] Soren Kierkegaard, "The Listener's Role In A Devotional Address," in *Purity of Heart Is To Will One Thing,* trans. with an introductory essay by Douglas V. Steere (New York: Harper & Row Publishers, 1956), 177-183.

[2] George Liddell and Robert Scott, "συμβάλλουσα," *A Greek-English Lexicon*, vol. 2 (Oxford: The Clarendon Press, 1940), 1674-1675. Public domain. Retrieved July 30, 2023. https://www.archive.org/details/1031364949_02.

[3] Emma Brockes, "Return of the Time Lord," Interview with Emma Brockes, The Guardian, September 27, 2005. Retrieved December 1, 2023. www.theguardian.com.

Chapter One

[1] Heiko A. Oberman, *Luther: a Man Between God and the Devil*, trans. Eileen Walliser-Schwarzbart (London: Yale University Press, 2006), 173.

[2] Fred D. Gealy, ed., *The Book of Worship for Church and Home* (Nashville, Tennessee: The Methodist Publishing House, 1965), 41. (note: the above book has been replaced by *The United Methodist Book OF Worship*, Nashville, Tennessee (United Methodist Publishing House, 1992, which does not include or suggest the use of Isaiah 35:4 in the committal service ritual.

[3] Paul D. Hanson, "Apocalypticism," in *The Interpreter's Dictionary of the Bible*, eds. Lloyd Richard Bailey, Sr., Victor Paul Furnish, Emory Stevens Bucke, supplementary volume (Nashville, Tennessee: Abingdon, 1976), 29. (note: all future volumes will be shown as *IDB for The Interpreter's Dictionary of the Bible*).

[4] Hanson, *IDB*, supplementary, vol.,33.

⁵Bruce Metzger, ed., The *Oxford Annotated Apocrypha: The Apocrypha of the Old Testament, Revised Standard Version* New York: Oxford University Press, 1965), xiii.

⁶ D. S. Russell, *The Method and Message of Jewish Apocalyptic* (Philadelphia: The Westminster Press, 1964), 29.

⁷ Michael Edward Stone, *Fourth Ezra*, ed. Frank Moore Cross (Minneapolis: Augsburg Fortress, 1990), 92-93.

⁸ Second Esdras of the *RSV Apocrypha* is also known as Fourth Ezra.

⁹ Clement of Alexandria, "The Stromata, or Miscellanies," in *Ante-Nicene Fathers*, ed. Alexander Roberts and James Donaldson, 2nd printing, vol. 2 (Peabody, Massachusetts: Hendrickson Publishing, 1995), 400.

¹⁰ Metzger, *Oxford Annotated Apocrypha,* ix-x.

¹¹ M. Gorg, "tohu wabohu," in *TDOT,* ed. Johannes Botterweck, Helmer Ringgren, Heinz-Josef Fabry, trans. David E. Green, vol. 15 (Grand Rapids, Michigan: William B. Eerdmans Publishing, 2015), 565-574.

¹² Otto Kaiser, *Isaiah 13-39: A Commentary* (Philadelphia: The Westminster Press, 1974), 359.

¹³ Arthur Koestler, "Is Man's Brain An Evolutionary Mistake," *Horizon: A Magazine of the Arts* 10, no. 4 (Spring 1968): 43.

¹⁴ H. G. Wells, *The Fate of Man* (New York and Toronto: Alliance Book Corporation, Longmans, Green and Co., 1939), 246-247.

¹⁵ Dietrich Bonhoeffer, *Creation and Fall: A Theological Interpretation of Genesis 1-3* (New York: Macmillan Publishing Co., Inc., 1974), 68.

¹⁶ Karl Barth, "The Pride and Fall of Man," in Church *Dogmatics,* trans. G. W. Bromiley, vol. 4, part 1 (1956; repr. Edinburgh: T. & T. Clarke, 1980), 495. All future citations will be shown as *CD* for *Church Dogmatics.*

¹⁷ Barth, "The Pride and Fall of Man," in *CD*, vol.4, part 1, 495.

[18] Walter Bauer, "συνωδίνω," *A Greek-English Lexicon of the New Testament and Other Early Christian Literature,* rev. and ed. William F. Arndt and F. Wilbur Gingrich, 4th revised and augmented ed. (Chicago: University of Chicago Press, 1957), 801. All future citations will be shown as *Greek-English Lexicon.*

[19] Martin Luther, *Commentary on Romans*, trans. J. Theodore Mueller (1954; repr. Grand Rapids, Michigan: Kregel Publications, 1976), 123-124.

[20] Ludwig Schmidt, "παράγω," in *Theological Dictionary of the New Testament,* ed. Gerhard Kittel, trans. Geoffrey Bromiley, vol. 1 (Grand Rapids, Michigan: William B. Eerdmans, 1964), 129-130. All future citations will be shown as TDNT for *Theological Dictionary of the New Testament.*

[21] Kaiser, *Isaiah 13-39,* 197.

[22] Blaise Pascal (1623-1662), "Section X: Typology, Thought #654," in *Pensées,* trans. W. F. Trotter (Grand Rapids, Michigan: Christian Classics Ethereal Library), 133. Retrieved December 18, 2022 from http://www.ccel.org/ccel/pascal/pensees.html.

[23] Georg Fohrer, "Σιών," in *TDNT,* ed. Gerhard Kittel and Gerhard Friedrich, trans. Geoffrey W. Bromiley, vol. 7 (Grand Rapids, Michigan: William B. Eerdmans, 1971), 312.

[24] Kaiser, *Isaiah 13-39,* 200.

[25] R. W. Funk, "The Wilderness." *Journal of Biblical Literature,* 78, no. 3 (September 1959): 206.

[26] S. Talmon, "midbar," in *TDOT,* ed. Johannes Botterweck, Helmer Ringgren and Heinz-Josef Fabry, trans. Douglas W. Stott, vol. 8 (Grand Rapids, Michigan: William B. Eerdmans, 1996), 91.

[27] S. Talmon, "Wilderness," *IDB,* supplementary vol., 946.

[28] S. Talmon, "midbar," *TDOT,* 102.

²⁹ John Lightfoot, *A Commentary on the New Testament from the Talmud and Hebraica: Matthew—1 Corinthians: Matthew—Mark, vol.3 (1859; repr; Peabody, Massachusetts: Hendrickson Publishers, 1997), 85.*

³⁰ Heinrich Schlier, "θλῖψις," in *TDNT*, ed. Gerhard Kittel, trans. Geoffrey W. Bromiley, vol. 3 (Grand Rapids, Michigan: William B. Eerdmans, 1965), 139-148.

³¹ Heinrich Schlier, "θλῖψις," in *TDNT*, vol. 3, 147.

³² Soren Kierkegaard, *Fear and Trembling and the Sickness Unto Death*, trans. Walter Lowrie (1941; repr. Princeton: Princeton University Press, 1974), 154.

³³ K. Koch, "derekh," in *TDOT*, ed. Johannes Botterweck and Helmer Ringgren, trans. Heinz-Josef Fabry, vol. 3 (Grand Rapids, Michigan: William B. Eerdmans Publishing, 1975), 271.

³⁴ Koch, "derekh," in *TDOT*, vol. 3, 271.

³⁵ Bauer, "ὁδός," *Greek-English Lexicon*, 556-557.

³⁶ Robert Frost, "The Road Not Taken," in *American Literature: Tradition and Innovation*, vol. 2, ed. Harrison T. Meserole, Walter Sutton, and Brom Weber (Lexington, Massachusetts: D. C. Heath and Company, 1969), 2859.

³⁷ Carl Sandburg, "Wilderness," in *Harvest Poems: 1910-1960*, (New York: Harcourt Brace &World, Inc., 1960), 47-48.

³⁸ T. S. Eliot, "The Waste Land," in *American Literature: Tradition and Innovation*, vol. 2, ed. Harrison T. Meserole, Walter Sutton, and Brom Weber (Lexington, Massachusetts: D. C. Heath and Company, 1969), 2965-2977.

³⁹ F. Scott Fitzgerald, *The Great Gatsby* (New York: Charles Scribner's Sons, 1925(, chapter 7, retrieved from www.gutenberg.org.

⁴⁰ Saint Augustine, "The Confessions of St. Augustine," in *Nicene and Post-Nicene Fathers: The Confessions and Letters of Augustine, with a Sketch of His*

Life and Work, ed. Philip Schaff, trans. J. G. Pilkington, 2nd printing, vol. 1 (Peabody, Massachusetts: Hendrickson Publishers, 1995), 45.

[41] Paul Tillich, *The Courage To Be* (1952; repr. New Haven and London:Yale University Press, 1979), 164-165.

[42] Saint Augustine, "Sermons on Selected Lessons of the New Testament, Sermon XCI (91)," in *Nicene and Post-Nicene Fathers: Sermon on the Mount, Harmony of the Gospels, Homilies on the Gospels*, ed. Philip Schaff, trans. R. G. MacMullen, 2nd printing, vol. 6 (Peabody, Massachusetts: Hendrickson Publishers, 1995), 532.

[43] John Hick, *Death and Eternal Life* (Louisville, Kentucky: Westminster/John Knox Press, 1994), 21.

[44] C. R. North, "chadhash; chodhesh," *TDOT*, ed. Johannes Botterweck and Helmer Ringgren, trans. David E. Green, vol. 4 (Grand Rapids, Michigan: William B. Eerdmans, 1981, 240.

[45] Origin, *Commentary on the Epistle to the Romans*, trans. Thomas P. Scheck (Washington, DC: The Catholic University of America Press, 2001), 161.

[46] Friedrich Büchsel, "λυτρόω," in *TDNT*, ed. Gerhard Kittel, trans. Geoffrey W. Bromiley, vol. 4 (Grand Rapids, Michigan: William B. Eerdmans, 1967), 340-351.

[47] Friedrich Büchsel, "ἀγοράζω/ἐξαγοράζω," in *TDNT*, ed. Gerhard Kittel, trans. Geoffrey W. Bromiley, vol. 1 (Grand Rapids: Michigan: William B, Eerdmans. 1974), 124-128.

[48] Rudolf Otto, *The Idea of the Holy*, trans. John W. Harvey (1923; repr., London: Oxford University Press, 1971), 8.

[49] William Faulkner, *Light In August* (London: Chatto and Windus, 1922), 111.

[50] William Wordsworth, "Ode: Intimations of Immortality from

Recollections of Early Childhood," in *Anthology of Romanticism*, ed. Ernest Bernbaum, 5th ed. (New York: The Ronald Press Company, 1948), 64-65.

[51] Alexander Pope, "An Essay on Man," in *World Masterpieces: Literature of Western Culture Since the Renaissance*, ed. Maynard Mack, vol. 2 (New York: W. W. Norton and Company, 1965), 191.

[52] Karl Barth and Edward Thurneysen, *Come Holy Spirit*, trans. George W. Richards, Elmer G. Homrighausen, and Karl J. Ernst (Grand Rapids, Michigan: William B. Eerdmans, 1978), 40.

[53] Walt Whitman, "Faces." In *Leaves of Grass*, ed. Harold W. Blodgett and Sculley Bradley (New York: W. W. Norton & Company, 1965). 463-467.

[54] James H. Charlesworth, ed., *The Old Testament and Pseudepigrapha*, vol. 1, *Apocalyptic Literature and Testaments* (Garden City, New York: Doubleday & Company, 1983), 196.

[55] Peggy Lee, "Is That All There Is?" 1969, track no. 1 on *Is That All There Is?* Capitol, 1969, Long Play album.

[56] Leonard Goppelt, "καταπίνω," *TDNT*, ed. Gerhard Kittel and Gerhard Friedrich, trans. Geoffrey W. Bromiley, vol.6 (Grand Rapids, Michigan: William B. Eerdmans, 1968), 158-159.

[57] James M. Houston, ed., *From the Works of Blaise Pascal: Mind on Fire* (Minneapolis, Minnesota: Bethany House Publishers, 1977), 13.

[58] Houston, *Works of Blaise Pascal,* 41.

[59] Houston, *Works of Blaise Pascal*, 41-42.

[60] Houston, *Works of Blaise Pascal*, 230.

[61] F. F. Bruce, *Paul: Apostle of the Heart Set Free* (Grand Rapids, Michigan: William B. Eerdmans, 1981), 309.

[62] Johannes Behm, "αρραβῶν," in *TDNT*, ed. Gerhard Kittel, trans. Geoffrey W. Bromiley, vol. 1 (Grand Rapids, Michigan: William B. Eerdmans, 1964),

475.

⁶³ Murray J. Harris, "The New Testament View of Life After Death." *Themelios* 11.2 (January 1986): 48; Murray J. Harris, "2 Corinthians 5:1-10: Watershed in Paul's Eschatology?" *Tyndale Bulletin* 22 (1971): 42; R. H. Charles, *A Critical History of the Doctrine of Future Life* (London: Adam and Charles Black, 1899), 394-397; Bruce, F. F. , *Paul: Apostle of the Heart Set Free* (Grand Rapids, Michigan: William B. Eerdmans, 1981), 309-313; Emil Brunner, *Eternal Hope*, trans. Harold Knight (Philadelphia: The Westminster Press, 1954), 106.

⁶⁴ Whitman, "The Mystic Trumpeter," in *Leaves of Grass*, 1965, 468-471.

⁶⁵ Saint Clement of Alexandria, "Exhortation to the Heathen, in *Ante-Nicene Fathers: Fathers of the Second Century*, ed. Alexander Roberts and James Donaldson, trans. W. L. Alexander, 2ⁿᵈ printing, vol. 2 (Peabody, Massachusetts: Hendrickson Publishers, 1995), 204.

⁶⁶ Saint Clement of Alexandria, "Exhortation to the Heathen," vol. 2, 204.

⁶⁷ Augustus Toplady, *Psalms and Hymns for Public and Private Worship* (London: E. and C. Dilby, 1776), 308-309.

⁶⁸ Ernst Fuchs, "σήμερον," *TDNT*, ed. Gerhard Kittel and Gerhard Friedrich, trans. Geoffrey W. Bromiley, vol. 7 (Grand Rapids, Michigan: William B. Eerdmans, 1971), 269-270.

⁶⁹ Alfred Plummer, *A Critical and Exegetical Commentary on the Gospel According to S. Luke,* 5ᵗʰ ed. (Edinburgh: T. & T. Clarke, 1922), 536.

⁷⁰ William Theodore Wiesner, *S. Ambrosii De Bono Mortis: A Revised Text with an Introduction, Translation, and Commentary* (Washington, DC: The Catholic University of America Press, 1970) 105.

Chapter Two

¹ Kaiser, *Isaiah 13-39*, 201.

² James P. Sullivan, "Oh, Say, but I'm Glad," 1930, public domain. Retrieved on December 29, 2022, from www.library.timelesstruths.org/music.

³ James Weldon Johnson, *God's Trombones: Seven Negro Sermons* (1929; repr., New York: The Viking Press, 1972), 17-20.

⁴ Saint Augustine, "Confessions," vol. 1, 45.

⁵ J. H. Hertz, ed., *The Pentateuch and Haftorahs: Hebrew Text, English Translation and Commentary*, vol. 2 (London: Oxford University Press, 1937), 106.

⁶ S. R. Driver, *The Book of Genesis*, 10th ed. (London: Methuen & Co., LTD, 1916), 265.

Chapter Three

¹ Johannes Behm, "μεταμορφόω," in *TDNT*, ed. Gerard Kittel, trans. Geoffrey W. Bromiley, vol.4 (Grand Rapids, Michigan: William B. Eerdmans, 1967), 755-759.

² Charles Wesley (1707-1788), "Love Divine, All Loves Excelling," *The Methodist Hymn Book With Tunes* (Letchworth, Great Britain: The Garden City Press, 1933), 381. Copyright for texts and lyrics in public domain.

³ Albrecht Oepke, "παρουσία, πάρειμι," in *TDNT*, ed. Gerhard Kittel and Gerhard Friedrich, trans. and ed. Geoffrey Bromiley, vol. 5 (Grand Rapids, Michigan: William B. Eerdmans, 1967), 859.

⁴ Bauer, *Greek-English Lexicon*, 635.

⁵ Albrecht Oepke, "παρουσία, πάρειμι," in *TDNT*, 867.

⁶ Justin Martyr, "The First Apology," 180; "Dialogue with Trypho," 202, 215, 258 in *Ante-Nicene Fathers*, ed. Alexander Roberts and James Donaldson, vol. 1 (1885; repr. Peabody, Massachusetts: Hendrickson Publishers, 1995). In these references, the Greek δύο παρουσίας is translated as "two advents," 180; "second advent," 202; and "two appearances," 258.

[7] C. K. Barrett, *The Holy Spirit and the Gospel Tradition* (London: SPCK, 1948), 160.

[8] Wilhelm Michaelis, *Der Herr verzeit nicht die Verheissung. Die Aussagen Jesu über die Nahedes Jungsten Tages* (Bern: BEG-Verlag, 1942), 101. (English trans. *The Lord Does Not Delay the Promise: The Statement of Jesus About the Nearness of Judgment Day.*)

[9] Adolf Diessemann, *Light From the Ancient East: The New Testament Illustrated by Recently Discovered Texts of the Graeco-Roman World*, 4th ed., trans. Lionel A. M. Strachan (New York and London: Harper and Brothers, 1908), 368.

[10] A. E. Brooke, *A Critical and Exegetical Commentary on the Johannine Epistles* (1912; repr., Edinburgh: T. & T. Clark. 1971), 65-67.

[11] Wolfgang Trilling, "ἁρπάζω," in *Exegetical Dictionary of the New Testament*, ed. Horst Balz and Gerhard Schneider, vol. 1 (Grand Rapids, Michigan: William B. Eerdmans Publishing Co., 1990), 156-157. All future volumes will be shown as *EDNT* for *Exegetical Dictionary of the New Teatament*.

[12] Barbara Rosser, *The Rapture Exposed* (Boulder, Colorado: Westview Press, 2004), 1.

[13] Paul Thigpen, *The Rapture Trap* (Westminster, Pennsylvania: Ascension Press, 2001); Carl E. Olsen, *Will Catholics Be Left Behind: A Critique of the Rapture and Today's Prophecy Preachers* (San Francisco: Ignatius Press, 2009); David Currie, Rapture: *The End-Times Error That Leaves the Bible Behind* (Nashua, New Hampshire: The Sophia Institute Press, 2004).

[14] Paul Thigpen, *The Rapture Trap* (Westminster, Pennsylvania: Ascension Press, 2001), 17.

[15] Alan Seeger (1888-1916), "I Have a Rendezvous with Death," Public Domain. Accessed February 10, 2023. poets.org/poem/i-have-rendezvous-deat

[16] Karl Barth, "The Doctrine of the Word of God," in *CD*, 2nd ed., ed. G. W. Bromiley and T. F. Torrance, trans. G. W. Bromiley, vol. 1, part 1 (Edinburgh: T. &T. Clark, 1975) 387.

Chapter Four

[1] George Adam Smith, *The Historical Geography of the Holy Land* (London: Holder and Staughton, 1894), 311-312.

[2] Wallenhorst Reuter, "qn; qina; qanna; quanno," in *TDOT*, ed. G. Johannes Botterweck, Helmer Ringgren, and Heinz-Josef Fabry, trans. David E. Green, vol. 13 (Grand Rapids, Michigan: William B. Eerdmans, 2004), 57.

[3] S. R. Driver, *A Critical and Exegetical Commentary on Deuteronomy* (New York: Charles Scribner's Sons, 1895), 357.

[4] Marcus Dods, *The Book of Genesis* (New York: A. C. Armstrong and Son, 1902), 12.

[5] Marcus Dods, *Genesis,* 12-13.

[6] Saint Augustine, "Confessions," vol. 1, 145.

[7] Saint Augustine, "Confessions," vol. 1, 147.

[8] Saint Augustine, "City of God," vol. 2, 250.

[9] David Daube, *The New Testament and Rabinnic Judaism* (Peabody, Massachusetts: Hendrickson Publishers, 1956), 273.

[10] David Daube, *The New Testament and Rabbinic Judaism*, 274-275.

[11] David Daube, *The New Testament and Rabbinic Judaism*, 279.

[12] Daube, *The New Testament and Rabbinical Judaism*, 271.

[13] Adolf Diessemann, *Light From the Ancient East*, 380-381.

[14] Karl Barth, "The Doctrine of Reconciliation," *CD*, ed. G. W. Bromiley and T. F. Torrance, trans. G. W. Bromiley, vol. 4, part 2 (Edinburgh: T.& T. Clark, 1958), 20-154.

[15] Karl Barth, "The Doctrine of Reconciliation," *CD*, vol. 4, part 2, 21.

[16] Karl Barth, "The Doctrine of Reconciliation," *CD*, vol. 4, part 2, 100.

[17] J. N. D. Kelly, *Early Christian Creeds*, 3rd ed. (New York & London: Continuum Books, 1972), 379.

[18] Justin Martyr (110-165), "Martyrdom of Ignatius," *Ante-Nicene Fathers*, ed. and trans. Alexander Roberts and James Donaldson, 2nd printing, vol. 1 (Peabody, Massachusetts: Hendrickson Publishers, 1995), 131.

[19] Justin Martyr, "Martyrdom of Ignatius," vol. 1, 130.

[20] Justin Martyr, "Martyrdom of Ignatius," 131.

[21] Martin Luther, *Luther's Works: The Christian in Society IV*, vol. 47 (Philadelphia: Fortress Press, 1971), 117.

[22] Martin Luther, *Luther's Works: The Christian in Society IV*, 112.

[23] Fyodor Dostoevsky (1821-1881), "Notes From Underground," trans. Constance Garnett, in *World Masterpieces: Literature of Western Culture Since the Renaissance*, vol. 2, gen. ed. Maynard Mack (New York: W. W. Norton & Company, Inc., 1965), 914-1002.

[24] Karl Barth, *The Epistle to the Romans*, 6th ed, trans. Edwyn Hoskyns (London: Oxford University Press, 1976), 263.

[25] Emil Brunner, *The Scandal of Christianity: The Gospel as Stumbling Block to Modern Man* (Richmond: John Knox Press, 1968), 110.

[26] John Donne (1572-1631), "Death's Duel," Public Domain. Accessed April 13, 2023. Ccel.org/ccel/donne/deaths_duel.i.html.

Chapter Five

[1] Flavius Josephus, *The Works of Flavius Josephus in Four Volumes*, "The Wars of the Jews," trans. William Whiston, vol. 1, book 5, chapter 5, section 6, (1974; repr. Grand Rapids, Michigan: Baker Book House, 1995), 23. All future references will be shown with abbreviated title and cited as: Josephus, *Works*, "Subtitle," Arabic numerals reflecting volume, book, chapter, section, page, e.g.,

Josephus, *Works*, "Wars of the Jews," 1.2.3.4.100.

² Josephus, *Works*, "Wars of the Jews," 1.5.13.7.419.

³ Josephus, *Works*, "Wars of the Jews," 1.5.9.3.469.

⁴ Josephus, *Works*, "Wars of the Jews," 1.6.10.4.470.

Chapter Six

¹ Rudyard Kipling (1865-1936), "Recessional." Public Domain. Accessed May 13, 2023. public-domain-poetry.com/rudyard-kipling/recessional-3440.

Chapter Seven

¹ W. F. Floyd (1791-1853), "My Times Are in Thy Hands," Public Domain. Accessed May 14, 2023, hymnary.org/text/my_times_are_in_thy_hand_my_god_i_wish?

² Norman D. Holcomb, Jr., *Who Killed Jesus? The Authority of the Sanhedrin at the Trial of Jesus* (Amazon Books 2024), 109.

Chapter Eight

¹ Saint Augustine, "Expositions on the Book of Psalms," in *Nicene and Ante-Nicene Fathers*, vol. 8 (1888; repr., Peabody, Massachusetts: Hendrickson Publishers, Inc., 1995), 487.

² Karl Barth, "The Doctrine of Reconciliation, in *CD*, trans. G. W. Bromiley, vol. 4, part 3, second half (Edinburgh: T. & T. Clark, 1962), 793.

³ Maltbie D. Babcock (1858-1901), "This Is My Father's World," Public Domain. Accessed May 14, 2023. hymnary.org/text/this_is_my_fathers_world_and_to_my.

Chapter Nine

¹ Harold S. Kushner, *When Bad Things Happen to Good People* (New York: Avon Books, 1983), 6.

Chapter Ten

¹ Oberman, *Luther*, 105.

Chapter Eleven

[1] Westminster Assembly (1643-1652), *The Assembly's Shorter Catechism, with the Scripture Proofs in Reference: with an Appendix on the Systematik Attention of the Young to Scriptural Knowledge*, by Hervey Wilbur (Newburyport, Massachusetts: Wm. B. Allen & Co., 1816).

Chapter Twelve

[1] Walter Chalmers Smith (1824-1908), "Immortal, Invisible, God Only Wise," Public Domain. Accessed May 14, 2023. hymnary.org/media/fetch/100827.

[2] Karl Barth, "The Doctrine of Reconciliation," in *CD*, trans. G. W. Bromiley, vol. 4, part 1 (1956; repr., Edinburgh: T. & T. Clark, 1980), 604.

Chapter Thirteen

[1] Henry Wordsworth Longfellow (1807-1882), "The Building of the Ship," [online resource], Maine Historical Society, in public domain, accessed June 3, 2023. http://www.hwlongfellow.org.

[2] Helmer Ringgren, "semen, samen, saman," in *TDOT*, ed. Johannes Botterweck, Helmer Ringgren, and Heinz-Josef Fabry, trans. David E. Green, vol. 15 (Grand Rapids, Michigan: William B. Eerdmans, 2015), 250.

[3] C. K. Barrett, *The Gospel According to St. John: An Introduction with Commentary and Notes on the Greek Text* (London: S. P. C. K., 1965), 398.

[4] Gustav Stählin, "φίλος, φίλη, φιλία," in *TDNT*, ed. Gerhard Friedrich and Geoffrey W. Bromiley, trans. Geoffrey W. Bromiley, vol. 9 (Grand Rapids, Michigan: William B. Eerdmans, 1974), 165.

Chapter Fourteen

[1] Philip Schaff and David S. Schaff, eds., *The Creeds of Christianity With a History and Critical Notes*, 6th ed., vol. 2, *The Greek and Latin Creeds* (Grand Rapids, Michigan: Baker Book House, 1996), 45-61.

² Richard Muller, *Dictionary of Latin and Greek Theological Terms* (Grand Rapids. Michigan: Baker Book House, 1985), 208.

³ Hugolinus Langkammer, "παντοκράτωρ," *EDNT*, ed. Horst Balz and Gerhard Schneider, trans. John W. Medendorp and Douglas W. Stott, vol. 3 (Grand Rapids, Michigan: William B. Eerdmans, 1993), 12.

⁴ Karl Barth, *Romans*, 359.

⁵ *History of Jack Horner*, Osborne Collection of Early Children's Books, Public Domain, Courtesy of Toronto Public Library. Accessed June 24, 2023. www.torontopubliclibrary.ca/digital-archive/license.jsp

⁶ Karl Barth, *Romans*, 359.

⁷ T. K. Abbott, *The Epistles to the Ephesians and Colossians* (1897; repr., Edinburgh: T. & T. Clark, 1974), 100.

⁸ Abbott, *Ephesians and Colossians*, 101.

⁹ John Calvin (1509-1564), *Commentaries on the Epistles of Paul to the Galatians and Ephesians*, trans. William Pringle (Edinburgh: The Calvin Translation Society, 1854), 19. Public Domain. Accessed from Internet Archives June 26, 2023. https://archive.org/details/calvinscommentar0000calv_z106.pdf

¹⁰ Gerhard Delling, "ὑπερβάλλω, ὑπερβαλλόντως, ὑπερβολή," in *TDNT*, vol. 8. 520-522; Bauer, "ὑπερβάλλω," *Greek-English Lexicon*, 848.

¹¹ Charles Wesley (1707-1788), "*O Love Divine, What Hast Thou Done*" (1742). Public Domain. Accessed June 27, 2023. www.hymnary.org/text/o_love_divine_what_hast_thou_done

¹²Charles Wesley (1707-1788), "*And Can It Be That I Should Gain*" (1738). Public Domain. Accessed June 27, 2023. www.hymnary.org/text/and_can_it_be_that_i_should_gain

¹³ Friedrich Hauck, "ὑπερεκπεπισσοῦ," in *TDNT*, vol. 6, 61-62.

¹⁴ Bauer, "ὑπερεκπεπισσοῦ," *Greek-English Lexicon*, 848.

¹⁵ Walter Grundmann, "δύναμαι, δύναμις," in *TDNT*, ed. Gerhard Kittel and Geoffrey W. Bromiley, trans. Geoffrey W. Bromiley, vol. 2 (Grand Rapids, Michigan: William B. Eerdmans, 1974), 284-317.

¹⁶ John Calvin, *Galatians and Ephesians*, 265-266.

¹⁷ Frank E. Graeff (1860-1919), *"Does Jesus Care?"* 1901). Public Domain. Accessed July 5, 2023. www.hymnary.org/text/docs_does_jesus_care.

Chapter Fifteen

¹ Rudyard Kipling (1865-1936), *"I Keep Six Honest Serving Men."* Public domain. Retrieved July 21, 2023. www.public-domain-poetry.com/rudyard-kipling.

² William Shakespeare (1564-1616). "The Tragedy of Macbeth," act 5, scene 5, lines 27-28. Public domain. Retrieved July 22, 2023. www.opensourceshakespeare.org.

³ Peter Geach, *Providence and Evil* (Cambridge: Cambridge University Press, 1977 (out of print), 124. Public domain. Retrieved July 24, 2023. www.archive.org/details/providenceevil0000geac/page/n5/mode/2up.

⁴ Geach, *Providence and Evil*, 124.

⁵ Geach, *Providence and Evil*, 128.

⁶ Joachim Jeremias (1900-1979), *New Testament Theology: The Proclamation of Jesus*, trans. John Bowden (New York: Charles Scribner's Sons, 1971), 184. Public domain. Retrieved July 24, 2023. www.archive.org/details/newtestamenttheo0000jere.

⁷ *Merriam-Webster.comDictionary*, s.v. "utopia," Retrieved July 24, 2023. https://www.merriam-webster.com/dictionary/utopia.

⁸ *Urban Thesaurus.orgThesaurus*, s.v. "utopia," July 24, 2023, https://urbanthesaurus.org/synonyms/utopia.

⁹ Thomas More (1478-1535), *Utopia*. Public domain. Retrieved July 28,

2023. www.gutenburg.org/files/2130-h.htm.

[10] Homer, trans. T. S. Norgate, "Of Sirens and of Dangerous Rocks," in *The Odyssey* (London: Williams and Norgate, 1863), book 12, 249-267. Public domain. Retrieved July 28, 2023. https://www.loc.gov/item/10000284.

[11] Karin Schönpflug, "Queer Utopia for a Feminist Economy: Gender and Sexuality," *Journal of the Center for Gender Studies*, ICU, vol. 16, no. 2 (2021): 1-30. Retrieved July 29, 2023. Subsite.icu.ac.jp/cgs/en/journal/cgs16.html.

[12] Schönpflug, 2.

[13] Schönpflug, 7.

[14] Schönpflug, 1-30.

[15] David Mikkelson, "Norman Thomas on Socialism," Snopes, September 26, 2009. Retrieved August 3, 2023. *Snopes*.com/fact-check/norman-thomas-on-socialism.

[16] Norman Thomas, *The Truth About Socialism* (New York: Socialist Party, 1943), 4. Public domain. Retrieved August 3, 2023. https://starslibrary.ucf.edu/prism/618.

[17] George Liddell and Robert Scott, "εὐ," *A Greek-English Lexicon*, vol. 1 (Oxford: The Clarendon Press, 1940), 704. Public domain. Retrieved July 30, 2023. https://www.archive.org/details/1031364949_0001.

[18] George Liddell and Robert Scott, "οὐ," *A Greek-English Lexicon*, vol. 2 (Oxford: The Clarendon Press, 1940), 1266. Public domain. Retrieved July 30, 2023. https://www.archive.org/details/1031364949_02.

[19] Mao Tse-Tung, *Selected Works of Mao Tse-Tung*, vol. 2. (Peking: Foreign Languages Press, 1965), 224.

[20] Mao Tse-Tung, 219.

[21] Igor Shafarevich, *The Socialist Phenomenon* (Shawnee, Kansas: Gideon House Books, 2019), 12.

²² Aleksandr Solzhenitsyn, foreword to *The Socialist Phenomenon*, by Igor Shafarevich (Shawnee, Kansas: Gideon House Books, 2019), 5-6.

²³ Aleksandr Solzhenitsyn, 6.

²⁴ Karl Marx (1818-1883), ed., Friedrich Engels, trans. Samuel Moore and Edward Aveling, *Capital: A Critique of Political Economy*, vol. 1, 1st English ed. (Moscow: USSR: Progress Publishing, 1877), 483. Public domain. Retrieved August 20, 2023. www.ia800503.us.archive.org/6/items/CapitalVolume1/Capital-Volume-1.pdf. Friedrich Engels (1820-1895), *Socialism: Utopian and Scientific*, trans. Edward Aveling (Chicago: Charles H. Herr & Company, 1908). Public domain. Retrieved August 20, 2023. www.archives.org/details/socialismutopian00engeuoft/page/20/mode/2up.

²⁵ Vladimer Ilich Lenin, *Lenin on Engels: On the 40th Anniversary of Engel's Death* (New York: International Publishers, 1935), 3. Public domain. Retrieved August 20, 2023. https://stars.library.ucf.edu/prism/544).

²⁶ Translation of inscriptions on the monuments in Alexandrovsky Garden in Moscow. The Center for Thomas More Studies at The University of Dallas).

²⁷ Shafarevich, 328.

²⁸ Karl Kautsky (1854-1938), *Thomas More and His Utopia* (New York: International Publishers, 1927), 249. Public domain. Retrieved August 21, 2023. www.archive.org/details/thomasmorehisutopia.

²⁹ Kautsky, 250.

³⁰ Jonathan Edwards (1703-1758), "Sinners in the Hands of an Angry God," in *Selected Sermons of Jonathan Edwards*, ed. H. Norman Gardiner (New York: The Macmillan Company, 1904). Public domain. Retrieved August 22, 2023. www.gutenberg.org>34632.

³¹ Edwards, 88.

³² Edwards, 88-89.

[33] J. Wächter, "sheol," in *TDOT*, ed. G. Johannes Botterweck, Helmer Ringgren, and Heinz-Josef Fabry, trans. Douglas W. Stott, vol. 14 (Grand Rapids, Michigan: William B. Eerdmans, 2004), 242.

[34] W. O. E. Oesterley, *Immortality and the Unseen World: A Study in Old Testament Religion* (New York: The Macmillan Company, 1921), 2. Public domain. Retrieved August 22, 2023. archive.org/details/immortalityunsee00oest/page/n15/mode/2up.

[35] T. H. Gaster, "Dead, Abode of the," *IDB*, vol. 1, A-D (Nashville: Abingdon Press, 1962), 787.

[36] John Gray, *I and II Kings*, 2nd ed., (Philadelphia: The Westminster Press, 1970), 102.

[37] The primary Greek texts were Erasmus (1550) Beza (1565), and Elzevir (1633). Muller, *Dictionary of Latin and Greek Theological Terms*, 298.

[38] Bruce M. Metzger, *The Text of the New Testament: Its Transmission, Corruption, and Restoration*, 2nd printing (New York: Oxford University Press, 1968), 106.

[39] M. J. Mulder, "topet," in *TDOT,* ed. G. Johannes Botterweck, Helmer Ringgren, and Heinz-Josef Fabry, trans. David E. Green, vol. 15 (Grand Rapids, Michigan: William B. Eerdmans, 2006), 753-758.

[40] Mulder, "topet," 754.

[41] Mulder, "topet," 754.

[42] "C'est la sortie qui condusait vers l'endroit Bethso don't parle Josephus: Betso representerait aloes le mot; lieu des ordures." My English translation: "This is the exit which led to the place Bethso of which Josephus speaks: Bethso would then represent the word 'garbage place." (Book not published in English.) Adolphe Neubauer, *La Geographie du Talmud* (Paris: A La Librairie Noevelle, 1968), 139-140. Public domain. Retrieved September 12, 2023. https://archive.org.lageographiedutalmud.

⁴³ Joachim Jeremias, *Jerusalem in the Time of Jesus: An Investigation into Economic and Social Conditions During the New Testament Period* (Philadelphia: Fortress Press, 1969), 17.

⁴⁴ Jeremias, *Jerusalem in the Time of Jesus*, 83.

⁴⁵ Flavius Josephus, *The Works of Flavius Josephus in Four Volumes*, trans. William Whiston, vol. 1, book 5, chapter 12, section 3-4, "The Wars of the Jews," (1974; repr. Grand Rapids, Michigan: Baker Book House, 1974), 412-413. All future references will be shown with abbreviated title and cited as: Josephus, *Works*: "Subtitle," Arabic numerals reflecting volume, book, chapter, section, page, e.g., Josephus, *Works*, "Wars," 1.5.12.3-4.412-413.

⁴⁶ Josephus, Works, "Wars," 1.5.12.3-4.413.

⁴⁷ R. H. Charles, *The Book of Enoch or 1 Enoch (Oxford*: The Clarendon Press, 1912), 13-25. Public domain. Retrieved September 21, 2023. http://archive.org/details/cu31924067146773.

⁴⁸ Hertz, *The Pentateuch and Haftorahs*, vol. 1. 19.

⁴⁹ Saint Augustine, "The City of God," vol. 2, 305.

⁵⁰ Jerome Neyrey, *2 Peter, Jude: A New Translation with Introduction and Commentary* (New York" Doubleday, 1993), 202.

⁵¹ Origen A.D. 185-254), "Against Celsus," in *The Ante-Nicene Fathers*, ed. Alexander Roberts and James Donaldson, trans. Frederick Cromby, vol. 4 (Peabody, Massachusetts: Hendrickson Publishers, 1995), 405.

⁵² Abdullah Yusuf Ali, ed. and trans., "Sura 69:35-37," in *The Holy Qur'an: English Translations of the Meaning and Commentary* (Saudi Arabia: The Ministry of Hajj and Endowments, 1993), 1810. All future references will come from this translation and will be shown as Sura number and page number, e.g., Sura 69:35-37, 1810.

⁵³ Philip Schaff, *History of the Christian Church*, vol. 4 (1910; repr. Grand Rapids, Michigan: William B, Eerdmans Publishing Company, 1995), 181.

⁵⁴ Schaff, 183-184.

⁵⁵ Robert M. Seltzer, *Jewish People, Jewish Thought: The Jewish Experience in History* (New York: Macmillan Publishing Company, Inc., 1980), 327.

⁵⁶ A. Jeffery, ed., *A Reader on Islamic Passages From Standard Arabic Writings Illustrative of the Beliefs and Practices of Muslims* (The Hague, the Netherlands: Mouton and Co., Publishers, 1962), 230.

⁵⁷ Jeffery, *A Reader on Islamic Passages*, 230.

⁵⁸ Jeffery, *A Reader on Islamic Passages*, 234.

⁵⁹ Jeffery, *A Reader on Islamic Passages*, 209.

⁶⁰ Jeffery, *A Reader on Islamic Passages*, 209.

⁶¹ Jeffery, *A Reader on Islamic Passages*, 231.

⁶² Jeffery, *A Reader on Islamic Passages*, 211.

⁶³ Edward Gibbon (1737-1794), *The History of the Decline and Fall of the Roman Empire*, vol.3 (verbatim repr. London: Frederich Warne and Co., n.d.). Public domain. Retrieved October 2, 2023. http://archive.org/details/History of decline12gibb.

⁶⁴ Massoud Ansari, *Psychology of Mohammad* (Washington, DC: Institute for Ethical and Clinical Hypnosis, 2007), 388. Public domain. Retrieved October 9, 2023. archive.org/details/PsychologyofMohammadDr.MassoudAnsari.

⁶⁵ Henry C. Sheldon, *History of the Christian Church: The Mediaeval Church*, vol. 2 (1895; repr. Peabody, Massachusetts: Hendrickson Publishers, 1994), 53.

⁶⁶ Gibbon, 175.

⁶⁷ Hans Kung, *Eternal Life? Life After Death as a Medical, Philosophical and Theological Problem*, trans. Edward Quinn (Garden City, New York: Doubleday & Company, Inc., 1984), 133.

⁶⁸ Saint Thomas Aquinas (1225-1274), "Of the Relations of the Saints Towards the Damned," in *The Summa Theologica*, trans. The Fathers of the English Dominican Province (London: Burns Oates & Washbourne, Ltd., 1922). Public domain. Retrieved October 16, 2023. www.domcentral.org/summa/summa-supp.html.

⁶⁹ Saint Gregory the Great, *The Dialogues of St. Gregory the Great* (London: Philip Lee Warner, n.d.), book 4, question 94, 211. Public Domain. Retrieved October 16, 2023. http://www.saintsbook.net>PopeSt.Gregory.

⁷⁰ Fyodor Dostoevsky (1821-1881), *The Brothers Karamazov*, trans. Constance Garnett (New York: The Modern Library, n.d.), book 4, chapter 4, 254.

⁷¹ Nicolas Berdyaev, *The Beginning and the End*, trans. R. M. French (New York: Harper & Brothers, 1952), 238. Public domain.

⁷² Boniface Ramsey, ed., Roland Teske, trans., *The Works of Saint Augustine: A Translation for the 21ˢᵗ Century*, vol. 2, ed. (Hyde Park, New York: New City Press, 2003), letter #100, 15.

⁷³ Ramsey, ed., *The Works of Saint Augustine*, letter #134, 206.

⁷⁴ Terence, "The Self-Tormentor," in *English Songs from Foreign Tongues* by Frederick W. Ricard (1819-1897), (New York: Charles Scribner's Sons, 1885), 25. Public domain. Retrieved October 20, 2023. www.archive.org.terrence>the selftormentor.

⁷⁵ Attributed to James Truslow Adams (1878-1949), an American Historian.

⁷⁶ Saint Augustine, "City of God," vol. 2, 282-283.

⁷⁷ Saint Augustine, "City of God," vol. 2 404.

⁷⁸ Saint Augustine, "City of God," vol. 2, 404.

⁷⁹ Martin Luther, "Secular Authority: To What Extent It Should Be Obeyed," in *Great Political Thinkers: Plato to the Present*, 4ᵗʰ ed. William

Ebbenstein, ed. (Hinsdale, Illinois: Dryden Press, 1969, 309.

[80] Luther, "Secular Authority." 314.

[81] Luther, "Secular Authority." 315.

[82] Ramsey, ed., *The Works of Saint Augustine*, letter #134, 206.

[83] Steven Runciman, *A History of the Crusades*, vol.3 (Cambridge: Cambridge University Press, 1954), 48. Public domain. Retrieved October 27, 2023. https://archive.org/details/dli.ernet502939.

[84] Nicolas Berdyaev, *Christian Existentialism*, trans. Donald A. Lowrie (London: George Allen and Unwin, Ltd., 1956), 205.

[85] Edward Taylor, ed. "The Soldier's Almanack, Bible And Prayer Book" in The History of Playing Cards, (London: John Camden Hotten, 1865), 442-444. Public domain. Retrieved October 28, 2023. https://archive.org>stream>streamEdwardS.Taylor.

[86] Erich Fromm, *Man For Himself: An Inquiry Into the Psychology of Ethics* (New York: Fawcett Premiere, 1947), 237.

[87] Fromm, *Man For Himself*, 236-237.

[88] Blaise Pascal, *Pascal's Pensées: Introduction by T. S. Eliot* (New York: E. P. Dutton & Co., Inc., 1958), #377, 102. https://www.gutenberg.org/files/18269/18269-h/18269-h.htm.

[89] Karl Barth and Edward Thurneysen, *Come Holy Spirit*, 13.

[90] Joseph Fitzmyer says that the KJV is supported by a "not unimpressive list of witnesses." Joseph A. Fitzmyer, *The Gospel According to Luke: A New Translation with Introduction and Commentary: I-IX* (New York: Doubleday, 1981), 830. G.B. Caird says that the longer text is "quite in keeping with the spirit of the incident." G.B. Caird, *Saint Luke* (Baltimore: Penguin Books, 1972), 141. Marcion (AD 85-160) includes the longer text in his gospel compilation which he brought to Rome in AD 140. Francois Bovon believes that

orthodox scribes opposed to Marcion omitted the verses. However, it can be argued that Marcion's copy was more likely to have been based on the original text than any text that was used at a later date. Francois Bovon, *Luke 2: A Commentary on the Gospel of Luke 9:51-19:27*, trans. Donald S. Deer (Minneapolis, Minnesota: Augsburg Fortress Press, 2002), 5.

[91] Walter Bruggemann, *1 & 2 Kings* (Macon, Georgia: Smyth & Helwys Publishing, Inc., 2000), 286.

[92] Gerhard von Rad, *Old Testament Theology*, vol. 2, trans. D.M.G. Stalker (New York: Harper & Row, Publishers, 1965), 14.

[93] K. Barth, "*laag, laeg/act arrogantly*," in *TDOT*, ed. Johannes Botterweck, Helmer Ringgren and Heinz-Josef Fabry, trans. Douglas W. Stott vol. 8 (Grand Rapids, Michigan: William B. Eerdmans, 1996), 10-14,

[94] St. Thomas Aquinas, *Catenae Aurea, Commentary on the Four Gospels, Collected Out of the Works of the Fathers*, new edition, vol.1, St. Matthew (Oxford and London: James Parker and Co., 1874), 103.

Conclusion

[1] Margaret Smith, *Muslim Women Mystics: The Life and Work of Rabi'a and Other Women Mystics in Islam* (Oxford, UK: Oneworld, 2001), 98.

[2] Saint Augustine, "Confessions" vol. 1, 45.

BIBLIOGRAPHY

Abbott, T. K. *The Epistles to the Ephesians and Colossians.* 1897. Reprint, Edinburgh: T. & T. Clark, 1974.

Augustine (354-430). "The Confessions of St. Augustine." *Nicene and Post-Nicene Fathers: The Confessions and Letters of Augustine, with a Sketch of His Life and Work.* Edited by Philip Schaff and Translated by J. G. Pilkington, 45-207. 2nd printing. Vol. 1. Peabody, Massachusetts: Hendrickson Publishers, 1995.

_____. "The City of God." *Nicene and Post-Nicene Fathers.* Edited by Philip Schaff and Translated by J. F. Shaw, 1-511. 2nd printing. Vol. 2. Peabody, Massachusetts: Hendrickson Publishers, 1995.

_____. "Sermons on Selected Lessons of the New Testament, Sermon XCI 91)." *Nicene and Post-Nicene Fathers: Sermon on the Mount, Harmony of the Gospels, Homilies on the Gospels.* Edited by Philip Schaff and Translated by R. G. MacMullen, 237-545. 2nd printing. Vol. 6. Peabody, Massachusetts: Hendrickson Publishers, 1995

_____. "Expositions on the Book of Psalms." *Nicene and Post-Nicene Fathers.* Edited by Philip Schaff, 1-683. 2nd printing. Vol. 8. Peabody, Massachusetts: Hendrickson Publishers, Inc., 1995.

Ali, Abdullah Yusu. Editor and Translator. *The Holy Qur'an: English Translations of the Meaning and Commentary.* Saudi Arabia: The Ministry of Hajj and Endowments, 1993. All future references to the Koran will come from this translation and will be shown as Sura number and page number, e.g., Sura 69:35-37, 1810.

Ansari, Massoud. *Psychology of Mohammad.* Washington, DC: Institute for Ethical and Clinical Hypnosis, 2007. Public domain. Retrieved October 9, 2023. archive.org/details/PsychologyofMohammadDr.MassoudAnsari.

Aquinas, Thomas (1225-1274). *Catenae Aurea, Commentary on the Four Gospels, Collected Out of the Works of the Fathers*. New Edition. Vol. 1, St. Matthew. Oxford and London: James Parker and Co., 1874.

_____. "Of the Relations of the Saints Towards the Damned." *The Summa Theologica*. Translated by The Fathers of the English Dominican Province. London: Burns Oates & Washbourne, Ltd., 1922. Public domain. Retrieved October 16, 2023. www.domcentral.org/summa/summa-supp.html.

Babcock, Maltbie D. (1858-1901). "This Is My Father's World," Public Domain. Accessed May 14, 2023. hymnary.org/text/this_is_my_fathers_world_and_to_my.

Barret, C. K. *The Holy Spirit and the Gospel Tradition*. London: SPCK, 1948.

_____. *The Gospel According to St. John: An Introduction with Commentary and Notes on the Greek Text*. London: S. P. C. K., 1965.

Barth, Karl. "laag, laeg/act arrogantly." *Theological Dictionary of the Old Testament*. Edited by Johannes Botterweck, Helmer Ringgren and Heinz-Josef Fabry and Translated by Douglas W. Stott, 10-14. Vol. 8. Grand Rapids, Michigan: William B. Eerdmans, 1996.

_____. "The Doctrine of the Word of God." *Church Dogmatics*. Edited by G. W. Bromiley and T. F. Torrance and Translated by G. W. Bromiley. 2nd Edition, Vol. 1, Part 1. Edinburgh: T. &T. Clark, 1975.

_____. "The Pride and Fall of Man." *Church Dogmatics*. Edited and Translated by G. W. Bromiley. 2nd Edition, Vol. 4, Part 1. 1956. Reprint, Edinburgh: T.& T. Clark, 1980.

_____. "The Doctrine of Reconciliation." *Church Dogmatics*. Edited and Translated by G. W. Bromiley. 2nd Edition, Vol. 4, Part 1. 1956. Reprint, Edinburgh: T. & T. Clark, 1980.

_____. "The Doctrine of Reconciliation." *Church Dogmatics*. Edited by G. W. Bromiley and T. F. Torrance and Translated by G. W. Bromiley. Vol. 4, Part 2. Edinburgh: T.& T. Clark, 1958.

_____. "The Doctrine of Reconciliation. *Church Dogmatics.* Edited and Translated by G. W. Bromiley. Vol. 4, part 3, second half. Edinburgh: T. & T. Clark, 1962.

_____. *The Epistle to the Romans*. 6th ed. Translated by Edwyn Hoskyns. London: Oxford University Press, 1976

Karl Barth and Edward Thurneysen. *Come Holy Spirit*. Translated by George W. Richards, Elmer G. Homrighausen, and Karl J. Ernst. Grand Rapids, Michigan: William B. Eerdmans, 1978.

Walter Bauer. "συνωδίνω." Edited by William F. Arndt and F. Wilbur Gingrich, 801. 4th revised and augmented ed. Chicago: University of Chicago Press, 1957.

_____. ὑπερβάλλω," *A Greek-English Lexicon of the New Testament and Other Early Christian Literature.* Edited by William F. Arndt and Wilbur Gingrich, 848. 4th revised and augmented ed. Chicago: University of Chicago Press, 1957.

Johannes Behm. "αρραβῶν." *Theological Dictionary of the New Testament*. Edited by Gerhard Kittel and Translated by Geoffrey W. Bromiley, 475. Vol. 1. Grand Rapids, Michigan: William B. Eerdmans, 1964.

_____. "μεταμορφόω." *Theological Dictionary of the New Testament*. Edited by Gerard Kittel and Translated by Geoffrey W. Bromiley, 755-759. Vol.4. Grand Rapids, Michigan: William B. Eerdmans, 1967.

Nicolas Berdyaev. *The Beginning and the End*. Translated by R. M. French. New York: Harper & Brothers, 1952. Public domain.

_____. *Christian Existentialism*. Translated by Donald A. Lowrie. London: George Allen and Unwin, Ltd., 1956.

Dietrich Bonhoeffer, *Creation and Fall: A Theological Interpretation of Genesis 1-3*. New York: Macmillan Publishing Co., Inc., 1974.

Bovon, Francois. *Luke 2: A Commentary on the Gospel of Luke 9:51-19:27*. Translated by Donald S. Deer. Minneapolis, Minnesota: Augsburg Fortress Press, 2002.

Brooke, A. E. *A Critical and Exegetical Commentary on the Johannine Epistles*. 1912. Reprint, Edinburgh: T. & T. Clark. 1971.

Brockes, Emma. "Return of the Time Lord." *The Guardian* (September 27, 2005). Retrieved December 1, 2023. www.the guardian.com.

Bruce, F. F. *Paul: Apostle of the Heart Set Free*. Grand Rapids, Michigan: William B. Eerdmans, 1981.

Bruggemann, Walter. *1 & 2 Kings*. Macon, Georgia: Smyth & Helwys Publishing, Inc., 2000.

Brunner, Emil. *Eternal Hope*. Translated by Harold Knight Philadelphia: The Westminster Press, 1954.

_____. *The Scandal of Christianity: The Gospel as Stumbling Block to Modern Man.* Richmond: The John Knox Press, Press, 1968.

Büchsel, Friedrich. "ἀγοράζω/ἐξαγοράζω." *Theological Dictionary of the New Testament*, Edited by Gerhard Kittel and Translated by Geoffrey W. Bromiley, 124-128. Vol. 1. Grand Rapids: Michigan: William B. Eerdmans. 1974.

_____. "λυτρόω." *Theological Dictionary of the New Testament.* Edited by Gerhard Kittel and Translated by Geoffrey W. Bromiley, 349-351. Vol. 4. Grand Rapids, Michigan: William B. Eerdmans, 1967.

Calvin, John (1509-1564). *Commentaries on the Epistles of Paul to the Galatians and Ephesians.* Translated by William Pringle. Edinburgh: The Calvin Translation Society, 1854. Public Domain. Accessed from Internet Archives June 26, 2023. https://archive.org/details/calvinscommentar0000calv_z106.pdf.

Clement of Alexandria, "Exhortation to the Heathen. *Ante-Nicene Fathers: Fathers of the Second Century.* Edited by Alexander Roberts and James Donaldson and Translated by W. L. Alexander, 163-206. 2nd printing. Vol. 2. Peabody, Massachusetts: Hendrickson Publishers, 1995.

Charles, R. H. *The Book of Enoch or 1 Enoch. Oxford*: The Clarendon Press, 1912. Public domain. Retrieved September 21, 2023. http://archive.org/details/cu31924067146773.

_____. *A Critical History of the Doctrine of Future Life.* London: Adam and Charles Black, 1899.

Charlesworth, James H., ed. *The Old Testament and Pseudepigrapha*, vol. 1, *Apocalyptic Literature and Testaments*. Garden City, New York: Doubleday & Company, 1983.

Currie, David. *Rapture: The End-Times Error That Leaves the Bible Behind.* Nashua, New Hampshire: The Sophia Institute Press, 2004.

Daube, David. *The New Testament and Rabbinic Judaism.* Peabody, Massachusetts: Hendrickson Publishers, 1956.

Delling, Gerhard. "ὑπερβάλλω, ὑπερβαλλόντως, ὑπερβολή." *Theological Dictionary of the New Testament.* Edited by Gerhard Kittel and Gerhard Friedrich and Translated by Geoffrey W. Bromiley, 520-522. Vol. 8. Grand Rapids, Michigan: William B. Eerdmans, 1972.

Diessemann, Adolf. *Light From the Ancient East: The New Testament Illustrated by Recently Discovered Texts of the Graeco-Roman World,* 4th ed. Translated by Lionel A. M. Strachan. New York and London: Harper and Brothers, 1908.

Dods, Marcus. *The Book of Genesis.* New York: A. C. Armstrong and Son, 1902.

Donne, John (1572-1631). "Death's Duel." Public Domain. Accessed April 13, 2023. Ccel.org/ccel/donne/deaths_duel.i.html.

Driver, S. R. *The Book of Genesis.* 10th ed. London: Methuen & Co., LTD, 1916.

Driver, S. R. *A Critical and Exegetical Commentary on Deuteronomy.* New York: Charles Scribner's Sons, 1895.

Dostoevsky, Fyodor (1821-1881). "Notes From Underground." Edited by Maynard Mack and Translated by Constance Garnett. *World Masterpieces: Literature of Western Culture Since the Renaissance.* Vol. 2. New York: W. W. Norton & Company, Inc., 1965.

_____. *The Brothers Karamazov*. Translated by Constance Garnett. New York: The Modern Library, n.d.

Edwards, Jonathan (1703-1758). "Sinners in the Hands of an Angry God." *Selected Sermons of Jonathan Edwards*. Edited by H. Norman Gardiner. New York: The Macmillan Company, 1904. Public domain. Retrieved August 22, 2023. www.gutenberg.org>34632.

Eliot T. S. "The Waste Land." *American Literature: Tradition and Innovation*. Edited by Harrison T. Meserole, Walter Sutton, and Brom Weber. Vol. 2. Lexington, Massachusetts: D. C. Heath and Company, 1969.

Engels, Friedrich (1820-1895). *Socialism: Utopian and Scientific*. Translated by Edward Aveling. Chicago: Charles H. Herr & Company, 1908. Public domain. Retrieved August 20, 2023. www.archives.org/details/socialismutopian00engeuoft/page/20/mode/2up.

Faulkner, William. *Light In August*. London: Chatto and Windus, 1922.

Fitzgerald, F. Scott. *The Great Gatsby*. New York: Charles Scribner's Sons, 1925. Public domain. Retrieved August 20, 2023. www.gutenberg.org.

Floyd, W. F. (1791-1853). "My Times Are in Thy Hands." Public Domain. Retrieved May 14, 2023. hymnary.org/text/my_times_are_in_thy_hand_my_god_i_wish?

Fohrer, Georg. *"Σιών." Theological Dictionary of the New Testament*. Edited by Gerhard Kittel and Gerhard Friedrich and Translated by Geoffrey W. Bromiley 292-319. Vol. 7. Grand Rapids, Michigan: William B. Eerdmans, 1971.

Fromm, Erich. *Man For Himself: An Inquiry Into the Psychology of Ethics*. New York: Fawcett Premiere, 1947.

Frost, Robert. "The Road Not Taken." *American Literature: Tradition and Innovation*. Edited by Harrison T. Meserole, Walter Sutton, and Brom Weber. Vol. 2. Lexington, Massachusetts: D. C. Heath and Company, 1969.

Fuchs, Ernst. "σήμερον." *Theological Dictionary of the New Testament*. Edited by Gerhard Kittel and Gerhard Friedrich and Translated by Geoffrey W. Bromiley, 269-275. Vol. 7. Grand Rapids, Michigan: William B. Eerdmans, 1971.

Funk, R. W. *"The Wilderness." Journal of Biblical Literature* 78, no. 3 (September 1959): 206.

Gaster, T. H. "Dead, Abode of the." *Interpreter's Dictionary of the Bible*. Edited by George A. Buttrick, Thomas s. Kepler, John Knox, Herbert G. May, Samuel Terrien, and Emory S. Bucke. Vol. 1, A-D. Nashville: Abingdon Press, 1962. All future Entries will be shown as *IDB* for *Interpreter's Dictionary of the Bible*.

Geach, Peter. *Providence and Evil*. Cambridge: Cambridge University Press, 1977, (out of print). Public domain. Retrieved July 24, 2023. www.archive.org/details/providenceevil0000geac/page/n5/mode/2up.

Gealy, Fred D., ed. *The Book of Worship for Church and Home* (Nashville, Tennessee: The Methodist Publishing House, 1965.

Gibbon, Edward (1737-1794). *The History of the Decline and Fall of the Roman Empire*. Vol.3. Verbatim Reprint. London: Frederich Warne and Co., n.d. Public domain. Retrieved October 2, 2023. http://archive.org/details/History of decline12gibb.

Goppelt, Leonard. "καταπίνω." *Theological Dictionary of the New Testament*. Edited by Gerhard Kittel and Gerhard Friedrich and Translated by

Geoffrey W. Bromiley 158-159. Vol.6. Grand Rapids, Michigan: William B. Eerdmans, 1968.

Gorg, M. "tohu wabohu." *Theological Dictionary of the Old Testament*. Edited by Johannes Botterweck, Helmer Ringgren, Heinz-Josef Fabry and Translated by David E. Green, 565-574. Vol. 15. Grand Rapids, Michigan: William B. Eerdmans Publishing, 2015.

Graeff, Frank E. (1860-1919). *"Does Jesus Care?"* 1901. Public Domain. Retrieved July 5, 2023. www.hymnary.org/text/docs_does_jesus_care.

Gray, John. *I and II Kings*. 2nd ed. Philadelphia: The Westminster Press, 1970.

Gregory the Great. *The Dialogues of St. Gregory the Great.* London: Philip Lee Warner, n.d. Public Domain. Retrieved October 16, 2023. http://www.saintsbook.net>PopeSt.Gregory.

Grundmann, Walter. "δύναμαι, δύναμις." *Theological Dictionary of the New Testament.* Edited by Gerhard Kittel and Geoffrey W. Bromiley and Translated by Geoffrey W. Bromiley 284-317. Vol. 2. Grand Rapids, Michigan: William B. Eerdmans, 1974.

Hanson, Paul D. "Apocalypticism." *Interpreter's Dictionary of the Bible.* Edited by Lloyd Richard Bailey, Sr., Victor Paul Furnish and Emory Stevens Bucke. Supplementary Volume. Nashville, Tennessee: Abingdon, 1976.

Harris, Murray J. "The New Testament View of Life After Death." *Themelios* 11.2 (January 1986): 48.

_____. "2 Corinthians 5:1-10: Watershed in Paul's Eschatology?" *Tyndale Bulletin* 22 (1971): 42.

Hauck, Friedrich. "ὑπερεκπερισσοῦ." *Theological Dictionary of the New Testament*. Edited by Gerhard Kittel and Geoffrey W. Bromiley and Translated by Geoffrey W. Bromiley, 61-62. Vol. 6. Grand Rapids, Michigan: William B. Eerdmans, 1968.

Hertz, J. H. ed. *The Pentateuch and Haftorahs: Hebrew Text, English Translation and Commentary*. Vol. 2. London: Oxford University Press, 1937.

Hick, John. *Death and Eternal Life*. Louisville, Kentucky: Westminster/John Knox Press, 1994.

History of Jack Horner. Osborne Collection of Early Children's Books. Public Domain. Courtesy of Toronto Public Library. Retrieved June 24, 2023. www.torontopubliclibrary.ca/digital-archive/license.jsp.

Holcomb, Jr., Norman D. *Who Killed Jesus? The Authority of the Sanhedrin at the Trial of Jesus*. 48HrBooks: Akron, Ohio, 2019.

Homer. Translated by T. S. Norgate. "Of Sirens and of Dangerous Rocks." *The Odyssey*. London: Williams and Norgate, 1863. Public domain. Retrieved July 28, 2023. https://www.loc.gov/item/10000284.

Houston, James M. ed. *From the Works of Blaise Pascal: Mind on Fire*. Minneapolis, Minnesota: Bethany House Publishers, 1977.

Jeffery, A. ed. *A Reader on Islamic Passages From Standard Arabic Writings Illustrative of the Beliefs and Practices of Muslims*. The Hague, the Netherlands: Mouton and Co., Publishers, 1962.

Jeremias, Joachim (1900-1979). *New Testament Theology: The Proclamation of Jesus*. Translated by John Bowden. New York: Charles Scribner's Sons, 1971. Public domain. Retrieved July 24, 2023. www.archive.org/details/newtestamenttheo0000jere.

_____. *Jerusalem in the Time of Jesus: An Investigation into Economic and Social Conditions During the New Testament Period*. Philadelphia: Fortress Press, 1969.

Johnson, James Weldon. *God's Trombones: Seven Negro Sermons*. 1929. Reprint, New York: The Viking Press, 1972.

Josephus, Flavius. *The Works of Flavius Josephus in Four Volumes*. Translated by William Whiston. Vol. 1. *The Wars of the Jews* and *Josephus and Masada*. Grand Rapids, Michigan: Baker Book House, 1974.

_____. *The Works of Flavius Josephus in Four Volumes*. Translated by William Whiston. Vol. 2. *The Life of Flavius Josephus* and *Antiquities of the Jews, Books 1-8*. Grand Rapids, Michigan: Baker Book House, 1974.

_____. *The Works of Flavius Josephus in Four Volumes*. Translated by William Whiston. Vol. 3. *The Life of Flavius Josephus* and *Antiquities of the Jews, Books 9-17*. Grand Rapids, Michigan: Baker Book House, 1974.

_____. *The Works of Flavius Josephus in Four Volumes*. Translated by William Whiston. Vol. 4. *Antiquities of the Jews, Books 18-20*. Grand Rapids, Michigan: Baker Book House, 1974.

Kaiser Otto. *Isaiah 13-39: A Commentary*. Philadelphia: The Westminster Press, 1974.

Kautsky, Karl (1854-1938). *Thomas More and His Utopia*. New York: International Publishers, 1927. Public domain. Retrieved August 21, 2023. www.archive.org/details/thomasmorehisutopia

_____. *Early Christian Creeds*. 3rd ed. New York & London: Continuum Books, 1972.

Kierkegaard, Soren (1813-1855). *Fear and Trembling and the Sickness Unto Death.* Translated by Walter Lowrie, 1941. Reprint, Princeton: Princeton University Press, 1974.

_____. "The Listener's Role In A Devotional Address," in *Purity Of Heart Is To Will One Thing.* Translated with an introductory essay by Douglas V. Steere. New York: Harper & Row Publishers, 1956.

Kipling, Rudyard (1865-1936). "*I Keep Six Honest Serving Men.*" Public domain. Retrieved July 21, 2023. www.public-domain-poetry.com/rudyard-kipling.

_____. "Recessional." Public Domain. Retrieved May 13, 2023. public-domain-poetry.com/rudyard-kipling/recessional-3440.

Koch, K. "derekh." *Theological Dictionary of the Old Testament.* Edited by Johannes Botterweck and Helmer Ringgren and Translated by Heinz-Josef Fabry, 270-273. Vol. 3. Grand Rapids, Michigan: William B. Eerdmans Publishing, 1975.

Koestler, Arthur. "Is Man's Brain An Evolutionary Mistake." *Horizon: A Magazine of the Arts* 10, no. 4 (Spring 1968): 43.

Kung, Hans. *Eternal Life? Life After Death as a Medical, Philosophical and Theological Problem.* Translated by Edward Quinn. Garden City, New York: Doubleday & Company, Inc., 1984.

Kushner, Harold S. *When Bad Things Happen to Good People.* New York: Avon Books, 1983.

Langkammer, Hugolinus. "παντοκράτωρ." *Exegetical Dictionary of the New Testamnt.* Edited by Horst Balz and Gerhard Schneider and Translated by

John W. Medendorp and Douglas W. Stott, 11-12. Vol. 3. Grand Rapids, Michigan: William B. Eerdmans, 1993.

Lee, Peggy. "Is That All There Is?" 1969, track no. 1 on *Is That All There Is?* Capitol, 1969, Long Play album.

Lenin, Vladimer Ilich. *Lenin on Engels: On the 40th Anniversary of Engel's Death.* New York: International Publishers, 1935. Public domain. Retrieved August 20, 2023. https://stars.library.ucf.edu/prism/544).

Liddel, George, and Robert Scott. "εὐ." *A Greek-English Lexicon.* Vol. 1. Oxford: The Clarendon Press, 1940. Public domain. Retrieved July 30, 2023. https://www.archive.org/details/1031364949_0001.

_____. "οὐ." *A Greek-English Lexicon.* Vol. 2. Oxford: The Clarendon Press, 1940. Public domain. Retrieved July 30, 2023. https://www.archive.org/details/1031364949_02.

_____. "συμβάλλουσα," *A Greek-English Lexicon*, vol.2

Lightfoot, John. *A Commentary on the New Testament from the Talmud and Hebraica: Matthew—1 Corinthians: Matthew—Mark. Vol.3 1859. Reprint, Peabody, Massachusetts: Hendrickson Publishers, 1997.*

Longfellow, Henry Wordsworth (1807-1882). "The Building of the Ship." [online resource], Maine Historical Society. Public domain. Retrieved June 3, 2023. http://www. hwlongfellow.org.

Luther, Martin. *Commentary on Romans.* Translated by J. Theodore Mueller, 1954. Reprint, Grand Rapids, Michigan: Kregel Publications1976.

_____. *Luther's Works: The Christian in Society IV.* Vol. 47. Philadelphia: Fortress Press, 1971.

_____. "Secular Authority: To What Extent It Should Be Obeyed." *Great Political Thinkers: Plato to the Present*. 4th ed. Edited by William Ebbenstein. Hinsdale, Illinois: Dryden Press, 1969.

Mao Tse-Tung, *Selected Works of Mao Tse-Tung*. Vol. 2. Peking: Foreign Languages Press, 1965.

Martyr, Justin (110-165). "The First Apology." *Ante-Nicene Fathers*. Edited and Translated by Alexander Roberts and James Donaldson, 159-187. 2nd printing. Vol. 1. 1885. Reprint, Peabody, Massachusetts: Hendrickson Publishers, 1995.

_____. "Dialogue With Trypho." *Ante-Nicene Fathers*. Edited and Translated by Alexander Roberts and James Donaldson, 194-270. 2nd printing. Vol. 1. 1885. Reprint, Peabody, Massachusetts: Hendrickson Publishers, 1995.

_____. "Martyrdom of Ignatius." *Ante-Nicene Fathers*. Edited and Translated by Alexander Roberts and James Donaldson, 127-131. 2nd printing. Vol. 1. 1885. Reprint, Peabody, Massachusetts: Hendrickson Publishers, 1995.

Marx, Karl (1818-1883). *Capital: A Critique of Political Economy*. Edited by Friedrich Engels and Translated by Samuel Moore and Edward Aveling. 1st English ed. Vol. 1. Moscow, USSR: Progress Publishing, 1877. Public domain. Retrieved August 20, 2023. www.ia800503.us.archive.org/6/items/CapitalVolume1/Capital-Volume-1.pdf.

Merriam-Webster.comDictionary, s.v. "utopia." Retrieved July 24, 2023. https://www.merriam-webster.com/dictionary/utopia.

Metzger, Bruce, ed. The *Oxford Annotated Apocrypha: The Apocrypha of the Old Testament, Revised Standard Version* New York: Oxford University Press, 1965.

_____. *The Text of the New Testament: Its Transmission, Corruption, and Restoration.* 2nd printing. New York: Oxford University Press, 1968.

Michaelis, Wilhelm. *Der Herr verzeit nicht die Verheissung. Die Aussagen Jesu über die Nahedes Jungsten Tages.* Bern: BEG-Verlag, 1942. English translation: *The Lord Does Not Delay the Promise: The Statement of Jesus About the Nearness of Judgment Day.*

Mikkelson, David. "Norman Thomas on Socialism." *Snopes*, September 26, 2009. Retrieved August 3, 2023. Snopes.com/fact-check/norman-thomas-on-socialism.

More, Thomas (1478-1535). *Utopia.* Public domain. Retrieved July 28, 2023. www.gutenburg.org/files/2130-h.htm.

Mulder, M. J. "topet." *Theological Dictionary of the Old Testament.* Edited by G. Johannes Botterweck, Helmer Ringgren, and Heinz-Josef Fabry and Translated by David E. Green, 753-758. Vol. 15. Grand Rapids, Michigan: William B. Eerdmans, 2006.

Muller, Richard. *Dictionary of Latin and Greek Theological Terms.* Grand Rapids, Michigan: Baker Book House, 1985.

North, C. R. "chadhash; chodhesh." *Theological Dictionary of the Old Testament.* Edited by Johannes Botterweck and Helmer Ringgren and Translated by David E. Green, 225-244. Vol. 4. Grand Rapids, Michigan: William B. Eerdmans, 1981.

Neubauer, Adolphe, *La Geographie du Talmud.* Paris: A La Librairie Noevelle, 1968. Public domain. Retrieved September 12, 2023. https://archive.org.lageographiedutalmud.

Neyrey, Jerome. *2 Peter, Jude: A New Translation with Introduction and Commentary*. New York" Doubleday, 1993.

Oberman. Heiko A. *Luther: a Man Between God and the Devil*. Translated by Eileen Walliser-Schwarzbart. London: Yale University Press, 2006

Oepke, Albrecht. "παρουσία, πάρειμι." in *Theological Dictionary of the New Testament*. Edited by Gerhard Kittel, Gerhard Friedrich and Geoffrey Bromiley and Translated by Geoffrey Bromiley, 858-871. Vol. 5. Grand Rapids, Michigan: William B. Eerdmans, 1967.

Oesterley, W. O. E. *Immortality and the Unseen World: A Study in Old Testament Religion*. New York: The Macmillan Company, 1921. Public domain. Retrieved August 22, 2023. archive.org/details/immortalityunsee00oest/page/n15/mode/2up.

Olsen, Carl E. *Will Catholics Be Left Behind: A Critique of the Rapture and Today's Prophecy Preachers*. San Francisco: Ignatius Press, 2009.

Origen (185-254). "Against Celsus." in *The Ante-Nicene Fathers*. Edited by Alexander Roberts and James Donaldson and Translated by Frederick Cromby, 395-669. 2nd printing. 1885. Reprint, Vol. 4. Peabody, Massachusetts: Hendrickson Publishers, 1995.

_____. Origin. *Commentary on the Epistle to the Romans*. Translated by Thomas P. Scheck. Washington, DC: The Catholic University of America Press, 2001.

Otto, Rudolf. *The Idea of the Holy*. Translated by John W. Harvey. 1923. Reprint, London: Oxford University Press, 1971.

Pascal, Blaise (1623-1662). *Pascal's Pensées: Introduction by T. S. Eliot.* New York: E. P. Dutton & Co., Inc., 1958. Retrieved December 18, 2022. https://www.gutenberg.org/files/18269/18269-h/18269-h.htm.

_____. "Section X: Typology, Thought #654." *Pensées*. Translated by W. F. Trotter. Grand Rapids, Michigan: Christian Classics Ethereal Library. Retrieved December 18, 2022. http://www.ccel.org/ccel/pascal/pensees.html.

Plummer, Alfred. *A Critical and Exegetical Commentary on the Gospel According to S. Luke.* 5th ed. Edinburgh: T. & T. Clarke, 1922.

Pope, Alexander. "An Essay on Man," in *World Masterpieces: Literature of Western Culture Since the Renaissance*. Edited by Maynard Mack. Vol. 2. New York: W. W. Norton and Company, 1965.

Ramsey, Boniface, ed. *The Works of Saint Augustine: A Translation for the 21st Century.* Translated by Roland Teske. Vol. 2. Hyde Park, New York: New City Press, 2003.

Reuter, Wallenhorst. "qn; qina; qanna; quanno." *Theological Dictionary of the Old Testament*. Edited by G. Johannes Botterweck, Helmer Ringgren, and Heinz-Josef Fabry and Translated by David E. Green, 47-58. Vol. 13. Grand Rapids, Michigan: William B. Eerdmans, 2004.

Ringgren, Helmer. "semen, samen, saman." *Theological Dictionary of the Old Testament*. Edited by Johannes Botterweck, Helmer Ringgren, and Heinz-Josef Fabry and Translated by David E. Green, 249-253. Vol. 15. Grand Rapids, Michigan: William B. Eerdmans, 2015.

Rosser, Barbara. *The Rapture Exposed*. Boulder, Colorado: Westview Press, 2004.

Runciman, Steven. *A History of the Crusades*. Vol. 3. Cambridge: Cambridge University Press, 1954. Public domain. Retrieved October 27, 2023. https://archive.org/details/dli.ernet502939.

Russell, D. S. *The Method and Message of Jewish Apocalyptic*. Philadelphia: The Westminster Press, 1964.

Sandburg, Carl. "Wilderness." *Harvest Poems: 1910-1960*. New York: Harcourt Brace & World, Inc., 1960.

Schaff, Philip. *History of the Christian Church*. Vol. 4. 1910. Reprint, Grand Rapids, Michigan: William B. Eerdmans Publishing Company, 1995.

Schaff, Philip, and David S. Schaff, ed., "Oecumenical Creeds." *The Creeds of Christianity With a History and Critical Notes*. 6th ed. 45-73. Vol. 2. Grand Rapids, Michigan: Baker Book House, 1996.

Schlier, Heinrich. "θλῖψις." *Theological Dictionary of the New Testament*. Edited by Gerhard Kittel and Translated by Geoffrey W. Bromiley, 139-148. Vol. 3. Grand Rapids, Michigan: William B. Eerdmans, 1965).

Schmidt, Ludwig. "παράγω." *Theological Dictionary of the New Testament*. Edited by Gerhard Kittel and Translated by Geoffrey Bromiley, 129-130. Vol. 1. Grand Rapids, Michigan: William B. Eerdmans, 1964.

Schönpflug, Karin. "Queer Utopia for a Feminist Economy: Gender and Sexuality." *Journal of the Center for Gender Studies*, ICU, 16, no. 2 (2021): 1-30. Retrieved July 29, 2023. Subsite.icu.ac.jp/cgs/en/journal/cgs16.html.

Seeger, Alan (1888-1916). "I Have a Rendezvous with Death." Public Domain. Retrieved February 10, 2023. poets.org/poem/i-have-rendezvous-deat

Seltzer, Robert M. *Jewish People, Jewish Thought: The Jewish Experience in History*. New York: Macmillan Publishing Company, Inc., 1980.

Shafarevich, Igor. *The Socialist Phenomenon*. Shawnee, Kansas: Gideon House Books, 2019.

Shakespeare, William (1564-1616). "The Tragedy of Macbeth." act 5, scene 5, lines 27-28. Public domain. Retrieved July 22, 2023. www.opensourceshakespeare.org.

Sheldon, Henry C. *History of the Christian Church: The Mediaeval Church*. Vol. 2. 1895. Reprint, Peabody, Massachusetts: Hendrickson Publishers, 1994.

Solzhenitsyn, Aleksandr. Foreword to *The Socialist Phenomenon*, by Igor Shafarevich. Shawnee, Kansas: Gideon House Books, 2019.

Smith, George Adam. *The Historical Geography of the Holy Land*. London: Holder and Staughton, 1894.

Smith, Margaret. *Muslim Women Mystics: The Life and Work of Rabi'a and Other Women Mystics in Islam*. Oxford, UK: Oneworld, 2001), 98.

Smith, Walter Chalmers (1824-1908). "Immortal, Invisible, God Only Wise." Public Domain. Retrieved May 14, 2023. hymnary.org/media/fetch/100827.

Stählin, Gustav. "φίλος, φίλη, φιλία." *Theological Dictionary of the New Testament.* Edited by Gerhard Friedrich and Geoffrey W. Bromiley and Translated by Geoffrey W. Bromiley, 113-171. Vol. 9. Grand Rapids, Michigan: William B. Eerdmans, 1974.

Stone, Michael Edward. *Fourth Ezra*. Edited by Frank Moore Cross. Minneapolis: Augsburg Fortress, 1990.

Sullivan, James P. "Oh, Say, but I'm Glad," 1930. Public domain. Retrieved on December 29, 2022. www.library.timelesstruths.org/music.

Talmon, S. "midbar." *Theological Dictionary of the Old Testament.* Edited by Johannes Botterweck, Helmer Ringgren and Heinz-Josef Fabry and Translated by Douglas W. Stott, 87-118. Vol. 8. Grand Rapids, Michigan: William B. Eerdmans, 1996.

_____. "Wilderness." *Interpreter's Dictionary of the Bible.* Edited by Lloyd Richard Bailey, Sr., Victor Paul Furnish and Emory Stevens Bucke. Supplementary Volume. Nashville, Tennessee: Abingdon, 1976.

Taylor, Edward, ed., "The Soldier's Almanack, Bible And Prayer Book." *The History of Playing Cards.* London: John Camden Hotten, 1865. Public domain. Retrieved October 28, 2023. https://archive.org>stream>

Terence. "The Self-Tormentor." *English Songs from Foreign Tongues* by Frederick W. Ricard (1819-1897). New York: Charles Scribner's Sons, 1885. Public domain. Retrieved October 20, 2023. www.archive.org.terrence>theselftormentor.

Thigpen, Paul. *The Rapture Trap.* Westminster, Pennsylvania: Ascension Press, 2001.

Thomas, Norman. *The Truth About Socialism.* New York: Socialist Party, 1943. Public domain. Retrieved August 3, 2023. https://starslibrary.ucf.edu/prism/618.

Tillich, Paul. *The Courage To Be.* 1952. Reprint, New Haven and London: Yale University Press.

Toplady, Augustus. *Psalms and Hymns for Public and Private Worship.* London: E. and C. Dilby, 1776.

Trilling, Wolfgang. "ἁρπάζω." in *Exegetical Dictionary of the New Testament*. Edited by Horst Balz and Gerhard Schneider, 156-157. Vol. 1. Grand Rapids, Michigan: William B. Eerdmans Publishing Co., 1990.

[1] *Urban Thesaurus.orgThesaurus*, s.v. "utopia." Retrieved July 24, 2023. https://urban thesaurus.org/synonyms/utopia

Von Rad, Gerhard. *Old Testament Theology*. Translated by D.M.G. Stalker. Vol. 2. New York: Harper & Row, Publishers, 1965.

Wächter, J. "sheol." *Theological Dictionary of the Old Testament*. Edited by G. Johannes Botterweck, Helmer Ringgren, and Heinz-Josef Fabry and Translated by Douglas W. Stott, 239-248. Vol. 14. Grand Rapids, Michigan: William B. Eerdmans, 2004.

Wells, H. G. *The Fate of Man*. New York and Toronto: Alliance Book Corporation, Longmans, Green and Co., 1939.

Wesley, Charles (1707-1788). *"And Can It Be That I Should Gain."* Public domain. Retrieved June 27, 2023. www.hymnary.org/text/and_can_it_be_that_i_should_gain.

_____. "Love Divine, All Loves Excelling." *The Methodist Hymn Book With Tunes.* Letchworth, Great Britain: The Garden City Press, 1933. Public domain.

_____. *"O Love Divine, What Hast Thou Done?"* Public Domain. Retrieved June 27, 2023. www.hymnary.org/text/o_love_divine_what_hast_thou_done.

Westminster Assembly (1643-1652*), The Assembly's Shorter Catechism , with the Scripture Proofs in Reference: with an Appendix on the Systematik Attention of the Young to Scriptural Knowledge*, by Hervey Wilbur Newburyport, Massachusetts: Wm. B. Allen & Co., 1816.

Whitman, Walt. "Faces." *Leaves of Grass*. Edited by Harold W. Blodgett and Sculley Bradley. New York: W. W. Norton & Company, 1965.

_____. "The Mystic Trumpeter." *Leaves of Grass*. Edited by Harold W. Blodgett and Sculley Bradley. New York: W. W. Norton & Company, 1965.

Wiesner, William Theodore. *S. Ambrosii De Bono Mortis: A Revised Text with an Introduction, Translation, and Commentary*. Washington, DC: The Catholic University of America Press, 1970.

Wordsworth, William, "Ode: Intimations of Immortality from Recollections of Early Childhood." *Anthology of Romanticism*. Edited by Ernest Bernbaum. 5th ed. New York: The Ronald Press Company, 1948.

INDEX

Abbott, T. K., 169, 267
Abel, 234
Abundant Life, 28, 94, 96, 99, 242
Adam, 25, 52, 77, 96, 98, 99, 185, 260, 263, 281, 295
Ahab, 240
Allahu Akbar, 224
Almighty, 57, 163, 187, 194, 244
Amos, 113, 114, 115, 116, 117
Amos 6:1-8, 113
Angel, 215
Ansari, Massoud, 217, 273
Apocalyptic Eschatology, 6
Apple Of God's Eye, 83
Apple Of The Eye, 79
Arabian Peninsula, 212, 217, 218
Autonomy, 11, 14, 17, 76, 86, 96, 108, 192
Babylon, 21, 135
Babylonian Captivity, 6, 34, 79, 184
Barrett, C. K., 69, 262, 266
Barth, 16, 41, 74, 89, 98, 99, 124, 146, 147, 164, 166, 168, 232, 255, 259, 263, 264, 265, 266, 267, 275, 276, 278, 279
Barth, Karl, 16, 41, 74, 89, 124, 146, 164, 196, 198, 232, 255, 259, 263, 264, 265, 266, 267, 270, 275, 278, 279, 287, 290
Becoming, iii, 66, 67, 68, 152, 176, 188, 190
Berdyaev, 220, 227, 274, 275, 280
Berdyaev, Nicolas, 220, 274, 275, 280
Bethel, 61, 62, 63
Bonhoeffer, Dietrich, 13, 255, 280
Bruce, F. F., 46, 259, 260
Bruggemann, Walter, 240, 276
Brunner, Emil, 99, 260, 264
Büchsel, Friedrich, 35, 258
Burns, Robert, 30
Cain, 234
Carousel Of Death, 5
Chadijah, 212
City of God, 223, 263, 272, 274, 277
Clement, 9, 50, 209, 255, 260, 281
Color, 21, 73
Color Charts, Endless Timelines, And Graphs, 73
Creed of Sirmium, 90
Dare to be provocative, vi
Daube, 83, 84, 263, 282
David, 26, 83, 113, 119, 120, 121, 157, 255, 258, 262,

263, 266, 269, 271, 282, 285, 291, 293, 294
Death, iv, v, 5, 6, 9, 10, 15, 19, 20, 21, 23, 24, 25, 28, 29, 31, 33, 37, 38, 40, 41, 43, 44, 45, 46, 47, 48, 49, 51, 52, 53, 54, 55, 56, 57, 58, 59, 60, 64, 65, 66, 70, 71, 73, 74, 75, 78, 82, 83, 84, 86, 88, 89, 90, 91, 92, 93, 94, 95, 96, 97, 99, 100, 101, 106, 120, 130, 133, 136, 151, 152, 154, 160, 164, 165, 168, 178, 198, 200, 201, 208, 212, 221, 228, 234, 236, 243, 245, 246, 249, 251, 253
Descartes, i
Deuteronomy, 76, 203, 263, 282
Diessemann, Adolf, 70, 262, 263
Dispensationalism, 72
Doctrine Of Two Ages, 8
Dods, Marcus, 81, 263
Domains And Environments Unknown To Us, 91
Donne, John, 100, 264
Dostoevsky, 97, 98, 220, 264, 274, 282
Dove, Christian, 225
Ecclesiastes 3:1-2, 54
Edwards, Jonathan, 198, 270, 283
Elijah, 70, 150, 151, 153, 162, 238, 239, 240, 241, 243

Eliot, T. S., 30, 257, 275, 293
End-Time Systems, 87
Ephesians 3:14-21, 161
Evil Impulses, 15
Ex Nihilo, 22
Exodus 14:10-12, 149
Faith-Based Life, 142
Faulkner, William, 39, 258
Feminine Utopia, 191
Fitzgerald, Scott, 31, 257
Fohrer, Georg, 22, 256
Founding Fathers, 115
Freud, Sigmund, 28
Fromm, Erich, 230, 275
Funk, Robert, 24
Garden of Eden, 22, 52, 76, 100
Geach, Peter, 183, 268
Gehenna, 183, 188, 201, 206, 208, 209, 213, 214, 219
Gender Equality Utopia, 191
Geography, 263, 295
Global Community, 99
God Has Made Not One World But Two, 10
God wills it!, 224
God's Ownership of His Creation, 77
Good And Evil, 14, 167
Grace, 16, 28, 52, 53, 63, 74, 90, 93, 95, 97, 101, 120, 133, 144, 145, 167, 168, 169, 187, 229, 230, 247, 253
Graeff, Frank, 177
Gray, John, 201, 271

Great White Throne of Judgment, 234
Green New Deal, 17
Groaning In Travail, 17, 18
Hawking, Stephen, v
Hertz., Rabbi J. H, 62
Hick, John, 33, 258, 286
Isaiah 34, 1, 5, 6, 10, 11, 19, 89
Isaiah 35, 3, 4, 5, 7, 10, 33, 36, 89, 254
Isaiah 43:1-7, 134
Islam, 212, 218, 276, 295
Jackson, Mahalia, 26
Jesus, i, ii, vii, 7, 11, 20, 21, 22, 23, 24, 25, 26, 28, 32, 33, 35, 36, 37, 38, 39, 41, 43, 44, 45, 46, 47, 48, 49, 50, 51, 52, 53, 56, 58, 59, 60, 66, 67, 68, 69, 71, 74, 77, 78, 82, 83, 84, 85, 86, 87, 88, 89, 90, 91, 93, 94, 95, 99, 100, 101, 102, 104, 105, 106, 107, 108, 110, 111, 117, 120, 121, 124, 136, 137, 138, 141, 145, 148, 152, 153, 154, 155, 156, 157, 158, 159, 161, 163, 164, 165, 166, 167, 171, 177, 178, 179, 180, 184, 186, 187, 189, 204, 205, 206, 209, 210, 212, 219, 220, 227, 228, 230, 234, 235, 236, 237, 238, 241, 242, 243, 244, 245, 246, 247, 249, 250, 253, 262, 265, 268, 272, 285, 286, 287, 291
Job, vi, 9, 24, 28, 127, 128, 129, 131, 132, 133, 159, 169, 174
John, iv, 7, 9, 11, 19, 22, 23, 24, 25, 26, 28, 29, 32, 33, 35, 37, 39, 45, 47, 49, 50, 60, 65, 66, 68, 69, 74, 77, 78, 83, 86, 88, 90, 92, 93, 94, 100, 107, 121, 153, 155, 164, 168, 169, 176, 179, 180, 184, 187, 201, 234, 235, 237, 238, 241, 244, 246, 247, 257, 258, 264, 266, 267, 268, 271, 275, 278, 281, 282, 284, 285, 286, 289, 292, 296
John, First, 19, 67, 68
Joseph, iv, 113, 191, 275
Josephus, 104, 106, 205, 264, 265, 271, 272, 287
Kaiser, Otto, 11, 21, 22, 255
Karl Marx And Friedrich Engels, 196
Kautsky, Karl, 198, 270, 287
Kierkegaard, iii, i, vii, 28, 254, 257, 288
Kierkegaard, Soren, iii, i, 254, 257, 288
Kingdom Of God, 22, 69
Kipling, Rudyard, 115, 181, 265, 268
Koestler, Arthur, 11, 255
Koran, 211, 213, 214, 218, 277

Language, v, 19, 21, 44, 60, 85, 193, 219, 233
Lenin, Vladimir, 196
Lightfoot, John, 257, 289
Little Jack Horner Syndrome, 167
Luke 21:5-6, 19, 23, 103
Luke 8:22-25, 149
Luke 9:49-56, 180
Luther, Martin, 4, 18, 96, 97, 137, 144, 202, 223, 256, 264, 274
Mao Tse-Tung, 194, 269, 290
Marine, 26, 110, 130, 147
Mark 13:1-2, 31, 102
Mark Of The Beast, 71, 87
Martyr, Justin, 69, 261, 264
Mary, iv, i, ii, iii, v, vii, 214
Matthew 24:1-2, 13, 35, 102
Metamorphosed, 67
Metamorphosis, 67, 70
Methuselah, 43
Metzger, Bruce, 8, 9, 255
Michaelis, Wilhelm, 69, 262
Midbar, 24, 256, 296
Mohammad, 212, 214, 215, 216, 217, 218, 273, 277
Monuments, 108, 110, 270
More, Thomas, 188, 191, 193, 195, 196, 268, 270, 287
Moses, 37, 70, 105, 141, 149, 151, 165, 203, 244
Myopia, 103, 104, 105, 107, 109, 112
Nationalism, 20, 21
Neubauer, Adolphe, 204, 271
New Thing, 34, 35, 38, 241
Noah, 15, 16, 21, 185
Norman, Thomas, 296
North, C. R., 34, 258
Occasions Of Fear And Anxiety, 65
Odysseus, 190, 191
Oepke, Albrecht, 292
Origen, 9, 272, 292
Origin, 35, 209, 258, 292
Otto, Rudolf, 258
Otto, Rudolf, 36, 38
Parable Of The Prompter, i
Paradise, 52, 82, 83, 87, 236
Parousia, 47, 68, 69, 70
Pascal, 45, 46, 231, 232, 233, 275, 293
Pascal, Blaise, ii, 21, 259, 275
Pascal, Blaise, 45
Pascal, Blaise, 256
Pascal, Blaise Pascal, 286
Paul, i, v, vi, vii, 5, 17, 18, 27, 31, 36, 38, 40, 42, 44, 45, 46, 47, 48, 49, 51, 52, 54, 55, 59, 60, 65, 67, 77, 78, 80, 84, 88, 92, 96, 98, 99, 105, 130, 133, 136, 145, 163, 164, 165, 166, 168, 169, 170, 172, 175, 177, 179, 186, 207, 209, 218, 220, 221, 222, 228, 229, 239, 245, 254, 258, 259, 260, 262, 267, 280, 281, 285, 296
Peter, 8, 19, 36, 46, 66, 90, 137, 170, 171, 183, 208,

209, 210, 220, 226, 236, 268, 272, 284, 292
Pharmacology, 13
Philosophers, i
Politics, 21, 72, 192, 197
Pondered, ii, iii, iv
Pondering, ii, iii, iv, v, vii, viii
Pope Gregory The Great, 220
Post-Millennial, 87
Potter, 185, 186
Pre-Millennial, 87
Prophetic Eschatology, 6, 7
Psalm 100, 123, 124, 125
Psalm 115, 139, 140
Psalm 130, 144, 145
Psalm 31:9-16, 118
Psalmist, iv, 41, 58, 73, 76, 79, 119, 120, 124, 125, 141, 142, 145, 147, 152, 176, 200
Psychology of Mohammad, 217
Public School System, 13
Queer Utopia, 191, 269, 294
Rabia Of Basra, 251, 252
Race, 11, 15, 21, 50, 80, 185
Rapture, 71, 72, 86, 87, 93, 248, 249
Re-Created World, 8, 35, 38, 41, 55, 63, 81, 83, 91, 94, 96, 100, 223
Re-Creation, 5, 16, 20, 22, 23, 31, 33, 34, 35, 36, 38, 42, 49, 50, 51, 54, 56, 58, 65, 89, 91, 95, 96, 228

Resurrection, 5, 34, 44, 45, 46, 47, 48, 49, 56, 68, 69, 70, 86, 88, 90, 96, 99, 100, 136, 212, 219, 234, 245, 251
Righteous Person, 146
Rock of Ages, 51
Roman Eagle, 225
Rosser, Barbara, 72, 262
Russell, D. S., 8, 255
Saint Ambrose, 53
Saint Augustine, 31, 32, 58, 81, 82, 123, 209, 221, 222, 223, 252, 257, 258, 261, 263, 265, 272, 274, 275, 276, 293
Saint Ignatius, 92, 93
Saint Thomas Aquinas, 219, 274
Sandburg, Carl, 30, 257
Satan, 26, 56, 63, 127, 128
Saul, 37, 119, 165, 166
Save The Planet, 17
Savior, 25, 44, 52, 56, 82, 86, 93, 121, 134, 164, 178, 187, 238, 253
Schaff, Philip, 212, 258, 266, 272, 277
Schema, 18
Scott, Walter Chambers, 145
Scylla And Charybdis, 190
Second Enoch, 42
Second Esdras, 9, 255
Second World Of God's Re-Creation, 34

Second-Coming, 47, 68, 69, 72, 86, 87, 93
Secular Government, 115
Seeger, Alan, 73, 262
Shafarevitch, 197
Sheol, 183, 188, 199, 200, 201
Shepherds, ii, iii
Shupe, Colonel David, 26
Socrates, i
Solzhenitsyn, Alexander, 195
St Irenaeus, 90
St. Ignatius, 90
St. Polycarp, 90
Talmon, 24, 256, 296
Tartarus, 183, 188, 208, 209, 210
Terence, 222, 274, 296
Tertullian, 90
The "Now" And The "Not Yet", 41
The Great But, 232
The Idea Of The Holy, 36, 258, 292
The Mystic Trumpeter, 49, 260, 298
The Self-Tormentor, 222, 274, 296
This World Is Passing Away, 18
Thomas, Norman, 192, 269, 291
Tilgath-Pileser, 114
Tillich, Paul, 31, 258, 296
Titus, 205
Tohu Wabohu, 10, 11, 12, 16, 24, 26, 79, 95, 255, 285
Topheth, 202, 203
Tribulation, 26, 27
Utopia, 97, 188, 193, 268, 290, 297
Utopian Socialism And Communism, 192
Valley Of Hennom, 203
Vessels Of Mercy, 164, 165, 166, 168
Vocabulary, 66, 70, 86, 87, 98, 159, 168, 234, 249
von Rad, Gerhard, 240, 276
Wasteland, 30, 32, 33
Wesley, Charles, 67, 261, 267
Whitman, Walt, 42, 49, 259
Wickedness Of Man, 15
Wilderness, 3, 20, 22, 23, 24, 25, 26, 28, 29, 30, 32, 33, 34, 76, 79, 89, 91, 95, 96, 98, 100, 105, 119, 129, 149, 150, 152, 175
Williams, Ted, 40
Wordsworth, William, 39, 258
Worrying, vii
Zechariah 2:8, 76

www.ingramcontent.com/pod-product-compliance
Lightning Source LLC
Chambersburg PA
CBHW041135110526
44590CB00027B/4024